Pranams to Sri Ganesha

SRI SAI SATCHARITRA

The Wonderful Life and Teachings
of Shirdi Sai Baba

By Hemadpant

Modern rendering by
Monika of Penukonda

The original *Sri Sai Satcharitra* was a long text written in Marathi by Sri Hemadpant. This new rendering has been adapted from the shortened English version which was translated by Sri Nagash Vasudev Gunaji.

This is offered to Bhagavan Shirdi Sai with infinite gratitude and humble pranams. May Baba bless everyone to experience his infinite love and living presence.

May the bells on Sai's ankles be heard dancing in your heart and may his leelas be sung in your ears for all time to come.

TABLE OF CONTENTS

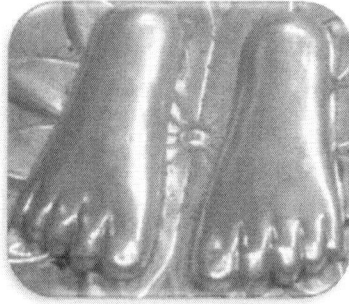

FOREWORD

This new rendering of the *Sri Sai Satcharitra* is humbly offered at the feet of Sri Shirdi Sai Baba, our beloved sadguru and our everything. It is through his grace that this work was inspired and completed. Without his grace, nothing is possible. He is watching over the entire universe and each and every one of us. To understand the mystery of Sai is our blessing and our way. Through listening to and meditating on his life and his leelas our false understanding is removed and we recognize that we are one with him and all that is. There is no greater bliss than to experience his love and living presence among us.

This modern rendering of the *Satcharitra* was begun over eight years ago in Penukonda, Andhra Pradesh, India at the Shiva Sai Mandir Ashram of Sri Kaleshwar, my guru and Shirdi Baba's disciple. It sprung out of a desire for others to know about the wonder that is Sai and for them to experience his living presence in their lives. Hemadpant wrote the original edition of Baba's life stories in Marathi, the language that Baba spoke. To him, we owe a great debt. Although not a writer, he was inspired in this undertaking by Baba himself. This is how the saints have their stories told, by those they choose as instruments and through which they write their stories. Hemadpant describes himself as ignorant and incapable of such a lofty task and, if it were not for Baba writing through him, it would have been impossible to accomplish such a task. This is also my feeling. Everything has to be laid at Baba's feet. The joy of being used by the divine force that is Baba is incomparable. To feel the force of his love and supreme wisdom guiding not only this task but all of life is true freedom and divine bliss.

I initially heard of Shirdi Baba when my first teacher, Swami Muktananda, spoke of him. Muktananda, a great siddha, had only two pictures on his personal altar: one of his guru Bhagawan Nityananda and one of Shirdi Baba. He, as with many saints, regard Shirdi Baba as the highest of saints. It is universally accepted among them that Baba is supremely great. He is the Paramaguru.

Although I had known of Shirdi Baba, my connection to him had not yet been awakened in this life until 1997. My first trip to Shirdi was in November of that year. Sri Kaleshwar had invited me to study with him in India. We were to meet in Shirdi, at Baba's samadhi. It was early in the evening that first day in Shirdi when we walked through the streets, still muddy from the monsoon rains, on the way to meditate in the Dwarkamai. This is where Baba had lived for more than sixty years. Sai bhajans blasted joyfully over the loud speakers, and crowds of beggars walked with us along the streets. I had imagined that Baba's samadhi would be serene like Ramana Maharshi's in Arunachala. But Baba's Samadhi is bustling, noisy, and filled with people, rich and poor, educated and uneducated, all equal in Baba's eyes. Hundreds of thousands of devotees visit each year.

We meditated in the Dwarkamai, the place where Baba's devotees used to sit to sing bhajans to him in the evenings. (Now it is enclosed in a simple open-air building with a tin roof.) Within moments of starting to meditate, the energy pulled me deeper and deeper as the world outside and inside dissolved into an indescribable peace and a continuously unfolding bliss. The connection to Baba was awakened.

Sri Kaleshwar connected his students first to his master, Shirdi Sai. Devotion to the guru is exemplified in our Parampara, our lineage. Baba loved his guru Venkusa and won his master's heart and everything his master had to give. His only spiritual practice was to love and serve his guru and fulfill his commands. Later, after Venkusa took mahasamadhi, his guru's consciousness was always in communication with him, especially at night when Baba slept on the brick that his master had given him as a final gift. Sri Kaleshwar's life was also totally dedicated to serving his master Shirdi Sai. He did so until his own mahasamadhi in March of 2012 at the age of thirty-nine, just a few months after Baba had given him permission to take samadhi.

Sri Kaleshwar brought many westerners into Baba's presence. He taught how to connect to Baba and how to understand the deeper inner significance of Baba's life, especially the energy mechanisms he was implementing in his inscrutable actions and advanced yogic practices like Kandhana Yoga and Dhauti Yoga, and how Baba commanded on the Kalachakra, the wheel of time, to help his devotees. Everything Baba did was for the sake of his devotees and all of humanity. He was born on Earth for that purpose. When he smoked his chillum he was burning the karmas of his devotees and balancing the vibrations of his own inner elements as he was burning those karmas. When he performed Dhauti Yoga, he vomited his intestines from his body, washed them in the river, and then hung them out to dry on a nearby tree. He wasn't just washing his intestines; he was washing the karmas of those he served. It was not symbolic; it was actual. Baba was suffering to pay for the karmas of his devotees. Baba, like Jesus, suffered on our behalf.

Over the fifteen years of his mission, Sri Kaleshwar taught his students how to understand Baba's state. Baba was an avadhut, living in the state of pure consciousness that cannot be understood by the normal mind—a bird that flies high in the sky cannot be understood by those walking on the earth below. An avadhut cannot be fully understood, only trusted. Faith is necessary.

The avadhut lives in the awareness of Aham Brahmasmi—everything is God. They are one with all of Creation. They are in the awareness of this ultimate reality even while living in a body. They are a little off from this planet. They are outside the boundaries of time and space yet are completely present to everything that is taking place. They have sankalpam siddhi—what they say happens. Whatever they say comes to pass. They have a special relationship with the Nature; they can command on the Nature. They can make the rain start and the wind stop or make fire appear out of the earth as Baba did with his miraculous stick. Or turn water into oil using the spit from his mouth. Baba was the supreme miraculous master, miracles happened spontaneously around him all the time. They are still happening today.

I was sitting with Sri Kaleshwar in the Dwarkamai in Shirdi in 1997, when he gave me a small red hardback copy of the *Satcharitra* and said, "Read it. It is important to your life." I really wanted to learn more about Baba's life but had a hard time reading the old style of English. Nine years later I received the message to render the book into modern English. I started editing. After an initial effort, it was put aside until now when it is finally completed in time for Shivaratri, 2014.

Reflecting on that time in the Dwarkamai almost seventeen years ago, I am smiling as I recognize just how Baba has guided my own life and the life of so many others. I am now living at a Dattatreya Temple in Mendocino County, California. The Datta Temple is a part of a larger healing center whose purpose it is to share the life and teachings of Shirdi Baba, Jesus, Babaji, Ramakrishna Paramahamsa, Ramana Maharshi, Sri Kaleshwar—our Paramapara. So, who can say what Baba has in store for each and every one of us?

Surprising as it may seem, our temple is not unique, there are other Baba temples springing up across the United States, Europe, and Asia. These temples are being established not only by Indians but by Westerners who have been touched by Baba. Baba would sometimes reveal to different devotees how many lifetimes they knew each other. How many lifetimes have we known him and been with him? He is Shiva, incarnated as a saptharishi, as Dattatreya, as Narasimha Swami, as Kabir, as Adi Shankaracharya and innumerable great souls throughout history, being born again and again to guide and protect humanity. He continues to be reborn whenever the dharma is forgotten, when conditions in the world worsen, and when we need his help.

What is not very known to the general world, though known to the inner world of the saints in India, is Baba's role in Jesus' life. According to the Indian saints Yogananda Paramahamsa, Swami Ram Tirtha, Swami (Papa Ramdas), Sri Kaleshwar, and ancient palm leaf manuscripts, Jesus lived in India. He spent his missing years in India learning and 'researching' with the saints and rishis, traveling throughout India to sacred temples and ancient power spots from the Himalayas to Mysore. Jesus was researching and discussing spiritual subjects with the soul during that incarnation that was Baba, and with other rishis and saints, who watched over Jesus when he went back to the Middle East to fulfill his divine mission. The saints and rishis were meditating on him, helping him on the consciousness level. Jesus was very special in the divine plan and Baba was part of the fulfillment of that plan. Now Baba and Jesus are guiding humanity to reach a new level of Divine Consciousness.

Sri Kaleshwar taught that the beginning of the millennium was a pivotal time in humanity's history. It was the beginning of a new consciousness yuga, the Sai Yuga. In the darkest night in our collective history, a new age of wisdom is emerging. During this time, it is possible to live in the state of consciousness that Baba described as Brahma Jnana, the awareness called Aham Brahmasi, everything is God, all is one.

The fastest growing spiritual movement in the world is the Sai Movement. This is happening not because there is any organization promoting Baba. It is simply by word of mouth and direct experience of Baba.

The beauty of Sai Baba's life is its simplicity. He was *Raja di Raja*, king among kings, *Yogi Raja*, king of the yogis, yet he was born in the simplest of life's circumstances, orphaned, and lived his life as a fakir, a holy beggar. He wore a simple torn robe, headscarf, and no shoes on his feet. He lived in a shelter that had no protection from the rain or wind, and each day begged for food. He owned nothing and wanted for nothing. He was only here to serve the people, those who were with him during that life and all those learning of him now. He exists out of place and time, he can appear anywhere at any time. Reports from those seeing Baba happen all the time, all over the world. He is all pervasive, ever present, ever taking care of us all. "I am a grandfather to all the people," Baba said to Sri Kaleshwar when he mysteriously appeared to awaken him as a young teenager. This kind of miraculous appearance is not unfamiliar in the leelas of Sai. It is his unique characteristic. He is Shiva, the Divine Father looking out for us all, protecting us, guiding us, loving us. All he asks is that we think of him. Remember him. Cast your problems to him; he will take care. Try to see and experience him for yourself. That is why this Sai Movement is spreading like a blazing fire throughout the world. He is blessing the world himself, directly to each person who looks to him.

The divine stories of Baba's life, his leelas, are inscrutable, miraculous and amazing. We can listen to the original stories of his life, and recognize that he is creating new stories now, new leelas in each of our lives. He is the director. He is the doer. Sri Kaleshwar loved to say that Baba creates the problem, then creates the solution. He is at work in each of our lives creating the situations we need to learn the spiritual qualities of faith, patience, devotion, humility and surrender. His message to all of us is the same as Jesus', love one another. His simple words to his devotees during his life who were both Muslim and Hindu—don't fight. He loved all equally and taught all are equal. He, as the sadguru, is here to remove the ignorance that you are different from him, that you are separate. You are not different from him. You are Divine. You are

God. After he fulfills your needs and desires, he creates faith in you and leads you to desiring what he truly has to give, the awareness of that ultimate reality, where there is no difference between you and another. You are the Supreme Consciousness, the same as he.

I am offering a prayer to Baba that this rendering of the *Satcharitra* will inspire people to read and listen to his stories. Everything can be gained by thinking on Baba. When we focus on him, he is there. He wants us to read his stories; that was his instruction to us. He demonstrated to his devotees over and over through his innumerable leelas that he was indeed omniscient. He knew everything about everyone, as he knows everything about each of us.

May Baba's blessings always be with you.

Monika of Penukonda
(Monika M. Taylor)
Divine Lineage Healing Center
Laytonville, California

   Monika worked closely with Sri Kaleshwar for fifteen years in Penukonda, India on the ancient knowledge. She was the editor of Sri Kaleshwar's books including: **Shirdi Sai Baba, The Universal Master, The Real Life and Teachings of Jesus Christ,** *and* **The Divine Mystery Fort.** *She is the author of* **Kaleshwar.** *She currently gives teachings, healings and shaktipat transmission around the world. Since Sri Kaleshwar's mahasamadhi in 2012, she has been in residence at the Divine Lineage Healing Center, in northern California. About her, Sri Kaleshwar said, "Monika belongs to the Divine Mother Kanaka Durga's feet. She is a Divine Ma on the planet. She'll walk and give a lot of wisdom and clarity to bloom wisdom. This lady will bless millions of people on the planet. She's going to do it. This is Swami Kaleshwar explaining her astrology."*

CHAPTER ONE

According to the ancient and revered custom, Hemadpant begins this work, the *Sai Satcharitra*, with salutations:

First, he gives homage to Lord Ganesh, to remove all obstacles and make the work a success, and it is Sri Sai Baba that is Lord Ganesh.

Next, to the Goddess Sarasvati, to inspire him to write the book, saying that Sri Sai Baba is one with the Goddess, and that he, himself, is singing his own life.

Then, to the gods Brahma, Vishnu, Shiva—the creating, sustaining, destroying deities—saying that Sri Sai Baba is one with them and he, as the great teacher, will carry us across the river of worldly existence.

Then, to his protecting deity Narayana Adinat, who manifested himself in Konkon, the land reclaimed from the sea by Parashuram, and to the Adi (original) deity of his family.

Then to Bharadwaja Muni, into whose clan he was born, and to the rishis Yajnavalkya, Bhrigu, Parashara, Narada, Veda Vyasa, Sanak, Sanandan, Sanat

Kumar, Shuka, Shounak, Vishwamitra, Vasistha, Valmiki, Vamadeva, Jaimini, Vaishampayan, Nava, Yogindra, etc. As well as to the modern saints, Nivritti, Jnanadev, Sopan, Muktabai, Janardan, Ekanath, Namdev, Tukaram, Kanha, Narahari, etc.

Then to his grandfather Sadashiv, his father Raghunath, his mother who left him in infancy, his paternal aunt who brought him up, and his loving elder brother.

Then, to the readers who, he prays, will give their whole and undivided attention to this work.

Then to his guru Sri Sainath, an incarnation of Sri Dattatreya, who is his sole refuge and who will make him realize that Brahman is the only reality and the world an illusion.

Finally, to all beings in whom the Lord God dwells.

GRINDING WHEAT TO STOP THE CHOLERA EPIDEMIC

It was sometime after 1910 when one fine morning I went to the masjid in Shirdi for *darshan* (seeing Divinity) of Sai Baba. I was wonderstruck to see the following phenomenon. After washing his mouth and face, Sai Baba began to make preparations for grinding wheat. He spread a sack on the floor then placed a hand-mill there. He drew up the sleeves of his *kafni* (robe) and put a few handfuls of wheat in the mill and started grinding it. I thought, 'What business does Baba have with grinding wheat when he possesses nothing, stores nothing and lives on alms?'

Others had thought the same thing but none had the courage to ask Baba what he was doing. Immediately, as the news of Baba grinding wheat spread into the village, men and women began to run to the masjid to watch Baba. Four bold women forced their way up from the crowd and pushed Baba aside, forcibly taking the handle in their hands, and started grinding and singing about Baba's *leelas* (divine plays).

At first Baba was enraged, but then seeing the women's love and devotion, he was much pleased and began to smile. While they were grinding, the women wondered what Baba was going to do with the big quantity of flour as Baba lived on alms. He had no house, no property, no children, none to look after and did not require any flour for making *roti* (flat bread). They thought that perhaps Baba would distribute the flour among them, as he was very kind. After they finished grinding, they put aside the handmill and divided the flour into four and each began to take some.

Baba, who was calm and quiet up until now, became wild and started abusing them saying, "Ladies, have you gone mad? Whose father's property are you looting? Have I borrowed any wheat from you so that you can safely take it now? Now please do this: take the flour and throw it along the village borders." On hearing this, the women felt ashamed and, whispering among themselves, left to go to the outskirts of the village and spread the flour as directed by Baba.

I asked people of Shirdi, "Why did Baba do this?" They replied that the cholera epidemic was spreading in the village and this was Baba's remedy against it; it was not wheat being ground but the cholera itself was being ground and pushed out of the village. From that time onward, the epidemic subsided and the people of the village were happy.

I was much pleased to know all this but at the same time my curiosity was aroused. I began to ask myself, 'What earthly connection is there between wheat flour and cholera? How is it related?' The incident seemed inexplicable. I thought I should write something about this and wanted to sing about Baba's sweet *leelas* (divine plays) to my heart's content. Thinking in this way about this leela, my heart was filled with joy and I was inspired to write Baba's life, the *Sai Satcharitra*.

As we know, with Baba's grace and blessing this work was successfully accomplished.

⚜

THE INNER MECHANISM OF BABA'S GRINDING

It was Baba's firm conviction that knowledge or self-realization is not possible unless as a prior act there is the grinding of all our impulses, desires, and karmas.

Apart from the meaning that the people of Shirdi made of this incident of grinding wheat, we think there was also a philosophical significance. Sai Baba lived in Shirdi for about 60 years and during this long period he did the business of grinding almost every day. However, it was not wheat alone, but the sins, the mental and physical afflictions and miseries of his innumerable devotees. The two stones of his mill consisted of *karma* (actions) and *bhakti* (devotion), karma being the lower stone and bhakti the upper one. The handle with which Baba worked the mill was *jnana* (knowledge). It was Baba's firm conviction that knowledge or self-realization is not possible unless as a prior act there is the grinding of all our impulses, desires, and karmas; as well as the three *gunas* (qualities)—*sattva* (purity), *raja* (activity) and *tamas* (inertia); and the *ahamkaara* (ego), which is so subtle and therefore so difficult to remove.

This reminds us of a similar story of Kabir, who seeing a woman grinding corn said to his guru, Nipathiranjana, "I am weeping because I feel the agony of being crushed in this wheel of worldly existence like the corn in the hand-mill."

Nipathiranjana replied, "Do not be afraid. Hold fast to the handle of knowledge as I do. Do not wander far from that but turn inward to the center and you are sure to be saved."

Pranams to Sri Sai

Peace Be to All

CHAPTER TWO

INSPIRATION FOR WRITING THIS WORK

I n the first chapter, I described Sai Baba's miracle of destroying the cholera epidemic by grinding wheat and throwing the flour on the outskirts of the village. To my great delight, I heard other miracles of Sai Baba which burst forth into this poetic work. I also thought that the descriptions of Sai Baba's miracles would be interesting and instructive to his devotees and remove their sins, and so I began to write about the sacred life and teachings of Sai Baba. The life of the saint is neither logical nor dialectical. It shows us the true and great path.

⚜

THE AUTHOR RECEIVES BABA'S GRACE
TO WRITE THIS BOOK

"Hearing my stories and teachings will create faith in devotees'
hearts and they will easily attain self-realization and bliss."

Hemadpant thought that he was not fit to undertake the work. He said, "I do not know the life of my intimate friend nor do I know my own mind, then how can I write the life of a saint or describe the nature of incarnations, which even the *Vedas* were unable to do? One must be a saint himself before he could know other saints, then how is it possible that I could describe their glory? To write the life of a saint is most difficult, one may as well try to measure the depth of the seven seas or enclose the sky with cloth. I knew that this was the most adventurous undertaking and might expose me to ridicule; I therefore invoked Sai Baba's grace."

The premier poet-saint of Maharashtra, Sri Jnaneshwar Maharaj, said that the Lord loves those who write the lives of saints. The saints also have a peculiar method of getting this service, which devotees long for, successfully accomplished. The saints inspire the work; the devotee becomes only an indirect cause or instrument to achieve the end.

For instance, in 1778 the poet Mahipati aspired to write the lives of saints. Saints inspired him and he wrote four books. Starting in 1878, Das Ganu wrote about the lives of modern saints in his books, composed sweet poems and wrote of the life and teachings of Sai Baba. Others also have written stories of Sai Baba's wonderful leelas. The question then arises, that while so many works regarding Sai Baba exist, why is it necessary to write this one?

The answer is plain and simple. The life of Sai Baba is as wide and deep as the infinite ocean. All can dive deep into it and take out precious gems of knowledge and *bhakti* (devotion) and distribute them to the world. The stories, parables, and teachings of Sai Baba are very wonderful. They will give peace and happiness to those who are afflicted with sorrow and weighed down by the suffering of this worldly existence, and also bestow knowledge and wisdom, both in worldly and spiritual domains. If these teachings of Sai Baba, which are as interesting and instructive as Vedic lore, are listened to and meditated upon, the devotees will get whatever they long for—union with *Brahman* (ultimate reality), mastery in eight-fold yoga, bliss of meditation and so on. So I thought that to put these stories together would be my best *upasana* (way to approach God). This collection would be most delightful to those simple souls whose eyes had not been blessed with Sai Baba's darshan. So, I set about collecting Sai Baba's teachings and words, the outcome of his boundless and natural self-realization.

It was Sai Baba who inspired me in this matter. In fact, when I surrendered my ego at his feet my path was clear and I knew he would make me very happy in this life and in the next.

I wanted Sai Baba's permission for this work so I requested Shama, Baba's most intimate devotee, to speak for me. He pleaded my cause and said to Baba, "He wishes to write your biography. Don't say that you are a poor begging *fakir* (ascetic), and there is no necessity to write it. If you agree and help him, he will write it, or rather, your grace will accomplish the work. Without your consent and blessing, nothing can be done successfully."

Sai Baba was moved by my request, blessed me by giving me *udi* (sacred ash) and placed his boon-bestowing hand on my head, saying:

Let him make a collection of stories and experiences, keeping notes and memos. I will help him. He is only an outward instrument. I will write my autobiography myself and satisfy the wishes of my devotees. He should get rid of his ego, surrender it at my feet. He who acts like this in life; I help the most. What of my life stories? I will serve him in all possible ways. When his ego is completely annihilated and there is no trace of it left, I shall enter into him and shall write my own life. Hearing my stories and teachings will create faith in devotees' hearts and they will easily attain self-realization and bliss. Let there be no insistence of establishing one's own view, no attempt to refute other's opinions, no discussions of pros and cons of any subject.

The word "discussion" reminded me of my promise to explain the story of my receiving the title Hemadpant, which I will now relate. I was on close friendly terms with Kakasaheb Dixit and Nanasaheb Chandorkar. They pressed me to go to Shirdi and have Baba's darshan and I promised them to do so. But something turned up preventing me from going to Shirdi. The son of a friend of mine fell ill. My friend tried all possible means, physical and spiritual, but the fever would not abate. He got his guru to sit by the bedside of his son but this too was of no avail.

Hearing this, I thought, 'What was the value of a guru, if he could not save my friend's son? If a guru can't do anything for us, why should I go to Shirdi at all?' Thinking this way, I postponed my trip to Shirdi. But the inevitable must happen and it happened in my case as follows.

Nanasaheb was waiting for a train bound for Bassein, but when a local train to Bandra arrived he got on that instead. In Bandra, he sent for me and arranged my trip to Shirdi. Nanasaheb's argument for my Shirdi trip was convincing and delightful, so I decided to start for Shirdi the same night. I packed my luggage and started for Shirdi. I booked a train to Dadar in order to catch a train for Manmad. As the train was about to leave, a Muslim rushed to my compartment and seeing all my bags, asked me where I was bound. I told him. He suggested I go straight to Boribunder instead as the train did not stop at Dadar. If this little miracle or leela had not happened, I would not have reached Shirdi the next day as planned and many doubts would have assailed me.

As fortune favored me, I reached Shirdi the next morning. Kakasaheb was waiting for me. After dismounting from the *tonga* (horse carriage), I was anxious to have Baba's darshan. The great devotee, Tatya, who had just come from the masjid, said that Baba was at the corner of Sathe's wada. This was in 1910, when it was the only place for lodging pilgrims. Kakasaheb told me to go for preliminary darshan then return to see Baba again at my leisure after having had a bath.

Hearing this, I ran and prostrated before Baba and my joy knew no bounds. I found even more than what Nanasaheb had described. All my senses were satisfied and I forgot thirst and hunger. The moment I touched Sai Baba's feet, I began a new lease on life. I felt very grateful to those who prompted and helped me to have his darshan. I considered them to be my true relatives and I cannot repay their debt. I remember and prostrate before them. In my experience, through Sai Baba's darshan our thoughts are changed, the force of previous actions is lessened and gradually dispassion towards worldly objects naturally arises. It is by the merit of actions in many past births that such darshan is received. And, through his darshan, the entire world assumes the form of Sai Baba.

NECESSITY FOR A GURU

On the first day of my arrival in Shirdi, Balasaheb Bhate and I had a discussion regarding the necessity of a guru. I argued, "Why should we lose our freedom and submit to someone else? When we have to do our duty, why is a guru necessary? One must try his best and save himself. What can the guru do for a man who does nothing but sleeps indolently?"

And so I pleaded free will while at the same time Balasaheb argued the other side—destiny—and said, "Whatever is bound to happen must happen. Even great men have failed. Man plans one way, but God arranges the opposite way. Brush aside your cleverness, pride and egoism. It won't help you." This discussion, with all its pros and cons, went on for an hour or so, and as usual no decision was arrived at. We had to stop the discussion, as we were exhausted. The net result of this was that I lost my peace of mind. I realized that unless strong body consciousness and egoism are present, there would be no discussion. In other words, it is egoism that breeds discussion.

Later when we went to the masjid, Baba asked Kakasaheb, "What was going on in Sathe's wada? What was the discussion about?"

Staring at me, Baba added, "What did Hemadpant say?"

Hearing these words I was much surprised. The masjid was at a considerable distance from Sathe's wada where the discussion was going on. How could Baba know our discussion unless he was omniscient and the inner ruler of all?

THE SIGNIFICANCE OF THE AUTHOR'S NAME

I began to think about why Sai Baba called me by the name Hemadpant. This word is a form of Hemadripant. Hemadripant was a well-known Minister of the kings Mahadev and Ramadev of Devgiri, of the Yadava dynasty. He was very learned, good-natured and the author of many books. He invented and started new methods of accounts and was the originator of the Marathi shorthand script. But I was quite the opposite, an ignoramus, with a dull, mediocre intellect. I could not understand why the name or title was conferred upon me. But thinking seriously upon it, I thought that the title was a dart to destroy my ego, so that I would always remain meek and humble. It was also a compliment paid to me for the cleverness in the discussion.

Note: Baba calling the author by the name Hemadpant was significant and prophetic, as he later looked after the management of Sai Samsthan very intelligently, kept all the accounts and was also the author of the Sai Satcharitra, which deals with such important spiritual subjects as jnana (knowledge), bhakti (devotion), dispassion, self-surrender and self-realization.

THE GURU GUIDES YOU

Hemadpant did not leave any words about what Baba said regarding the subject of the necessity of a guru guiding you. But Kakasaheb published his notes regarding this matter:

The day after Hemadpant's meeting with Sai Baba, Kakasaheb went to Baba and asked whether he should leave Shirdi. Baba said yes.

"Baba, where to go?"

Baba said, "High up."

"What is the way?"

Baba said, "There are many ways leading there. There is also a way from here (Shirdi). The way is difficult. There are tigers and wolves in the jungles on the way."

"But Baba, what if we take a guide with us?" I (Kakasaheb) asked.

Baba answered, "Then there is no difficulty. The guide will take you straight to your destination so you will avoid wolves, tigers and ditches on the way. If there is no guide, there is the danger of you being lost in the jungle or falling into ditches."

Hemadpant was present on this occasion and thought this was the answer Baba gave to the question whether a guru was necessary. He took this as a hint that no discussion of whether man is free or bound is of any use in spiritual matters. On the contrary, to reach the real *Paramatma* (Absolute) is possible only as the result of the teachings of the guru.

This is illustrated in the instances of great avatars like Rama and Krishna, who had to surrender to their gurus, Vasishtha and Sandipani, for self-realization and the only virtues necessary for progress are faith and patience.

Pranams to Sri Sai

Peace Be to All

CHAPTER THREE

BABA'S PROMISE

"Believe me, if anybody sings my leelas I will give him infinite joy and everlasting happiness."

As described in the previous chapter, Sai Baba gave his complete approval to the writing of the *Sai Satcharitra* and said, "I fully agree with you regarding the writing of *Satcharitra*. You do your duty. Don't be afraid in the least. Steady your mind and have faith in my words. If my leelas are written, *avidya* (ignorance) will vanish and if they are listened to with reverence and attention, the consciousness of worldly existence will decrease, and strong waves of devotion and love will rise up. If one dives deep into my *leelas* (divine plays), he will get precious jewels of knowledge."

Hearing this, the author was very pleased, and immediately became confident and fearless, and knew the work was bound to be a success. Then turning to Shama, Sai Baba said:

If a man utters my name with love, I shall fulfill all his wishes and increase his devotion. If he sings earnestly of my life and my deeds, I shall surround him in front and back and on all sides. Those devotees who are attached to me heart and soul will naturally feel happiness when they hear these stories. Believe me, if anybody sings my leelas I will give him infinite joy and everlasting happiness. It is my special characteristic to free any person who surrenders completely to me, who worships me faithfully, who remembers me and meditates on me constantly. How can they who utter my name, worship me, think of my stories and my life, and always remember me, be conscious of worldly objects and sensations? I shall rescue my devotees from the jaws of death. If my stories are listened to, diseases will be healed. So, hear my stories with respect. Think and meditate on them and assimilate them. This is the way of happiness and contentment. The pride and egoism of my devotees will vanish and the mind of the listeners will find peace. If the devotee has wholehearted and complete faith, they will become one with the Supreme Consciousness. The simple remembrance of my name as 'Sai, Sai' will do away with sins of speech and hearing.

GOD ASSIGNS EACH PERSON DIFFERENT WORK

The Lord entrusts different works to different devotees. Some are given the work of building temples and *maths* (organizations), or *ghats* (cremation grounds) on rivers. Some are made to sing the glories of God. Some are sent on pilgrimages. But I was allotted the work of writing the *Satcharitra*. Being a jack-of-all-trades but master of none, I was quite unqualified for this job. Then why should I undertake such a difficult job? Who can describe the true life of Sai Baba? His grace alone can enable one to accomplish this difficult work. So, when I took the pen in hand, Sai Baba took away my egoism and wrote his stories himself. The credit of relating these stories goes to him and not to me. Though Brahmin by birth, I lacked the vision of *shruti* (revelation) and *smriti* (remembrance) and was not at all capable of writing the *Satcharitra*. But the grace of the Lord makes a dumb man talk and enables a lame man to cross a mountain. He alone knows how to get things done as he likes. Neither the flute nor the harmonium knows how the sounds are produced. This is the concern of the player. The oozing of the *chandrakant* (moonstone) jewel and the surging of the sea are not due to the jewel and the sea but to the rise of the moon.

BABA'S STORIES — BEACONS OF LIGHT

Lighthouses are constructed at various places in the sea to enable the boatmen to avoid rocks and dangers and make them sail safely. Sai Baba's stories serve a similar purpose in the ocean of worldly existence. They surpass nectar in sweetness and make our worldly path smooth and easy to traverse. Blessed are the stories of the saints. When they enter our hearts through the ears, body consciousness, egoism and the sense of duality vanish. When they are stored in the heart, doubts fly away, pride of the body leaves and wisdom is gained in abundance.

The description of Baba's pure life and the hearing of it with love will destroy the sins of the devotee and, therefore, this is a simple *sadhana* (spiritual practice) for attaining salvation. The sadhana for the Krita Age was *shamadama* (tranquility of mind and body), for the Treta Age, sacrifice, for Dwapara Age, worship, and for the current Kali Age, it is the singing of the name and glory of the Lord.

This sadhana is open to anyone of the four *varnas* (castes). The other sadhanas—yoga, *tyaga* (sacrifice), *dhyana* (meditation) and *dharana* (concentration)—are very difficult to practice. But singing and hearing the stories and the glory of the Lord is very easy. We have only to turn our attention towards them. The listening and singing of the stories will remove attachment to the senses and their objects, will make the devotees dispassionate, and ultimately lead them to self-realization. With this end in view, Sai Baba made me, or helped me, to write his stories, the *Satcharitra*.

The devotees may easily read and hear these stories of Sai Baba and while doing so meditate on him, his form, and attain devotion to guru and God, and detachment and self-realization. In the preparation and writing of this work, *Satcharitra*, it is Sai Baba's grace that accomplished everything, making use of me as a mere instrument.

Baba's Motherly Love

Everyone knows how a cow loves her infant calf. Her udder is always full and when the calf wants milk from her udder, out comes the milk in an unceasing flow. Similarly, a human mother knows the wants of her child and automatically feeds it at her breast. In cases of dressing and adorning the child, the mother takes particular care to see this is well done. The child cares nothing about this, but the mother's joy knows no bounds when she sees her child beautifully dressed and adorned. The love of the mother is unusual, extraordinary and unconditional, and has no parallel. Sadgurus feel this motherly love towards their disciples. Sai Baba had this same love towards me. I will give an instance of it.

In 1916, I retired from government service. The pension that was settled in my case was not sufficient to maintain my family decently. On Guru Purnima day of that year, I went to Shirdi with other devotees. There, of his own accord, Anna Chinchanikar prayed to Baba on my behalf, "Please look kindly on him. The pension he gets is quite insufficient. His family is growing. Give him some other appointment. Remove his anxiety and make him happy."

Baba replied, "He will get some other job, but now he should serve me and be happy. His plate will be ever full and never empty. He should turn all his attention towards me and avoid the company of atheists, unbelieving and wicked people. He should be meek and humble towards all and worship me with his heart and soul. If he does this, he will get eternal happiness."

Rohilla

The story of the Rohilla illustrates Sai Baba's all embracing love. Rohilla, tall, well built and strong as a bull, came to Shirdi wearing a long *kafni* (robe) and was enamored of Sai. Day and night he used to recite *Kalma*, verses from the Koran, in a loud and harsh tone and shout, "Allah Ho Akbar!" (God is Great!) Most of the people of Shirdi were working in the fields by day and were welcomed with Rohilla's harsh cries and shouts when they returned to their homes at night. They couldn't get any sleep and were very troubled and inconvenienced. They suffered this nuisance in silence for some days.

When they could stand it no longer, they approached Baba and requested that he check Rohilla and stop the nuisance. Baba did not pay attention to their complaint. On the contrary, he asked the villagers to mind their own business and not Rohilla. He told them that Rohilla had a very bad wife who tried to trouble both Rohilla and him. But hearing Rohilla's prayers, she dared not enter and so they were both at peace and happy.

In fact, Rohilla had no wife but what Baba meant by wife was *durbuddhi* (bad thoughts). As Baba liked prayers and cries to God better than anything else, he took the side of Rohilla and asked the villagers to wait and suffer the nuisance which would end in due course.

❧

THE GURU IS SEATED IN YOUR HEART

One day at noon after the *Aarati* (offering of a flame and devotional song to God), the devotees were returning to their lodgings when Baba gave the following beautiful advice:

Be wherever you like, do whatever you choose. But remember this well—that all you do is known to me. I am the inner ruler of all and am seated in your hearts. I envelop all creatures in the movable and immovable world. I am the controller, the wirepuller of the show of this universe. I am the Mother, the origin of all beings, the harmony of three *gunas* (qualities), the propeller of the senses, the creator, preserver and destroyer. Nothing will harm him who turns his attention towards me, but *Maya* (illusion) will lash or whip him who forgets me. All the insects, ants and the visible, movable and immovable world, are my body.

Hearing these beautiful and precious words, I at once decided to serve no man but my guru. But Baba's reply to Anna Chinchanikar's request (which was really mine) that I would get a job began to revolve in my mind and I began to think whether it would really happen. As future events show, Baba's words came true. I did get a government job that was of short duration. After that, I became free and devoted myself completely to the service of my guru Sai Baba.

Before concluding this chapter, I request the readers to let go of such obstacles as indolence, sleep, wandering of mind, and attachment to senses, and turn their whole and undivided attention to these stories of Sai Baba. Let their love be natural. Let them know the secret of devotion. Let them not exhaust themselves with other sadhanas. Let them stick to this one simple remedy—listening to Sai Baba's stories. This will destroy their ignorance and will secure liberation. A miser may stay at various places but he always thinks of his buried treasure. In this way, let Sai Baba be enthroned in the hearts of all.

Pranams to Sri Sai

Peace Be to All

CHAPTER FOUR

I n the last chapter, I described the circumstances which led me to write the *Sri Satcharitra*. Let me now describe the coming of Baba to Shirdi.

MISSION OF THE SAINTS

Lord Krishna says in the *Bhagavad Gita*, "Whenever there is a decay of *dharma* (righteousness) and a rise in unrighteousness, I manifest myself. For the protection of the virtuous, the destruction of the vicious and the establishment of righteousness, I manifest myself in age after age." This is the mission of the Lord and the sages and saints who are his representatives. They appear at appropriate times and work in their own way to set matters right by their words and action, including when:

Spiritual preceptors are not respected but are dishonored.

There is no respect for spiritual teachings.

People think themselves very learned.

People partake of forbidden foods and intoxicating drinks.

People indulge in malpractices under the guise of spirituality.

People of different sects fight among themselves.

Brahmins fail to do their spiritual practices.

Yogis neglect their meditation.

People think that wealth, children and wife are their sole concern and turn away from the path of liberation.

The sages and saints serve as beacons of light and show the true path for us to follow. In this way, many saints such as Nivritti, Jnanadev, Muktabai, Namdev, Gora, Gonayi, Ekanath, Tukaram, Narahari, Narsi Bhai, Sajan Kasai, Sawata, Ramdas and others appeared at various times to show the way to the people. And so, Sri Sai Baba came to Shirdi.

Shirdi—A Holy Gathering Place

The banks of the Godavari River in the Ahmednagar District are very fortunate; they have given birth and refuge to many a saint, prominent among them being Jnaneshwar. Shirdi also falls in the Ahmednagar District. After crossing the Godavari River at Kopargaon, one finds the way to Shirdi. When you go nine miles you come to Nimgaon, from there Shirdi is visible. Shirdi is as famous and well known as other holy places on the banks of Krishna River. As Damaji blessed Mangalvedha and caused it to flourish, as Ramdas blessed Sajjangad, and Sri Narasimha blessed Sarasvatiwadi, so did Sainath bless and make Shirdi flourish.

Baba's Personality

Rich or poor were the same to him. He did not know or care for honor or dishonor. He was the Lord of all beings.

It is on account of Baba that Shirdi grew in importance. Let us see what sort of a person Sai Baba was. He conquered *samsara* (worldly bondage), which is very difficult and hard to cross. Peace and mental calm was his ornament and he was the repository of all wisdom. He was the home for *Vaishnava* (Vishnu) devotees, he was the most generous, and was the quintessence of all essences. He had no love for perishable things and was always engrossed in self-realization, which was his sole concern. He felt no pleasure in the things of this world or in the world beyond. His heart was as clear as a mirror and his speech always rained nectar. Rich or poor were the same to him. He did not know or care for honor or dishonor. He was the Lord of all beings. He spoke freely and mixed with all people, saw the acting and dancing of Nautch girls and heard gajjal songs. Still, he swerved not an inch from *samadhi* (advanced state of consciousness, where the mind is merged in the Self). The name of *Allah* (God) was always on his lips. While the world was awake, he slept, and while the world slept he was vigilant. Inside, he was as calm as the deep sea. His *ashram* (hermitage) could not be determined, nor could his actions be definitely determined. Though he lived in one place, he knew all the transactions of the world. His *darbar* (inner circle) was imposing. Daily he told hundreds of stories, still he swerved not an inch from his silence. Whether he leaned against the wall in the *masjid* (mosque) or walked towards Lendi and the Chavadi, he was always abiding in the Self. Though a *siddha* (perfected one), he acted like a *sadhaka* (spiritual practitioner). He was modest, humble, egoless, and pleased all. Such was Sai Baba.

As Sai Baba's feet walked on the soil of Shirdi, it attained extraordinary importance. As Jnaneshwar elevated Alandi, and as Ekanath did to Paithan, so Sai Baba raised Shirdi. Blessed are the leaves of grass and stones of Shirdi for they could easily kiss the holy feet of Sai Baba. To devotees, Shirdi became another Pandharpur, Jagannath, Dwarka, Benaras, Rameshwar, Badrikedar, Nasik, Tryambakeshwar, Ujjain, Maha Kaleshwar or Mahabaleshwar Gokarn. Contact with Sai Baba in Shirdi was like our *Veda* and *Tantra*. It quieted our *samsara* (worldly bondage) and made self-realization easy.

The *darshan* (seeing) of Sri Sai was our yoga *sadhana* (spiritual practice), and talking with him removed our sins and karmas. Shampooing his legs was our bath in Triveni Prayag, and drinking the holy water from his feet destroyed our desires. To us, his commands were *Vedas*, and accepting his *udi* (sacred ash) and *prasad* (blessed food) was all purifying. He was our Sri Krishna and Sri Rama who gave solace. He was our *Parabrahma* (Absolute Reality). He was beyond the pair of opposites, never dejected nor elated. He was always engrossed in his Self as existence, consciousness and bliss. Shirdi was his center, but his field of action extended far and wide. Sai Baba's fame spread far and people from afar came to take his darshan and be blessed. By mere darshan, the minds of people, whether pure or impure, would at once become quiet. They received the same unparalleled joy that devotees had at Pandharpur by seeing Lord Vithal. This is not an exaggeration. Consider what a devotee says in this respect.

❧

STATEMENT OF AN OLD DEVOTEE

An old devotee named Goulibuva, who was about 95 years old, was a pilgrim of Pandharpur, the center of worship for Lord Vithoba. He stayed for eight months at Pandharpur and four months on the banks of the Ganges River. He had a donkey to carry his luggage and a disciple as his companion. Every year when he made his trip to Pandharpur he came to Shirdi to see Baba, whom he loved most. He used to stare at Baba and say, "This is Vithal incarnate, the merciful Lord of the poor and helpless." He attested that Sai Baba was real Vithoba.

❧

LORD VITHAL APPEARS

Sai Baba was very fond of remembering and singing God's name. He always uttered *Allah Malik* (God is One; God is the Sole Proprietor; God is Lord) and made others sing God's name continuously in his presence, day and night, for seven days. This is called *namasaptah*. Once he asked Das Ganu to do the namasaptah. Das Ganu replied that he would do it provided that Lord Vithal would appear at the end of the seventh day! Then Baba, placing his hand on his chest, assured him that Lord Vithal would appear but the devotee must be sincere and devoted. The Dankapuri of Takurnath, the Pandhari of Vithal, and the Dwarka of Krishna are all in Shirdi. One need not go far to see Dwarka. Will Vithal come here from some outside place? He is here. Only when the devotee is bursting with love and devotion will Vithal manifest himself in Shirdi.

After the saptah was over, Vithal did manifest himself in the following manner. Kakasaheb was sitting in meditation after his bath when he saw Lord Vithal in a vision. When he went for Baba's darshan at noon, Baba asked him directly, "Did Vithal come? Did you see him? He is a very absentee fellow, catch him firmly otherwise he will escape if you are a little inattentive." This happened in the morning and by noon there was another Lord Vithal darshan. A vendor had come from outside to sell pictures of Vithal. This picture exactly matched the image that appeared in Kakasaheb's vision. On seeing this, and remembering Baba's words, he was very surprised and delighted. He bought a picture of Vithal and placed it in his shrine for worship.

BABA LEADS MAN TO WORSHIP

How fond Baba was of Vithal worship is illustrated in Bhagwantrao Kshirsagar's story. Bhagwantrao's father was a devotee of Lord Vithoba and made annual trips to Pandharpur. He also had an image of Lord Vithoba that he worshipped at home. After his death, the son had stopped all forms of the family's worship to Vithoba. When Bhagwantrao came to Shirdi, Baba immediately said about him, "His father was my friend so I dragged the son here. Because he never offered *naivaidya* (offering of food) he starved Vithal and me. So I brought him here. I shall scold him now and have him start to do worship."

BABA GIVES MIRACLE BATH TO DAS GANU

The Hindus think that a bath in the Prayag, the confluence where the Ganga and Yamuna Rivers meet, is very meritorious. Thousands of pilgrims go there for a sacred bath. Once, Das Ganu thought that he should go to Prayag for a bath and came to get Baba's permission. Baba replied, "It is not necessary to go so far. Our Prayag is here, believe me." Then wonder of wonders! When Das Ganu placed his head on Baba's feet, out flowed streams of Ganga and Yamuna water from both of Baba's toes. Seeing this miracle,

Das Ganu was overwhelmed with feelings of love and adoration and was full of tears. He was so inspired he burst into a song in praise of Baba and his leelas.

⚜

BABA'S FIRST APPEARANCE IN SHIRDI — THE FOUR FLAMES AND HIS GURU'S SAMADHI

No one knew the parents, birth, or birthplace of Sai Baba. Many inquiries were made, many questions were put to Baba and others, but no satisfactory information has yet been obtained. Practically, we know nothing about these matters. Namdev and Kabir were not born like ordinary mortals. They were found as infants in mother-of-pearls. Namdev was found on the bank of Bhimrathi River, and Kabir on the bank of Bhagirathi River. Similar was the case with Sai Baba. For the sake of *bhaktas* (devotees), he first manifested himself as a young lad of sixteen under a neem tree in Shirdi. Even then he seemed to be full with the knowledge of Brahman. He had no desire for worldly objects even in dreams. He kicked out *Maya* (illusion) and *mukti* (liberation) was serving at his feet.

One old woman of Shirdi, the mother of Nanasaheb Chopdar, described him then. This young lad, fair, smart and very handsome, was first seen under the neem tree, seated in an *asana* (lotus posture). The people of the village were wonderstruck to see such a young lad practicing austerities, not minding heat or cold. By day he associated with none, by night he was afraid of no one. People wondered from where this young lad had turned up. His form and features were so beautiful that a mere look endeared him to all. He went to no one's door, always sat near the neem tree. Outwardly, he looked very young but his actions demonstrated he was truly a great soul. He was the embodiment of dispassion and a mystery to all.

One day, it so happened that the God Khandoba possessed the body of a devotee. People began to ask him, "*Deva* (God), please who is this blessed son's father and from where did he come?"

The God Khandoba asked them to bring a pickaxe and dig in a particular place. When it was dug, bricks were found underneath a flat stone. When the stone was removed, a corridor in which four *samayis* (lights) were burning led to a cellar where cow-mouth shaped structures, wooden boards, and necklaces were seen. Khandoba said, "This lad practiced penance here for 12 years." Then the people began to question the lad about this. He diverted them by telling them that it was his guru's holy spot and requested them to guard it well. The people then closed the corridor as before. As ashwattha and audumbar trees are held sacred, Baba regarded the neem tree at this holy spot as equally sacred and loved it most. Mhalsapati and other Shirdi devotees regard this site as the *samadhi sthana* (burial place) of Baba's guru and prostrate before it.

RESTING PLACES FOR DEVOTEES ARE BUILT IN SHIRDI

Hari Vinayak Sathe bought the surrounding space around the neem tree and erected a big building. This *wada* (pilgrim dwelling) initially was the only resting place for pilgrims who flocked to Shirdi. A platform was built around the neem tree and lofts with steps were constructed. Under the steps, there is a niche facing south and devotees sit on the platform facing north. It is believed whoever burns incense there on Thursday and Friday evenings will, by God's grace, be happy.

After some years, Dixit's wada was also constructed. Kakasaheb Dixit, who was the Solicitor of Mumbai, had gone to England and injured his leg in an accident there. The injury could not be healed by any means. Nanasaheb advised him to go see Baba. So he went to see Sai Baba in 1909 but requested him to cure the lameness of his mind rather than that of his leg. He was so happy from Baba's darshan that he decided to reside in Shirdi. So he built a wada for himself and other devotees. The foundation of this building was laid on December 10, 1910. On this day, two other important events took place. Dadasaheb Khaparde was given permission to return home, and the night Aarati in the Chavadi commenced. The wada was complete and became inhabited on Ramanavami Day (Lord Rama's birthday) in 1911, with due rites and formalities.

Another wada, a palatial building, was built by the famous millionaire, Mr. Buti of Nagpur. A lot of money was spent on this building but it was well utilized, as Sai Baba's body is now resting there. It is now called the Samadhi Mandir. The site of this Mandir formerly had a garden which was watered and looked after by Baba. And so, three wadas were built. Of these, Sathe's wada was most useful to all in the early days.

Pranams to Sri Sai

Peace Be to All

CHAPTER FIVE

BABA'S RETURN TO SHIRDI WITH
CHAND PATIL'S WEDDING PARTY

I shall now describe how Sai Baba returned to Shirdi after a temporary disappearance. In a village called Dhoop in the Aurangabad District, there lived a well-to-do Muslim gentleman named Chand Patil. While making a trip to Aurangabad he lost his mare. For two long months he made a diligent search but there was no trace of his lost mare. Disappointed, he returned from Aurangabad with the saddle on his back.

He came upon a mango tree under which sat what appeared to him to be a very odd fellow. This fellow had a scarf on his head, wore *kafni* (long robe) and had a *satka* (short stick) under his arm and was preparing to smoke a *chillum* (pipe). On seeing Chand Patil pass by, this fellow called out and asked him to have a smoke and rest a little. The fellow asked him about the saddle. Chand Patil replied that it was for his mare which was lost some time ago. The unusual fellow asked him to make a search in the gully close by.

Chand Patil went and, wonder of wonders, found the mare! He realized that this *fakir* (ascetic) was not an ordinary man, but an *avalia* (a great saint). He returned to the fakir with the mare. The chillum was ready but two things were missing—fire to light the pipe and water to wet the piece of cloth through which smoke is drawn up. The fakir took his prong and thrust it forcibly into the ground and out came a live burning coal which he put in the pipe. Then he dashed his stick on the ground and water began to ooze from the earth. The cloth was wetted with that water, then wrung out and wrapped around the pipe. Everything was complete. The fakir smoked the chillum and then gave it to Chand Patil. On seeing all this, Chand Patil was wonderstruck. He then invited the fakir to come to his home and accept his hospitality.

Next day, the fakir went to Patil's house and stayed there for some time. Patil was the village officer of Dhoop. His nephew was to be married and the bride was from Shirdi. So Patil made preparations to start for Shirdi for the marriage. The fakir also accompanied the marriage party. The marriage ceremony went without a hitch. Then the party returned to Dhoop, except for the fakir, who alone stayed in Shirdi and remained there forever.

HOW BABA RECEIVES THE NAME SAI

When the marriage party came to Shirdi, it stopped at the foot of a banyan tree in Mhalsapati's field, near Khandoba's temple. The carts were loosened in the open courtyard of the temple and the members of the party descended one by one, including the fakir. Mhalsapati saw the young fakir getting down and hailed him, "*Ya Sai!*" (Welcome holy one!) Others also addressed him as Sai and from that day onwards he became known as *Sai Baba* (holy father).

CONTACT WITH OTHER SAINTS

Sai Baba began to stay in a deserted *masjid* (mosque). A saint named Devidas had been living in Shirdi many years before Baba came there. Baba liked his company. Sometimes he stayed with him in the Maruti temple or in the Chavadi. Sometimes Baba lived alone. Then another saint named Jankidas came by. Baba spent most of his time talking with him or Jankidas came to Baba's residence. Also, a householder saint, Gangagir, always frequented Shirdi. When he first saw Baba carrying pitchers of water to water the garden, he was amazed and said, "Blessed is Shirdi that it got this precious jewel. This man is carrying water today but he is not an ordinary fellow. As this land of Shirdi was lucky and meritorious, it has secured this jewel."

One famous saint by the name Anandnath, a disciple of Akkalkot Maharaj, came to Shirdi with some people from Shirdi. When he saw Sai Baba, he said out loud, "This is a precious diamond in reality. Though he looks like an ordinary man; he is not a *gar* (ordinary stone) but a diamond. You will realize this in the near future." Saying this, he returned to Yeola. This was said while Baba was a youngster.

BABA GROWS A GARDEN

In his young days, Sai Baba grew hair on his head and never had his head shaved. He dressed like an athlete. When he went to Rahata, three miles from Shirdi, he brought back with him small plants of marigold, jai and jui. After cleaning them, he planted and watered the plants. A devotee by the name Vaman Tatya supplied him with two earthen pitchers daily. With these, Baba used to water the plants. He drew water from the well and carried the pitchers on his shoulders. In the evening, the pitchers were kept at the foot of the neem tree. As soon as they were placed there they broke, as they were made of raw earth and not baked. Next day, Tatya supplied two fresh pitchers. This went on for three years. Through Baba's labor a flower garden grew. On this site now stands Baba's Samadhi Mandir, which is frequented and used by so many devotees.

PADUKAS UNDER THE NEEM TREE

A devotee of Akkalkot Maharaj by the name Bhai Alibagkar worshipped the photo of Akkalkot Maharaj. He thought of going to the town of Akkalkot to take darshan of the *padukas* (sandals) of the Maharaj and offer his worship there. But before he left, he had a vision in his dream. Akkalkot Maharaj appeared in the vision and said to him, "Now Shirdi is my resting place, go there and offer your worship." So Bhai changed his plan and came to Shirdi. He stayed for six months and worshipped Baba and was happy. In 1912, as a reminder of this vision experience, he prepared padukas and installed them under the neem tree on the auspicious day of Shravan with due ceremonies and formalities conducted by Dada Kelkar and Upasani.

⚜

COMPLETE VERSION OF PADUKAS UNDER THE NEEM TREE

Before the tree was bitter, but Baba's presence made it sweet, and transformed it into a kalpa vriksha (wish-fulfilling tree).

B.V. Deo, a great devotee of Sai Baba, made inquiries about the padukas and published a full version of the paduka story. It ran as follows:

In 1912, Dr. Ramarao Kothare of Mumbai came to Shirdi for Baba's darshan. The doctor's compounder and his friend, Bhai Alibagkar, accompanied him. The compounder and Bhai became intimate with Sagun Naik and G.K. Dixit. They all decided there should be a memorial of Sai Baba coming to Shirdi and sitting under the holy neem tree. They thought of making padukas of some rough stones and installing them under the neem tree. Then Bhai's friend suggested letting Dr. Ramarao Kothare know, as he would create a nice design for the padukas. As all liked the proposal, Dr. Kothare was informed. Dr. Kothare came to Shirdi and drew a design for the padukas. He went to Upasani Maharaj, who lived at Khandoba's temple, and showed him the plan. Upasani Maharaj made many improvements, drew lotuses, flowers, a conch, disc and mace and suggested that the following *sloka* (verse) regarding the neem tree's greatness and Baba's yogic powers be inscribed.

The verse went as follows:

Sada Nimbarvrikshasya Mooladhivasat Dhasravinam Tiktampi-apriyam Tam Tarum Kalpavrikshadhikam Sadhayantam Namameeshvaram Sadgurum Sai Natham.

Translation:

I bow to Lord Sai Nath, who always stays at the foot of the neem tree and makes it ooze *amruta* (healing nectar). Before the tree was bitter, but Baba's presence made it sweet, and transformed it into a *kalpa vriksha* (wish-fulfilling tree).

Upasani's suggestions were accepted and carried out. The padukas were made in Mumbai and sent to Shirdi. Baba said that they should be installed on *Shravan Purnima* (full moon in August). On that day at 11 a.m., G.K. Dixit brought them on his head from Khandoba's temple to the Dwarkamai in a procession. Baba touched the padukas, saying these are the feet of the Lord, and asked the people to install them under the neem tree.

A day before, Pastha Shet, a Parsi devotee of Mumbai, sent Rs.25 by money order. Baba gave it for the installation of the padukas. The total expense of installation came to Rs.100, out of which Rs.75 was collected through donations. For the first five years, G.K. Dixit worshipped the padukas daily and then this was done by Laxman Jakhadi. In the first five years, Dr. Kothare sent Rs.2 per month for lighting and also sent money for the railing around the padukas. The roofing and the expense of bringing the railing from the station to Shirdi was paid by Sagun Meru Naik. Eventually, Jakhadi did the worship and Sagun Naik offered the *naivaidya* (blessed food) and lit the evening lamps.

In 1912, Bhai Krishnaji stopped in Shirdi for the installation of the padukas on his way to the village of Akkalkot. He was a devotee of Akkalkot Maharaj and wanted to go to Akkalkot after taking Baba's darshan. He asked Baba's permission for this. Baba said, "Oh, what is there in Akkalkot? Why do you go there? The Maharaj of that place is here, myself." Hearing this, Bhai did not go to Akkalkot. After the installation of the padukas, he came to Shirdi off and on.

B.V. Deo concluded that Hemadpant did not know these details from the article. Had he known them, he would have depicted them in the Satcharitra.

BABA WRESTLES WITH A DEVOTEE NAMED TAMBOLI

To return to the stories of Baba. There was a wrestler in Shirdi named Tamboli. He and Baba did not agree on certain things and fought in a wrestling bout. In this, Baba was defeated. From then onwards, Baba changed his dress and mode of living. He put on a *kafni* (robe), wore a waistband and covered his head with a piece of cloth. He took a piece of sack cloth for his seat, a sack cloth for his bed and was content with wearing torn rags. He always said, "Poverty is better than kingship, far better than lordship. The Lord is always the brother of the poor."

Gangagir was also very fond of wrestling. Once when he was wrestling, a feeling of dispassion suddenly came over him. He heard the voice of an adept saying that he should wear out his body playing with God. So he too gave up *samsara* (worldly bondage) and turned to God realization. He established a math on the banks of the river near Puntambe and lived there with disciples.

BABA LIVED SIMPLY

Sai Baba did not mix with the people. He only gave answers when asked. By day, he always sat under the neem tree. Sometimes he sat under the shade of a babul tree near the stream at the outskirts of the village. In the afternoon, he used to walk at random and at times go to Nimgaon. There he frequented the house of Balasaheb Dengale. Baba loved Balasaheb.

Balasaheb's younger brother, Nanasaheb, had no son though he had married a second wife. Balasaheb sent Nanasaheb to take darshan of Sai Baba. After some time, through Baba's grace, Nanasaheb had a son. From that time onwards, people began to come in numbers to see Sai Baba and his fame began to spread. From that time, Nanasaheb, Keshav Chidamber and many others began coming to Shirdi.

Pranams to Sri Sai

Peace Be to All

CHAPTER SIX

Ramanavami Festival and the masjid repairs: the author makes some preliminary remarks about the *sadguru* (true guru).

THE POWER OF THE GURU'S TOUCH &
OUR SURRENDER TO HIM

"There will never be any shortage or scarcity of food and clothes in my devotee's home. It is my special characteristic that I always look to and provide for the welfare of those devotees who worship me wholeheartedly with their minds ever fixed on me."

Where the sadguru is helmsman, he is sure to carry us safely and easily beyond the ocean of worldly existence. The word sadguru brings to mind Sai Baba. He appears to me, as if standing before me and applying *udi* (sacred ash) to my forehead and placing his blessing on my head. Joy fills my heart and love overflows through my eyes. Wonderful is the power of the touch of the guru's hand. The subtle body consisting of thoughts and desires that cannot be burned by world-dissolving fire can be dissolved by the mere touch of the guru's hand.

Karmas from many past births are purified and washed away. Even those who feel annoyed when they hear religious and Godly talk, attain calmness. Seeing Sai Baba's handsome form chokes our throat with joy, makes the eyes overflow with tears, and overwhelms the heart with emotion. It awakens 'I am He' (oneness with the Divine) in us and manifests the joy of self-realization. It dissolves the distinction of 'I and you' and makes us one with the supreme Reality.

When I read scriptures, I am reminded of my sadguru at every step. Sai Baba assumes the form of Rama or Krishna and makes me listen. When I sit to listen to *Bhagavad Gita*, Sai becomes Krishna from head to toe and sings the *Bhagavad Gita* or *Uddhava Gita* for the welfare of devotees. When I start to chitchat, I immediately think of Sai's stories which enable me to give suitable illustrations. When I start to write anything, I cannot compose even a few words or sentences. But when Baba makes me write, I go on writing and writing to no end. When the disciple's egoism pops up, he presses it down with his hand. He gives him his own power, makes him gain his goal, and satisfies and blesses him. If anyone bows before Sai and surrenders heart and soul to him, then spontaneously all the chief aims of life—*dharma* (righteousness), *artha* (wealth), *kama* (desire) and *moksha* (liberation)—are easily attained. Each of the four paths to God—*karma* (action), *jnana* (knowledge), *yoga* and *bhakti* (devotion)—lead us to God. Of these, the path of bhakti is thorny and full of pits and ditches, and difficult to traverse. If you rely on your sadguru you will avoid the ditches and thorns and walk straight to the destination. So says Sai Baba.

After philosophizing about the self-existent Brahman, His power (Maya) to create this world, and the world He created and how all these three are ultimately one and the same, the author quotes Baba's promise guaranteeing the welfare of *bhaktas* (devotees):

There will never be any shortage or scarcity of food and clothes in my devotee's home. It is my special characteristic that I always look to and provide for the welfare of those devotees who worship me wholeheartedly with their minds ever fixed on me. Lord Krishna has also said the same in the *Gita*. So, strive not for food and clothes. If you want anything, beg the Lord. Leave aside worldly honors and try to win the Lord's grace and blessings and be honored in his Court. Do not be deluded by worldly honor. The form of the deity should be firmly fixed in your mind. Let the senses and mind be always devoted to the worship of the Lord. Let there be no attraction for any other thing. Fix the mind in remembering me always so that it does not wander to the body, wealth and home. Then it will be calm, peaceful and carefree. This is the sign of the mind well engaged in good company. If the mind is wandering, it is not well merged.

After quoting these words, the author goes on to relate the story of the Ramanavami Festival in Shirdi. As Ramanavami is the greatest festival celebrated at Shirdi, another fuller account of it was later published and a summary of both accounts is attempted here.

❦

BABA INITIATES THE FAIR IN SHIRDI

Gopalrao Gund was the Circle Inspector at Kopergaon and a great devotee of Baba. He had three wives but no children. Through Baba's blessings, a son was born to him, and in his joy from this an idea came to celebrate an *urus* (fair). In 1897, he placed it for consideration before Tatya Patil, Dada Patil and Shama. They all approved of the idea and got Baba's permission and blessings for it. Then application was made for the Collector's sanction to celebrate the fair but permission was refused. But as Sai Baba had blessed it, they tried again, and ultimately succeeded in getting the Collector's permission. After consulting with Baba, they fixed the fair to be celebrated on *Ramanavami Day* (Lord Rama's birthday). But it seems that Baba had a bigger end in mind—the unification of two festivals, Muslim and Hindu, and ultimately the unification of these two communities. As future events show, this was achieved.

Though the permission was obtained, other difficulties cropped up. Water was scarce in Shirdi. There were two wells in the village. The one in use dried up, and the water from the second well was brackish. Baba threw flowers into the brackish water and it turned sweet. But the water from this well was insufficient, so Tatya arranged to carry water from another well a considerable distance away. Then temporary shops had to be constructed and wrestling bouts arranged.

Damu Anna Kasar of Ahmednagar, who had also been unhappy in the matter of progeny though he had married two wives, was blessed by Sai Baba with sons as well. His friend, Mr. Gund, asked him to supply a flag for the procession. Mr. Gund also got Nanasaheb to supply an embroidered flag. Both these flags were taken in a procession through the village and finally fixed at the two corners of the masjid, which Baba called the "Dwarkamai." This is being done even now.

⚜

THE SANDAL PROCESSION—HINDUS & MUSLIMS SIDE BY SIDE

In addition to the Hindu ceremonies at the fair, another procession was begun at this time. The idea of a *sandalpaste* (paste made from grinding pieces of sandalwood into a powder; this paste is considered to be very pure and able to pull cosmic energy, and is used in worship of the Divine) procession came from Amir Dalal, a Muslim *bhakta* (devotee). The procession was held in honor of great Muslim saints. Sandalwood paste and burning incense were put on *thalis* (flat plates) and carried in the front of the procession. A music band accompanied the procession through the village then returned to the masjid. The contents of the plates were thrown on the *nimbar* (niche) and the walls of the masjid. This work was managed by Mr. Dalal for the first three years, and then later by his wife. So on that day, two processions went side by side with the flags held by the Hindus and the sandalpaste carried by the Muslims. These processions are still going on.

⚜

PREPARING FOR THE FAIR

This day was very dear and sacred to the devotees of Sai Baba. Most of them turned out on the occasion and took a leading part in the management of the fair. Tatya looked to all outward affairs while the internal management was left entirely to Radhakrishna Mai, a female devotee of Baba. Her residence was full of guests whose needs she had to look after and she also made all arrangements for the fair. She willingly washed out, cleaned, and whitewashed the entire masjid. Its walls and floor were blackened and full of soot from Baba's ever-burning *dhuni* (sacred fire). To do that, she worked every other night while Baba slept in the Chavadi. She had to take everything out, including the dhuni, and after thoroughly cleaning and whitewashing everything, replaced everything as it was before. Feeding the poor, which was so dear to Baba, was also an important part of the fair. Cooking on a grand scale and preparing various sweet dishes was done at Radhakrishna Mai's house with some wealthy devotees taking a lead in that effort.

THE EVOLUTION OF THE FAIR INTO THE RAMANAVAMI FESTIVAL

The celebrations went on in this way and the fair gradually increased in importance until 1912, when a change took place. That year, a devotee, Krishnarao Bhishma, came for the fair with Dadasaheb Khaparde and was staying at the Dixit wada. While lying on the verandah, when Bhisma saw Kaka Mahajani going to the masjid with puja materials, a thought arose in his mind that there is something providential in the fact that this fair is celebrated in Shirdi on Ramanavami Day. Since this day is very dear to Hindus, why not begin the Ramanavami Festival, which celebrates the birth of Sri Rama, on this day along with the fair? Kaka Mahajani liked the idea and so it was arranged to get Baba's permission. The main difficulty was how to secure a *haridas* (kirtan leader) who would perform *kirtan*, singing the glories of the Lord. But Bhishma solved the difficulty. He said that his *Rama Akhyan* (composition on Rama's birth) was ready, and he would do the kirtan, while Mahajani would play the harmonium. It was also arranged to have *sunthavada* (sugared ginger) as *prasad* (blessed food) prepared by Radhakrishna Mai. Then they immediately left for the masjid to get Baba's permission.

Baba, who knew all things including what had transpired, asked Mahajani what was going on in the wada. Being somewhat disturbed, Mahajani could not catch the meaning of the question and remained silent. Then Baba asked Bhishma, who explained the idea for celebrating the Ramanavami Festival and asked for Baba's permission. Baba gave it gladly. Everyone rejoiced and began making preparations for the Ramanavami Festival.

The next day the masjid was decorated with flags. A cradle was supplied by Radhakrishna Mai and placed in front of Baba's seat, then the proceedings started. Bhishma stood up for kirtan and Mahajani began playing the harmonium. Sai Baba called Mahajani. He hesitated, having a doubt whether Baba would allow the festival to go on. But when he went, Baba asked him what was going on and why the cradle was placed there. He answered that the Ramanavami Festival had commenced and the cradle was put there for that purpose. Baba took a garland from the *nimbar* (niche) and placed it around Mahajani's neck and sent another garland for Bhishma. Then they commenced the kirtan.

When it came to a close, sounds of "Victory to Rama" went up, and *kum kum* (red powder) was thrown all round, amidst band and music. Everybody was overjoyed when suddenly roaring was heard. The red powder, which had been liberally thrown all around, went into Baba's eyes. Baba got wild and began to scold and abuse loudly. People were frightened by this scene and left quickly. Those intimate devotees who knew Baba well took this scolding and outpouring as blessings in disguise. They thought that when Rama was born it was right for Baba to get wild and enraged in order to kill Ravana and his demons, in the form of egoism and wicked thoughts. Besides, they knew that whenever a new thing was undertaken in Shirdi it was usual for Baba to get wild and angry, so they kept quiet.

As Radhakrishna Mai was afraid and thought that Baba might break the cradle, she asked Mahajani to get the cradle back. But when he went to loosen and unfasten the cradle, Baba asked him not to remove it. After some time, Baba became calm and that day's program, including *mahapuja* (the great worship) and Aarati, was finished. Later on, Mahajani asked Baba for permission to remove the cradle. Baba refused, saying that the festival was not yet finished.

The next day, another kirtan and the Gopal Kala ceremony were performed. In the Gopal Kala ceremony, an earthen pot containing parched rice mixed with curds is hung and broken after the kirtan. The contents are distributed to all by Lord Krishna and his cowherd friends. After this, Baba allowed the cradle to be removed. While the Ramanavami Festival was going on, the procession of the two flags by day and of the sandalpaste by night went off with the usual pomp and show. From this time onwards, the '*Urus* (fair) of Baba' was transformed into the Ramanavami Festival.

From the following year, the events in the Ramanavami program began to increase. Radhakrishna Mai started a *namasaptah* (singing the glory of God's name continuously for seven days and nights). For this, all devotees took turns. She also joined in, sometimes early in the morning. But the difficulty of getting a *haridas* (kirtan leader) was felt again. But five or six days before the festival, Mahajani accidentally ran across Balabuva Mali, who was known as modern Tukaram, and got him to do the kirtan that year. In 1914, Balabuva Satarkar was unable to act as a haridas due to the plague in his own town, so he came to Shirdi. Kakasaheb received Baba's permission and Satarkar sang kirtan and was compensated for his labor. After 1914, Baba solved the difficulty of getting a new haridas every year by permanently entrusting the function to Das Ganu Maharaj. From then on, he performed kirtan for the festivals admirably.

Since it first began in 1912, the festival grew gradually each year. During festival time, Shirdi looked like a beehive full of men. Shops began to increase. Celebrated wrestlers took part in wrestling bouts. Feeding of the poor was done on a grand scale. The hard work and sincere efforts of Radhakrishna Mai turned Shirdi into a *sansthan* (state).

Many things were presented to Baba: a beautiful horse, palanquin, chariot, many silver items, pots, buckets, pictures, mirrors and elephants for the procession. Although these things increased enormously, Baba ignored all of it and maintained his simplicity as before.

It is to be noted that both the Hindus and Muslims worked in unison in both processions. During the entire festival history there has been no quarrel between them. Early on, there were about 5,000 to 7,000 attendees, but that figure went up to 75,000 in some years. There was never any outbreak of violence, nor any epidemics.

THE COMMUNITY REPAIRS THE MASJID

Another important idea inspired Gopal Gund, which was to get the masjid in order. In order to carry out the repairs, he collected and prepared the stones. Nanasaheb and Kakasaheb completed the pavement work. First, Baba was unwilling to allow them to do these works, but with the intervention of Mhalsapati, permission was given. The pavement was completed in one night. In the masjid, Baba took a small *gadi* (cushion) for his seat, discarding the usual piece of sackcloth he had used until then. In 1911, the *sabha mandap* (courtyard) was also put in order with great labor and effort. The open space in front of the masjid was very small and inconvenient. Kakasaheb wanted to extend it and put a roof on it. At great expense, he got iron posts, pillars and trusses and started the work. At night, all the devotees worked hard and fixed the posts.

But when Baba returned from the Chavadi next morning, he uprooted them all and threw them out. Once it so happened that Baba had gotten very excited, grabbed a pole and began to shake and uproot it, and with the other hand caught Tatya by the neck. He grabbed Tatya's head cloth, struck a match, set it on fire and threw it in a pit! At that time, Baba's eyes flashed like burning coals. None dared to look at him. Everyone was terribly frightened. Baba took out a rupee from his pocket and threw it there, as if it were an offering on an auspicious occasion. Tatya was also very frightened. None knew what was going to happen to Tatya and none dared interfere.

Bhagoji Shinde, Baba's devotee with leprosy, made a bold advance but was pushed out by Baba. Madhavrao was also treated the same way and pelted with brick pieces. All those who tried to intercede were similarly dealt with. After some time, Baba's anger cooled down. He sent for a shopkeeper and got an embroidered headcloth from him. Baba then tied it on Tatya's head as if he were being given a special honor. Everyone was wonderstruck to see Baba's strange behavior. They were at a loss to know what had enraged Baba so suddenly, what led him to attack Tatya, and why his anger suddenly cooled down. Baba was sometimes very calm and quiet and talked sweetly with love, but then, with or without any cause, he became enraged. Many such incidents may be related; I do not know which to choose and which to omit. Therefore, I mention them as they occur to me.

Pranams to Sri Sai

Peace Be to All

CHAPTER SEVEN

BABA'S ACTIONS WERE A MYSTERY

Such a person was Sai Baba, who saw no difference between castes or human beings.

B aba knew all yogic practices. He was well versed in the six processes including *Dhauti Yoga* (removing and cleaning the intestines), *Kandhana Yoga* (separating his limbs and re-joining them), and *samadhi* (advanced state of consciousness). If you think he was a Hindu, he looked like a Muslim. If you think him to be a Muslim, he looked like a pious Hindu. No one knew whether he was a Hindu or a Muslim. He celebrated the Hindu festival of Ramanavami with all due formalities, and at the same time permitted the sandal procession of the Muslims. He encouraged wrestling bouts in this festival and gave good prizes to winners. When the *Gokul Ashtami* (Hindu festival) came, he had the Gopal Kala ceremony duly performed, and on *Id*, the Muslim festival, he allowed Muslims to say their *namaj* (prayers) in his masjid.

Once during the Moharum festival, some Muslims proposed to construct a *tabut* (Muslim religious symbol) in the masjid, keep it there for some days and afterwards take it in procession through the village. Baba allowed the tabut to stay for four days, and on the fifth day removed it from the masjid without the least compunction.

If we say that he was a Muslim, his ears were pierced according to Hindu fashion. If you think that he was a Hindu, he advocated the practice of circumcision, though according to Nanasaheb, who observed him closely, he was not circumcised. If you call him Hindu, he lived in a masjid. If Muslim, he always had a *dhuni* (sacred fire) and things which are contrary to the Muslim religion, such as grinding on the hand mill, blowing of the conch, ringing of bells, offering to the fire, bhajans (devotion singing), giving of food, and worshipping Baba's feet with water. If you think he was a Muslim, the best of *Brahmins* (orthodox Hindus) and *Agnihotris* (Hindu fire sect), leaving aside their orthodox ways, fell prostrate at his feet. Those who went to make inquiries about his nationality were rendered speechless and were captivated by his darshan. No one could decide definitively whether Sai Baba was a Hindu or a Muslim (Mhalsapati, who always slept with Baba in the masjid and Chavadi, said that Baba told him that he was a Brahmin from Pathari and was handed over to a fakir in his infancy; this was shared when men from Pathari had come, and Baba was inquiring about some men from that place). This is no wonder; for he who completely surrenders himself to the Lord by getting rid of egoism and body consciousness becomes one with Him, and has nothing to do with questions of caste or nationality. Such a person was Sai Baba, who saw no difference between castes or human beings. He took meat and fish with *fakirs* (ascetics) but did not grumble when dogs touched the dishes with their mouths.

Such a unique and wonderful incarnation was Sai Baba. On account of the merits in my past birth, I had the good fortune to sit at his feet and enjoy his blessed company. The joy and delight I derived was incomparable. In fact, Sai Baba was pure consciousness and *ananda* (bliss). I cannot sufficiently describe him, his greatness or uniqueness. He was established in his own Self. Many *sanyasis* (renunciates), *sadhakas* (spiritual practitioners) and all sorts of men aspiring for liberation came to Baba. He walked, talked and laughed with them and always uttered, "Allah Malik" (God is One/God is the Sole Proprietor). He never liked discussion or arguments. He was always calm and controlled, though irritable at times, always preaching Vedanta. Until the end, nobody knew who Baba was. Both princes and poor people were treated alike by him. He knew the innermost secrets of all, and when he gave expression to them, all were surprised. Although he was the repository of all knowledge, he feigned ignorance. He disliked honor. Such were the characteristics of Baba. Though he had a human body, his deeds testified to his Godhood. Everyone in Shirdi considered him to be the Lord incarnated.

BABA'S MIRACLES

Fool that I am, I cannot describe Baba's miracles. He had almost all the temples in Shirdi repaired. Through Tatya, the temples of Shani, Ganapati, Shankar Parvati, the village deity, and Maruti were put in order. Baba's charity was remarkable. The money he used to collect as *dakshina* (offerings) was freely distributed, Rs.20 to some, Rs.15 or 50 to others, everyday. The recipients received this as charity and Baba wished that it be used properly.

People immensely benefited by having Baba's darshan. Some became healthy and hearty. Wicked people were turned into good ones. Leprosy was cured in some cases. Many had their desires fulfilled, some blind men had their sight restored without any drops or medicine being put in their eyes, and some who were lame were able to walk. No one could see the limit to Baba's greatness. His fame spread far and wide and pilgrims from all directions flocked to Shirdi. Baba always sat near the *dhuni* (sacred fire), and in meditation, sometimes going without a bath. He used to tie a white turban on his head and wear a clean *dhotar* (cloth) round his waist, and a shirt on his body. This was his dress in the beginning.

He started practicing medicine in the village, examining patients and giving medicines. He was always successful and so became famous as a doctor. A curious case is narrated here. One devotee's eyes were quite red and swollen. No doctor was available in Shirdi so some devotees took him to Baba. Other doctors would use ointments, collyrium, cow's milk and camphorated drugs in such cases, but Baba's remedy was quite unique. He pounded some nuts and cardamom together and made two balls, put one on each eye of the patient and wrapped a bandage around the eyes. Next day, the bandage was removed and water was poured in a stream over the eyes. The inflammation subsided and the pupils became white and clear. Though the eyes are very delicate, the remedy caused no irritation but instead removed the disease of the eyes. Many such cases were cured and this is only one instance.

BABA'S YOGA PRACTICES

Baba knew all the processes and practices of yoga. Two of them are described here:

Dhauti Yoga: Every third day, Baba walked a considerable distance from the masjid to the well near the banyan tree, washed his mouth and had a bath. On one occasion, he was seen to vomit out his intestines, clean them inside and outside and place them on a tree for drying. There are people in Shirdi who actually saw this and have testified to this fact. Ordinary dhauti is done with a moistened piece of linen, three inches wide and 22-½ inches long. This piece of cloth is gulped down the throat and allowed to remain in the stomach for about half an hour and then taken out. But Baba's dhauti was quite unique and extraordinary.

Kandhana Yoga: In this practice, Baba removed the limbs from his body and left them at different places in the masjid. Once, a gentleman went to the masjid and saw Baba's limbs lying around in separate places. He was terrified. His first thought was to run to the village officers to inform them Baba had been murdered and hacked to pieces. But he feared he would be held responsible as he was the first informant and knew something of the affair. So he kept silent. But next day when he went to the masjid, he was very much surprised to see Baba healthy, hearty and as sound as before. He thought that what he saw the previous day was only a dream.

Baba had practiced yoga since his infancy and nobody knew or guessed the proficiency he attained. He charged no fees for his cures and became renowned and famous by virtue of his merits.

He restored health to many a poor and suffering person. This famous doctor of doctors cared not for his own interests, but always worked for the good and welfare of others, though he suffered unbearable and terrible pain many a time in the process. One such instance I give below, which will show the all pervasive and most merciful character of Sai Baba.

BABA SAVES CHILD THROUGH HIS DHUNI

In the year 1910, Baba was sitting warming himself near his dhuni on the Diwali holiday. He was pushing firewood into the dhuni, which was burning brightly. A little later, instead of pushing logs, Baba pushed his arm into the dhuni. His arm was burned immediately. Madhava and Shama watched this happen. Immediately they ran to Baba and Madhava clasped Baba from behind by his waist and pulled him backwards forcibly, then asked, "Deva, why have you done this?"

Then Baba came to his senses and replied, "The wife of a blacksmith at a distant place was working the bellows of a furnace when her husband called her. Forgetting that her child was on her waist, she got up hastily and the child slipped into the furnace. I immediately thrust my hand into the furnace and saved the child. I do not mind my arm being burned. I am glad that the life of the child is saved."

BABA REFUSES DOCTOR TREATMENT FOR HIS BURN

On hearing the news of Baba's arm being burned, Nanasaheb rushed to Shirdi accompanied by the famous Dr. Parmanand of Mumbai with his medical kit consisting of ointments, lint and bandages. He requested Baba to allow Dr. Parmanand to examine the arm and dress the burn wound. This was refused. Ever after, the burned arm was then dressed by the leper devotee, Bhagoji Shinde. His treatment consisted of massaging the burned part of Baba's arm with ghee and then placing a leaf over it and wrapping it tightly with bandages. Nanasaheb asked Baba many a time to unfasten the bandages and get the wound examined, dressed, and treated by Dr. Parmanand, with the intent for it to heal quickly. Dr. Parmanand himself made similar requests but

Baba put it off saying that Allah was his doctor and did not allow his arm to be examined.

Although Dr. Paramanand's medicines did not see the light of day in Shirdi, he had the good fortune of having Baba's darshan. Only Bhagoji was allowed to treat the arm daily. After some days, the arm healed and everyone was happy. Still, we do not know whether any trace of pain was left or not. Every morning, Bhagoji went through his program of loosening the bandages, massaging the arm with ghee and tightly bandaging it again. This went on till Baba's *samadhi* (death). Baba, a perfect *siddha* (perfected one) as he was, did not really want this treatment, but out of love to his devotee allowed Bhagoji's service to go on uninterrupted. When Baba started for Lendi, Bhagoji held an umbrella over him and accompanied him. Every morning, when Baba sat near the post close to the dhuni, Bhagoji was present and started his service. Bhagoji was a sinner in his past birth. He was suffering from leprosy, his fingers had shrunk, his body was full of pus and smelling badly. Though outwardly he seemed so unfortunate, he was really very lucky and happy, for he was the premier servant of Baba and had the benefit of his company.

BABA SUFFERS FOR HIS DEVOTEES

I shall now relate another instance of Baba's wonderful *leela* (divine play). Mrs. Khaparde was staying at Shirdi with her young son for some days. One day her son got a high fever, which then developed into bubonic plague. The mother was very frightened and uneasy. She thought of leaving for her village and went to Baba in the evening to ask him permission while he was making his evening rounds near the wada (now the Samadhi Mandir). She informed him in a trembling tone that her dear young son was down with plague. Baba spoke kindly and softly to her, saying that the sky is beset with clouds but they will dissolve and everything will be smooth and clear. So saying, he lifted his *kafni* (robe) up to the waist and showed everyone there four fully developed boils, as big as eggs, and added, "See, how I have to suffer for my devotees. Their difficulties are mine." Seeing this unique and extraordinary deed, the people were shown how the saints suffer for their devotees. The heart of the saints is softer than wax, it is soft, in and out, as butter. They love their devotees without any idea of gain and regard them as their true relatives.

BABA'S LOVE FOR HIS DEVOTEES

I shall now close this chapter after relating a story illustrating how Baba loved his devotees and anticipated their wishes and movements. Nanasaheb, who was a great devotee of Baba, was the Revenue Collector in Khandesh. His devotion to Baba bore fruit, as he received a transfer to Pandharpur, which he regarded as *bhuvaikuntha,* heaven on earth. As Nanasaheb had to take charge there immediately, he left at once without even writing or informing anybody in Shirdi. He wanted to give a surprise visit to Shirdi, his Pandharpur, to see and *pranam* (bow) to his Vithoba (Baba), and then proceed. Nobody knew of Nanasaheb's departure for Shirdi except Baba, whose eyes were everywhere.

As soon as Nanasaheb was a few miles outside of Shirdi, there was a stir in the masjid. Baba was sitting and talking with Mhalsapati, Appa Shinde and Kashiram when suddenly he said, "Let all four of us sing bhajans, the doors of Pandharpur are open. Let us sing happily." They began to sing the words of the song together, "I have to go to Pandharpur and stay on there, for it is the house of my Lord."

Baba was singing and the devotees followed. Soon after, Nanasaheb came with his family, pranammed before Baba and requested Baba to accompany them to Pandharpur and stay with them there. This request was not necessary, as the devotees told Nanasaheb that Baba was already in the mood for going to Pandharpur and staying there. Hearing this Nanasaheb was moved and fell at Baba's feet. Then getting Baba's permission, udi and blessings, Nanasaheb left for Pandharpur.

Pranams to Sri Sai

Peace Be to All

CHAPTER EIGHT

IMPORTANCE OF HUMAN BIRTH

In this wonderful universe, God has created billions of creatures including gods, demigods, insects, beasts and men, inhabiting heaven, hell, Earth, ocean, sky and other intermediate regions. Of these, those souls whose merits predominate go to heaven and live there until they enjoy the fruits of their actions. When this is done, they are cast down. Those souls whose sins or demerits predominate go down to hell and suffer the consequences of their misdeeds for as long a time as they deserve. When their merits and demerits balance each other, they are born on Earth as human beings and are given a chance to work for their liberation. Ultimately, when both their merits and demerits are gone completely, they receive their deliverance and become free. To put the matter in a nutshell, souls get their rebirths according to their deeds and intelligence.

❧

THE GOOD FORTUNE OF BEING HUMAN

As we all know, four things are common to all the creatures—food, sleep, fear and sexual union. In the case of man, he is endowed with a special faculty—knowledge—with which he can attain self-realization that is impossible in any other birth. It is for this reason that Gods envy man's good fortune and aspires to be born as men on Earth to get their final deliverance.

Some say that there is nothing worse than the human body, which is full of filth, mucus, phlegm and dirt, and which is subject to decay, disease and death. This is no doubt true to a certain extent. But in spite of these drawbacks and defects, the special value of the human body is that man has the capacity to acquire knowledge. It is only on account of the human body that one sees, through knowledge, the perishable and transitory nature of the body and of the world. One then develops aversion to sensory enjoyments and can discriminate between the real and unreal, and so attains self-realization. If we reject or neglect the body because it is filthy, we lose the chance for realization. If we are attached to it, and run after sensory enjoyments, we go to hell. Therefore, the proper course for us to pursue is the following: the body should neither be neglected nor cherished, but should be properly cared for, just as a traveler on horseback takes care of his horse on the way to his destination to return home. Therefore, the body should be used to attain self-realization, which is the supreme goal of life.

It is said that although God created various creatures, He was not satisfied, for none of them was able to know and appreciate His work. So He had to create a special being—man—and endow him with a special faculty, knowledge. When He saw that man was able to appreciate his leela—God's marvelous work and intelligence—He was highly pleased and satisfied. So really it is good luck to get a human body, and best yet to have the path to surrender to Sai Baba's feet.

BE EVER ALERT TO ACHIEVE THE OBJECT OF OUR LIVES

Realizing how precious human life is, and knowing that death is certain and may snatch us at any time, we should be ever alert to achieve the aim of our life. We should not delay but make every possible effort to attain our goal. Just as a widower is most anxious to get himself married to a new bride, or just as a king leaves no stone unturned to seek his lost son, so with all sincerity and speed we should strive to attain our end, self-realization. Casting aside lethargy and laziness, warding off drowsiness, we should meditate day and night on the Self. If we fail to do this, we reduce ourselves to the level of beasts.

THE BENEFIT OF SEEKING A SAINT OR SADGURU

His movements and simple talks give us silent advice. The virtues of forgiveness, peace, detachment, charity, compassion, egolessness, and control of mind and body are demonstrated practically to disciples by such pure and holy company.

The most effective and speedy way to reach our goal is to approach a saint, sage or *sadguru* (true guru) who has attained God-realization. What cannot be achieved by hearing spiritual lectures and study of spiritual books is easily obtained in the company of such worthy souls. Just as the sun gives light that all the stars put together cannot do, so the sadguru alone imparts spiritual wisdom that all the sacred books and lectures cannot impart. His movements and simple talks give us silent advice. The virtues of forgiveness, peace, detachment, charity, compassion, egolessness, and control of mind and body are demonstrated practically to disciples by such pure and holy company. This enlightens their minds and lifts them up spiritually. Sai Baba was such a sadguru. Though he acted like a fakir, he was always engrossed in the Self. He loved all beings as he saw Divinity in them. He was not elated by pleasures nor depressed by misfortunes. A king and a pauper were the same to him. He whose glance could turn a beggar into a king, used to beg for food from door to door in Shirdi. Let us now see how he did it.

⚜

BABA BEGGED FOR HIS FOOD

Blessed are the people of Shirdi, in front of whose houses Baba stood as a beggar and called, "Oh Mother, give me a piece of bread," then spread out his hand to receive. In one hand he carried a *tumrel* (tinpot) and in the other a *choupadari* (rectangular piece of cloth). Each day he went door to door and visited certain houses. Liquid or semi-liquid things such as soup, vegetables, milk or buttermilk were received in the tinpot, while cooked rice, bread and solid things were taken in the cloth. Baba's tongue knew no taste as he had acquired control over it. So how could he care for the taste of the different things collected together? Whatever things he got in his cloth and in the tinpot were mixed together and eaten by Baba to his heart's content. Whether particular things were tasty or not was not noticed by Baba, as his tongue was devoid of the sense of taste altogether.

Baba begged till noon but his begging was very irregular. Some days he went a few rounds, on other days up to noon. The food collected was thrown in an earthen pot. Dogs, cats and crows freely ate from it and Baba never drove them away. The woman who swept the floor of the masjid took 10 or 12 pieces of bread to her house and nobody prevented her from doing so. How could he, who even in dreams never warded off cats and dogs by harsh words and signs, refuse food to poor helpless people? Blessed indeed is the life of such a noble person! In the beginning, people in Shirdi took him for a mad fakir. He was known in the village by this name. How could one who lived on alms by begging a few crumbs of bread be revered and respected? But this fakir was very generous of heart and hand, detached and charitable. Though he looked unpredictable and restless from outside, he was firm and steady inside. His way was inscrutable. In Shirdi, there were a few kind and blessed people who recognized and regarded him as a great soul. One such instance is given below.

BAYAJABAI ROAMS THROUGH THE WOODS TO FEED BABA

Every noon, Tatya's mother, Bayajabai, used to go to the woods with a basket on her head containing bread and vegetables. She roamed in the jungles for about three miles, trampling over bushes and shrubs in search of the mad fakir, and after hunting him down, fell at his feet. The fakir sat calm and motionless in meditation while she placed a leaf before him, spread out the food, bread, and vegetables and fed him forcibly. Wonderful was her faith and service. Every day at noon she roamed in the jungles and forced Baba to partake of lunch. Her service, or austerity, by whatever name we call it, was never forgotten by Baba until his *mahasamadhi* (death). Remembering fully what service she rendered, Baba benefited her son magnificently. Both the son and the mother had great faith in the fakir, who was their God. Baba often said to them that, "Fakir is the real Lordship, as it is everlasting, and so-called Lordship is transient." After some years, Baba stopped going into the woods, began to live in the village and took his food in the masjid. From that time on, Bayajabai's troubles of roaming in the jungles ended.

SHARING HIS MASJID WITH TATYA AND MHALSAPATI

Blessed are the saints in whose heart the Lord dwells, and fortunate, indeed, are the devotees who get the benefit of the company of such saints. Two such fortunate souls were Tatya and Mhalsapati, who shared the company of Sai Baba. Baba loved them both equally. These three people slept in the masjid with their heads towards the east, west and north and with their feet touching one another at the center. Stretching their beds, they lay on them, chit chatting and gossiping about many things till late at night. If any one of them showed signs of sleep, others would wake him up. For instance, if Tatya began to snore, Baba at once got up and shook him from side to side and pressed his head. If it was Mhalsapati, he hugged him close, stroked his legs and kneaded his back. It was this way for 14 years that Tatya, having left his parents at home, slept in the masjid on account of his love for Baba. How happy and never to be forgotten were those days! How to measure that love and how to value the grace of Baba! After the passing away of his father, Tatya took charge of his household's affairs and then began to sleep at home.

BABA'S DEVOTEE KHUSHALCHAND OF RAHATA

Baba loved Kote Patil. He equally loved Chandrabhanshet Marwadi of Rahata. After Marwadi's death, Baba loved his nephew Khushalchand equally or even perhaps more, and watched out for his welfare day and night. Sometimes in a bullock cart, at other times in a carriage with intimate friends, Baba went to Rahata. People of that village came out, with band and music, received Baba at the gate of the village and prostrated before him. Then he was taken into the village with great pomp and ceremony. Khushalchand took Baba to his house, seated him on a comfortable seat and fed him a good lunch. They talked freely and happily for some time, then Baba returned to Shirdi, giving happiness and blessings to all. Shirdi is midway between Rahata in the south and Nimgaon in the north. Baba never went beyond these places. He never saw any railway train nor travelled by it. Still, he knew the exact arrival and departure times of all trains. Devotees who acted according to Baba's instructions regarding their departure fared well, while those who disregarded them suffered many a mishap and accident. More about this and other matters will be revealed in the next chapter.

Pranams to Sri Sai

Peace Be to All

CHAPTER NINE

A t the end of the last chapter, it was mentioned that the devotees who obeyed Baba's orders at the time of taking his leave fared well, while those who disobeyed them suffered many a mishap. This statement will be amplified and illustrated with a few striking examples in this chapter.

⚜

NO PERMISSION TO LEAVE SHIRDI WITHOUT BABA'S BLESSING

One special peculiarity of a pilgrimage to Shirdi was that no one could leave Shirdi without Baba's permission. If he did, he invited untold sufferings. But if anyone was asked to leave Shirdi, he could stay there no longer. Baba gave certain suggestions or hints when devotees went to bid goodbye and take leave. These suggestions had to be followed. If they were not followed, accidents were sure to befall those who acted contrary to Baba's directions. A few instances are given below.

TATYA IGNORES BABA'S ADVICE

Once Tatya was going by *tanga* (horse carriage) to the Kopargaon bazaar. He came in haste to the masjid, saluted Baba (putting hands in prayer to express devotion and respect), and said that he was going to the Kopargaon bazaar. Baba said, "Don't hurry, stop a little. Go to the bazaar but don't go out of the village." On seeing his anxiety to go, Baba asked him to at least take Shama with him. Not listening to this direction, Tatya immediately drove his tanga. One of the two horses was very active and restless. After passing the well, the horse began to run wildly and sprained its waist and fell down. Tatya was not very hurt but was reminded of Mother Sai's direction. On another occasion, while proceeding to Kolhar village, he disregarded Baba's direction and drove in a tanga, which met with a similar accident.

CONSEQUENCES OF DISOBEYING BABA'S ORDERS

One European gentleman came to Shirdi with a letter of introduction from Nanasaheb and an object in mind. He was comfortably accommodated in a tent. He wanted to kneel before Baba and kiss his hand. He tried three times to step into the masjid but Baba prevented him from doing so. He was asked to sit in the open courtyard below and take Baba's darshan from there. Not pleased with the reception he got, he wanted to leave Shirdi at once and came to say goodbye. Baba asked him not to hurry but to go the next day. People also requested that he follow Baba's direction. Not listening to all this, he left Shirdi in a tanga. The horses ran fine at first, but when they passed the well, a bicycle came in front of them, which frightened them so they started running fast. The tanga was turned upside down and the gentleman fell and was dragged for some distance. He was immediately rescued, but had to go and stay in the Kopargaon hospital for the treatment of his injuries. Because of such experiences, everyone learned the lesson that those who disregarded Baba's instruction met with accidents in one way or another, and those who obeyed them were safe and happy.

Why Baba Begged

Now to return to the question of mendicancy. A question may arise in the minds of some that if Baba was such a great person—God in fact— why should he have to use a begging bowl his whole life? This question may be considered from two standpoints. First, we must ask who are the people who have a right to live by the begging bowl? Our *Shastras* say that those who have become free from the three main desires of children, wealth, and fame are fit to live by begging alms. They cannot make cooking arrangements and eat at home. The duty of feeding them rests on the shoulders of householders. Baba was neither a householder nor hermit. He was a *sannyasi* (renunciate) from boyhood. His firm conviction was that the universe was his home. He was the Lord Vasudev, the supporter of the universe and the imperishable Brahman. So he had the full right to use a begging bowl.

The second consideration is from the standpoint of *panchasoon*, the five sins and their atonement. In order to prepare food, the householders have to go through five actions: pounding, grinding, washing pots, sweeping and cleaning and lighting hearths. These processes cause the destruction of small insects and creatures, which causes householders to incur karma. In order to atone for this, our *Shastras* prescribe six kinds of sacrifices:

Brahma Yajna: offering to Brahma
Veda Dhyana: study of the Vedas
Pitra Yajna: offering to the ancestors
Deva Yajna: offerings to the Gods
Bhoota Yajna: offerings to beings
Manushya Atithi Yajna: offerings to men or uninvited guests

If these sacrifices are done, the mind is purified which helps people to get knowledge and self-realization. By going from house to house, Baba reminded the residents of their sacred duty. Fortunate were the people who got the lesson from Baba at their home.

❧

DEVOTEES EXPERIENCE GIVING OFFERINGS TO BABA

Now to return to another interesting subject. Lord Krishna has said in the *Bhagavad Gita*, "Whosoever devoutly offers a leaf, a flower, a fruit or water to me, of that pure-hearted man, I accept that heartfelt offering." In Baba's case, if a devotee really longed to offer something to him but forgot, Baba reminded him about the offering and made him present it. Baba then accepted it and blessed the devotee. A few instances are given below.

❧

THE TARKHAD FAMILY EXPERIENCE

Babasaheb Tarkhad was a staunch devotee of Sai Baba. His wife and son loved Baba equally, even more so perhaps. He suggested that his wife and son go and spend the son's vacation in Shirdi. But the son was unwilling to go and leave his home in Bandra, as he thought that the worship of Sai Baba's portrait in his home would not be properly attended to. Although it was not his father's predilection to worship Baba's picture, he promised to do it exactly as the son was doing. So mother and son left for Shirdi one Friday night.

The next day, Mr. Tarkhad got up early, took his bath and before proceeding with the puja, prostrated himself before the shrine and said, "Baba, I am going to perform the puja exactly as my son has been doing, but please don't let it be a mere drill." After he performed the puja, he offered a few pieces of sugar as *naivedya* (offering), which were then distributed at lunchtime.

That evening and again on Sunday, everything went well. The following Monday also went well. Mr. Tarkhad, who had never performed *puja* (worship) like this in all his life, felt great confidence in himself that everything was going quite satisfactorily according to the promise he gave to his son. On Tuesday, he performed the morning puja as usual and left for work. When he came home at lunchtime, he found that sugar prasad was not distributed with the meal. He asked the cook, who told him that no offering was made that morning, and that he had completely forgotten to perform that part of the puja. After hearing this, Mr. Tarkhad left his seat and prostrated himself before the shrine. He expressed his regret and at the same time chided Baba about the lack of guidance to do exactly what his son had done. Then he wrote a letter to his son stating the facts and requested him to lay it before Baba's feet and ask his pardon for his neglect.

This happened in Bandra at Tuesday noon. At about the same time, when the noon Aarati was just about to commence in Shirdi, Baba said to Mrs. Tarkhad, "Mother, I have been to your house in Bandra looking for something to eat. I found the door locked. Somehow I entered inside and found, to my regret, that Bhau (Mr. Tarkhad) had left nothing for me to eat. So I have returned from there without eating anything."

She did not understand, but the son understood that there was something wrong with the puja in his home and asked Baba's permission to go home. Baba refused but allowed him to perform the puja there. The son then wrote a letter to his father stating all that had taken place at Shirdi and implored his father not to neglect the puja at home. Both these letters crossed each other and were delivered to the respective parties the next day. Is this not astonishing?

BABA IS ALL KNOWING

"All creatures are one with me. I am roaming in their forms. He who sees me in all these creatures is my beloved."

Let us now take up the case of Mrs. Tarkhad. She offered three things, *bharit* (roasted brinjal eggplant, mixed curds and spice), *kacharya* (pieces of brinjal fried in ghee), and *peda* (sweetmeat ball). Let us see how Baba accepted them.

Once Mr. Purandare, a great devotee of Baba's, started for Shirdi with his family. Mrs. Tarkhad went to Mrs. Purandare and gave her two eggplants and requested that when she went to Shirdi, to prepare bharit with one eggplant and kacharya with the other and serve them to Baba. After reaching Shirdi, Mrs. Purandare went to the masjid with her dish of bharit just as Baba was about to start his meals. Baba found the bharit very tasty so he distributed it to everyone and said that now he wanted kacharyas. A word was sent to

Radhakrishna Mai that Baba wanted kacharyas. She was in a fix, as it was not the season for brinjals. How to get brinjals? An inquiry was made about who brought the bharit, and it was found that Mrs. Purandare was also entrusted with serving kacharyas. Then everybody understood the significance of Baba's inquiry about kacharyas, and was wonderstruck at his all-pervasive knowledge.

In December 1915, Govind Balaram Mankar wanted to go to Shirdi to perform the funeral rituals for his father. Before he left, he came to see Mr. Tarkhad, whose wife wanted to send something with him to Baba. She searched the whole house but found nothing except a *peda* (sweetmeat) that had already been offered as naivedya. The boy, Govind, was in mourning. Even so, out of great devotion to Baba, she sent the sweetmeat with him, hoping that Baba would accept and eat it. Govind went to Shirdi and saw Baba, but forgot to take the sweetmeat with him. Baba simply waited. When Govind again went to Baba in the afternoon, he went without the sweetmeat. Baba could wait no longer and asked him directly, "What did you bring for me?"

"Nothing," was the reply.

Baba asked him again. The same reply came forth. Then Baba asked him, "At the time of your starting, didn't Mrs. Tarkhad give some sweetmeat to you to give me?"

The boy then remembered. He felt embarrassed, asked Baba's pardon, then ran to his lodging and brought the sweetmeat to give to Baba. As soon as Baba got it in his hand he put it into his mouth and gulped it down. And so, the devotion of Mrs. Tarkhad was recognized and accepted. In this case, it was proven that, 'As men believe in me, so do I accept them.' (*Bhagavad Gita*).

BABA IS FED THROUGH ALL MOUTHS

Once, Mrs. Tarkhad was staying in Shirdi. At noon, meals were ready and dishes were being served when a hungry dog turned up and began to cry. Mrs. Tarkhad immediately got up and threw it a piece of bread, which the dog gulped with great relish. In the afternoon, when she went to the masjid Baba said to her:

Mother, you have fed me sumptuously. My *pranas* (life forces) have been satisfied. Always act like this and you will remain in good standing. Sitting in this masjid, I shall never, ever speak untruth. Take pity on me like this. First give bread to the hungry, and then eat yourself. Note this well.

At first, she could not understand the meaning of what Baba said. So she replied, "Baba, how could I feed you? I am dependent on others and receive my food from them." Then Baba replied:

Eating that lovely bread I am completely content and am still belching. The dog that you saw before your meal, and to which you gave the piece of bread, is one with me. All creatures are one with me. I am roaming in their forms. He who sees me in all these creatures is my beloved. So abandon the sense of duality and distinction and serve me as you did today.

Drinking these nectar-like words, she was moved, her eyes were filled with tears, her throat was choked and her joy knew no bounds.

SEE GOD IN ALL BEINGS

'See God in all beings' is the moral of this chapter. The *Upanishads,* the Gita, and the *Bhagwat* all urge us to perceive God or Divinity in all creatures. By the example given at the end of this chapter and others too numerous to mention, Baba practically demonstrated to us how to put the *Upanishad* teachings into practice. In this way, Baba stands as the best exponent or teacher of the *Upanishad* doctrines.

Pranams to Sri Sai

Peace Be to All

CHAPTER TEN

ALWAYS REMEMBER BABA

Always remember Baba with love, for he was always engrossed in doing good to all, and was always abiding in the Self. To remember only him is to solve the mystery of life and death. This is the best and easiest of sadhanas as it involves little effort. Just a little exertion brings great rewards. So as long as our senses are sound, we should practice this sadhana minute by minute. All other gods are illusory. The guru is the only God. If we believe in sadguru's holy feet, he can change our fortune for the better. If we serve him, we become free from *samsara* (worldly bondage). We need not study any philosophy like the *Nyaya* and the *Mimansa*. If we make him our helmsman, we can easily cross over the ocean of all our suffering and sorrows. As we trust a helmsman to go across the rivers and seas, so we have to trust our sadguru in order to go over the ocean of worldly existence. What the sadguru looks for is the intense feeling and devotion of his devotees and endows them with knowledge and eternal bliss.

In the last chapter, Baba's mendicancy, devotees' experiences and other subjects are dealt with. Let the readers now hear where and how Baba lived, how he slept and how he taught.

BABA'S CURIOUS WAY OF SLEEPING

Let us first see where and how Baba slept. Nanasaheb brought Baba a wooden plank, four cubits in length and one span in breath, for sleeping on. Instead of keeping the plank on the floor and sleeping there, Baba tied it like a swing to the rafters of the masjid using old rags and slept on it there. The rags were so thin and worn out that it was a wonder how they could support the weight of the plank itself, let alone the weight of Baba. But somehow or other it was Baba's leela that the worn out rags sustained the plank with Baba on it. On each of the four corners of this plank, Baba lit earthen lamps and kept them burning the whole night. It was a sight for the Gods to see Baba sitting or sleeping on this plank! It was a wonder to all how Baba got up and down from the plank. Out of curiosity, many tried to observe his process of mounting and dismounting the plank but none succeeded. When crowds began to gather to watch this wonderful feat, Baba broke the plank into pieces and threw it away. Baba had all eight *siddhic* (supernatural) powers at his command but never practiced nor craved them. They came to him naturally as a result of his perfection.

BABA'S DIVINE NATURE

Always remember Baba with love, for he was always engrossed in doing good to all, and was always abiding in the Self. To remember only him is to solve the mystery of life and death. This is the best and easiest of sadhanas as it involves little effort.

Though Sai Baba looked like a man, over three and half cubits in length, still he dwelt in the hearts of all. Inwardly, he was detached and unconcerned, but outwardly, he longed for everyone's welfare. Inwardly he was disinterested; yet outwardly he appeared full of desires for the sake of his devotees. Inwardly he was the abode of peace; outwardly he looked restless. Inwardly he had the state of *Brahman* (Ultimate Reality); outwardly he acted like a devil. Inwardly he loved *advaita* (oneness), outwardly he got entangled with the world. Sometimes he looked on all with affection, and at other times he threw stones. Sometimes he scolded them, then at times he embraced them and was calm, composed, tolerant and well balanced.

Whatever his actions were, he was always abiding in the Self and always loved his devotees. He sat on one seat and never traveled. He always carried a small stick in his hand. He was calm and free from thought. He never cared for wealth and fame and lived on begging. Such a life he led. He always uttered, Allah Malik—God is One. Eternal and all embracing was his love for his devotees. He was the storehouse of self-knowledge and full of divine bliss. Such was the divine form of Sai Baba, boundless, endless and at one with all of the Creation. Incarnated in Baba was the one principle that envelops the whole universe, from stone pillar to Brahman. The truly meritorious and fortunate received this treasure chest in their hands, while others who did not know the real worth of Sai Baba, or took him to be a mere human being, were truly unfortunate.

HIS STAY IN SHIRDI & PROBABLE BIRTHDATE

No one knew the parents and exact birthdate of Sai Baba, but his age can be determined approximately by his stay in Shirdi. Baba first came to Shirdi when he was a young man of 16 and stayed for three years, then suddenly disappeared. He reappeared near Aurangabad when he was about 20 years old and returned to Shirdi with the marriage party of Chand Patil. He stayed in Shirdi continuously for 60 years, after which Baba took his mahasamadhi in the year 1918. From this we can say that Baba's birth year is approximately 1838.

BABA'S MISSION

Saint Ramadas (1608-1681) flourished in the 17th century and to a great extent fulfilled his mission of protecting cows and Brahmins against the

Muslims. But within two centuries after him, the split between the two communities, Hindus and Muslims, widened again, and Sai Baba came to bridge the gap. His constant advice to everyone was this:

Rama, the God of the Hindus and *Rahim*, the God of the Muslims, are one and the same. As there is not the slightest difference between them, why should their devotees quarrel amongst themselves? Children, join hands and bring both communities together, act sanely and then you will gain your goal of national unity. It is not good to dispute and argue. So don't argue, don't oppose one another. Always consider your interest and welfare. The Lord will protect you. Yoga, sacrifice, austerities, and knowledge are the means to attain God. If you do not succeed in this through whatever means, vain is your birth. If anyone does any evil to you, do not retaliate. If you can do something, do some good to others.

This, in short, was Sai Baba's advice to all. This will stand in good stead both in material and spiritual matters.

❧

BABA AS SADGURU

There are gurus and gurus. There are many so-called gurus, who go about from house to house with cymbals and *vina* (one stringed instrument) in their hands and make a show of their spirituality. They blow *mantras* (sacred words) into the ears of their disciples and extract money from them. They profess to teach devotion and spirituality to their disciples, but are themselves immoral and irreligious. Baba never thought of making the least show of his devotion. He had no body consciousness but had great love for his disciples.

There are two kinds of gurus, the first, *niyat* (appointed), and the second, *aniyat* (unappointed). The aniyat, or unappointed, gurus develop good qualities through their advice, purify our hearts and set us on the path of self-realization. But it is contact with the niyat, the appointed guru, who dispels our sense of duality and establishes us in unity by making us realize, 'I am That.' There are various gurus imparting different kinds of worldly knowledge to us, but he who fixes us in our true nature, the Self, and carries us beyond the ocean of worldly existence, is a sadguru. Baba was such a sadguru. His greatness is indescribable. If anybody went to take his darshan, he, without being asked, would give every detail of the person's past, present and future life. He saw divinity in all beings. Friends and foes were the same to him. Detached and balanced, he helped everyone, even evildoers. He was the same in prosperity and adversity. No doubt ever touched him. Though he possessed a human body, he was not in the least attached to his body. Though he looked embodied, he was beyond the body—free in this very life.

Blessed are the people of Shirdi who worshipped Baba as their God. While eating, drinking and working in their backyards and fields and doing various household works, they always remembered Baba and sang his glory. They knew no other God except Baba. How to speak of the love, the sweetness of the love of the women of Shirdi! They were quite ignorant but their pure love inspired them to compose poems or songs in their simple rural language. While not learned in letters, still one can discern real poetry in their simple songs. It is not intelligence, but love, that inspires real poetry. Real poetry is the manifestation of true love, and this can be seen and appreciated by intelligent listeners. Collection of these folk songs is desirable and, Baba willing, some fortunate devotee may undertake the task of collecting and publishing them.

BABA'S HUMILITY

The Lord, or Bhagawan, is said to have six qualities: fame, wealth, non-attachment, knowledge, grandeur and generosity. Baba had all these. He incarnated in flesh for the sake of the bhaktas. Wonderful was his grace and kindness! He drew the devotees to him, or how else could one have known him. For the sake of his devotees, Baba spoke such words as the Goddess of speech dare not utter. Here is an example. Baba spoke very humbly, "I am a slave of slaves; I am in your debt. I am fulfilled by your darshan. It is a great favor that I see your feet. I am but an insect in your excreta. I consider myself blessed." What humility is this? If anybody thinks that by publishing this, any disrespect is shown to Baba, we beg his pardon and to atone for this we sing and chant Baba's name.

Though Baba seemed outwardly to enjoy sense objects, he had not the least taste for them, or even the consciousness of enjoying them. Though he ate, he had no taste. Though he saw, he never felt any interest in what he saw. Regarding passion, he exhibited perfect self-control. He was not attached to anything. He was pure consciousness, the final resting place of desire, anger, envy and all other feelings. In short, he was detached, free and perfect. A striking instance may be illustrated in the following statement.

Baba Takes Orders from His Devotee Nanavalli

There was in Shirdi a very peculiar and odd fellow named Nanavalli. He looked after Baba's work and affairs. Once he approached Baba, who was seated on his seat, and asked him to get up, as he wanted to occupy it. Baba got up at once and left the seat. After sitting there awhile, Nanavalli got up and asked Baba to take his seat again. Then Baba sat down and Nanavalli fell at his feet, and went away. Baba did not show the slightest displeasure in being dictated to and ousted. Nanavalli loved Baba so much that he breathed his last breath on the 13th day after Baba took his mahasamadhi.

The Easiest Path Is the Company of Saints

Though Baba acted outwardly like an ordinary man, his actions showed extraordinary intelligence and skill. Whatever he did was done for the good of his devotees. He never prescribed any *asana* (yoga posture), breathing technique or practice to his bhaktas, nor did he blow any mantra into their ears. He told them to leave off all cleverness and always remember, 'Sai, Sai.' "If you do that," he said, "all your chains will be removed and you will be free." Sitting between five fires, sacrifices, chanting, and eight-fold yoga are possible for Brahmins only. They are of no use to the other classes.

The function of the mind is to think; it cannot remain for a minute without thinking. If you give it a sense object, it will think about that. If you give it to a guru, it will think about the guru. You have heard most attentively the greatness and grandeur of Baba. This is the natural remembrance of Sai. Hearing the stories of saints is not as difficult as the other sadhanas mentioned earlier. These stories remove all fear of samsara and take you on the spiritual path. So listen to these stories, meditate on them, and assimilate them. If this is done, everyone will become pure and holy. You may attend to your worldly duties, but give your mind to Baba and his stories, and then he is sure to bless you. This is the easiest path, but why don't all take to it? The reason is that without God's grace, we do not have the desire to listen to the stories of saints. With God's grace everything is smooth and easy. Hearing the stories of saints is, in a way, keeping their company.

The importance of the company of saints is very great. It removes our body consciousness and egoism, completely destroys the chain of birth and death, cuts all the knots of the heart, and takes us to God who is pure consciousness. It certainly increases our non-attachment to sense objects, makes us indifferent to pain and pleasure, and leads us on the spiritual path. If you have no other sadhana, such as uttering God's name, worship or devotion, but wholeheartedly take refuge in the saints, they will carry you safely across the ocean of worldly existence. It is for this reason that the saints manifest themselves in this world. Even sacred rivers such as the Ganges, Godavari, Krishna and Kaveri, which wash away the sins of the world, desire that the saints come to take a bath in their waters and purify them. Such is the grandeur of the saints. It is on account of the store of merit in past births that we have attained the feet of Sai Baba.

We conclude this chapter with meditation on Baba's form. He is the beautiful and handsome Sai, standing on the edge of the masjid and distributing udi to each and every bhakta, with a view to his welfare. He thinks the world is not important, and is ever engrossed in supreme bliss. Before him we humbly prostrate ourselves.

Pranams to Sri Sai

Peace Be to All

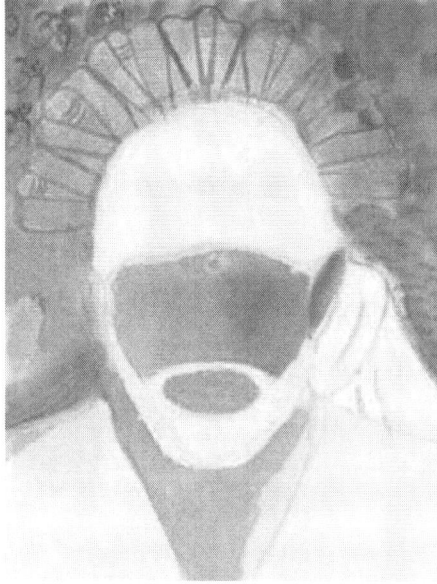

CHAPTER ELEVEN

I n this chapter let us now describe the *saguna* Brahman Sai. How he was
worshipped and how he controlled the elements.

❧

HUMBLE PRANAMS TO SAI, THE ALL PERVASIVE SADGURU

> *This indescribable shakti or power of God, known as pure
> existence, consciousness and bliss, incarnated in the form of Sai
> Baba in Shirdi.*

There are two aspects of God or Brahman, the *nirguna* and the *saguna*.
The nirguna is formless, while the saguna is with form, though both express
the same Brahman. Some prefer to worship the formless, some the form. As
stated in the *Bhagavad Gita*, the worship of the form is easy and preferable. As
man has a form, it is natural and easy for him to worship God with a form.
Our love and devotion do not develop unless we worship the form of God for
a period of time, and as we advance it leads us to the meditation of *nirguna*

(formless) Brahman. So let us start with saguna worship. Image, altar, fire, light, sun, water, Brahman are the seven objects of worship, but the sadguru is better than all these.

Let us, on this occasion, bring to our mind the form of Sai, who was detachment incarnate, and who was the resting place for his wholehearted devotees. Our faith in his words is the seat of asana; and our *sankalpam* (intention) is the abandonment of all our desires. Some call Baba a *Bhagvad bhakta* (devotee of the Lord) and others call him was a *maha bhagwat* (a great devotee), but to us he was God incarnate. He was extremely forgiving, never irritable, straight, soft, tolerant and content beyond comparison. Though he looked embodied and having a form, he was really beyond the body, emotionless, detached and internally free. The Ganges on its way to the sea cools and refreshes the creatures affected with heat, gives life to the crops and trees, and quenches the thirst of many. Similarly, saints like Baba, while they live their own life, give solace and comfort to all. Lord Krishna has said, "The saint is my soul, my living image. I am he and he is my pure form (being)." This indescribable *shakti* or power of God, known as pure existence, consciousness and bliss, incarnated in the form of Sai Baba in Shirdi. The *Shruti* (Taittiriya Upanishad) describes Brahman as bliss. This we read of or hear daily in books but the devoted experienced this Brahman or bliss in Shirdi.

Baba, the support of all, required no prop or support from anyone. He always used a piece of sackcloth for his seat. His bhaktas covered his small beautiful bed and placed a bolster as a rest for his back. Baba respected the feelings of his devotees and allowed them to worship him as they liked. Some waved fans before him, some played musical instruments, some washed his hands and feet, some others applied scent and sandalpaste, some gave betel nut with leaves and other things, and some offered naivedya. But though he looked like he was living in Shirdi, he was present everywhere. This all-pervasiveness of his was experienced daily by his devotees. Our humble prostrations to this all-pervasive sadguru.

SANDALPASTE TO BABA'S FOREHEAD

Dr. Pandit, a friend of Tatya's, came to Shirdi for Baba's darshan. After pranamming to Baba, he stayed in the masjid for some time. Baba asked him to go see Dadabhat Kelkar. He went to Dadabhat and was well received. Then Dababhat left his house for *puja* (worship) with Dr. Pandit accompanying him. Until then, no one had dared to apply sandalpaste to Baba's forehead. Only Mhalsapati would apply it to his throat. But this simple-hearted devotee took Dabadhat's dish of puja materials, took the sandalpaste and drew a *tripundra* (three horizontal lines) on Baba's forehead. To the surprise of all, Baba kept silent, not uttering a single word.

That evening Dababhat asked Baba, "How is it that you object to sandalpaste being applied to your forehead by others but you allowed Dr. Pandit to do so?" Baba replied that Dr. Pandit believed him to be the same as his own guru, Kaka Puranik. When he applied the paste to his forehead, he was doing it to his guru, so he could not object. On inquiry, Dr. Pandit did feel it was his guru's forehead that he was marking with sandalpaste.

Though Baba allowed the devotees to worship him as they pleased, he still acted in a strange way at times. Sometimes he threw the puja dish and was wrath incarnate and no one could approach him. Sometimes he scolded the devotees, and at other times he looked softer than wax, a statue of peace and forgiveness. Although sometimes he seemed to shake with anger and his red eyes rolled round and round, he was internally a stream of affection and motherly love. Immediately he would call out his devotees and say that he was never really angry with them. It was impossible for him to neglect the devotees' welfare, just as it was impossible for mothers to kick their children and for the sea to turn back the rivers flowing into it. He was the slave of his devotees. He stood by them and responded to them whenever they called and always longed for their love.

❦

PATIENCE PAYS

There was no knowing when Baba would accept a devotee. That depended on his sweet will. This story illustrates this point. A Muslim gentleman named Sidik Falke came to Shirdi after making a pilgrimage to Mecca and Madina. He lived in the Chavadi, facing north, and sat in the open courtyard of the masjid. For nine months, Baba ignored him and did not allow him to step into the masjid. Falke was disconsolate and did not know what to do. Someone advised him not to be disappointed, but to try to approach Baba through Shama, a close and intimate devotee. He said that as Shiva is approached through his servant Nandi, so Baba should be approached through Shama. Falke liked the idea and appealed to Shama to intercede for him. Shama agreed, and when the time was right, he approached Baba and asked, "Baba, why don't you allow the old *Haji* (one who has made a pilgrimage to Mecca) to step into the masjid while so many people freely come and go taking your darshan? Why can't you bless him once?"

Baba replied, "Shama, you are too young to understand things. If the fakir (God) does not allow it, what can I do? Without His grace, who will climb into the masjid? Well, go to him and ask him whether he will come to the narrow footpath near the well."

Shama went and returned with an affirmative answer. Then Baba said to Shama, "Ask him whether he is willing to pay me the sum of Rs. 40,000 in four installments."

Shama went and returned with the answer that he was willing to pay even 40 lakhs.

Again Baba said to Shama, "We are going to butcher a goat in the masjid, so ask him whether he would like to have mutton, haunch or the testicles of the goat."

Shama returned with the answer that Haji would be happy to receive even a small crumb from Baba's mudpot. Hearing this Baba got excited and threw away the earthen jars and immediately went to Haji, lifted his own kafni up in his arms and said, "Why do you brag and fancy yourself great and pose as an old Haji? Do you read *Koran* like this? You are proud of your pilgrimage to Mecca, but you do not know me." Being scolded like this confounded Haji.

After that Baba went back to the masjid, purchased a few baskets of mangoes and sent them to Haji. Then Baba took Rs.55 from his pocket and placed them into Haji's hand. From that time on, Baba loved Haji, invited him for meals, and Haji came into the masjid whenever he liked. At times, Baba gave him some rupees. This is how Haji was brought into Baba's court.

BABA'S CONTROL OVER THE ELEMENTS

We shall close this chapter after describing two incidents showing Baba's control over the elements.

Once, at evening time, there was a terrible storm at Shirdi. The sky was overcast with thick black clouds. The winds began to blow forcibly. The clouds roared, lightning flashed, and the rains began to descend in torrents. In a short time, the whole place was flooded with water. All the creatures, birds, beasts and men became terribly frightened and all flocked to the masjid for shelter. There are many local deities in Shirdi but none came to their help. So everyone prayed to Baba, their God, who was fond of their devotion, to intercede and quiet the storm. Baba was much moved. He came out and standing at the edge of the masjid, addressed the storm in a loud and thunderous voice, "Stop! Stop your fury and be calm." In a few minutes the rains subsided, the winds ceased to blow and the storm ended. Then the moon rose in the sky and the people returned to their homes happy.

On another occasion, the fire in the dhuni began to burn brightly and its flames were seen to reach the rafters above. The people who were sitting in the masjid did not know what to do. They dared not ask Baba to pour water or do anything to quench the flames. But Baba soon came to realize what was happening. He took up his *satka* (short stick) and dashed it against a pillar saying, "Get down! Be calm." At each stroke of the satka, the flames lowered and slowed down. In a few minutes, the dhuni became calm and normal.

This is our Baba, an incarnation of God. He will bless any man who prostrates and surrenders himself to him. Who reads the stories of this chapter daily with faith and devotion will soon be free from all calamities. Not only this, but by always being attached and devoted to Sai, he will very soon achieve God realization. All his desires will be fulfilled and then, being desireless, he will attain the Supreme. Amen.

Pranams to Sri Sai

Peace Be to All

CHAPTER TWELVE

N ow let us see in this chapter how devotees were received and treated by Baba.

⚜

SAINTS LOVE ALL BEINGS EQUALLY

For the sake of devotees, he spent his stock of merits and was ever alert to help them. But the devotees could never approach him unless he meant to receive them. If their turn did not come, Baba did not remember them and his leelas could not reach their ears.

We have seen before that the purpose or object of divine incarnation is to protect the good and destroy the wicked. But the mission of the saints is quite different. To them the good and the wicked are the same. First, they feel for wrongdoers then set them on the right path. They are like the *agasti* (destroyer) of *bhavasagara* (the ocean of worldly existence) or like the sun to the darkness of ignorance. The Lord dwells in the saints. In fact, they are not different from Him.

Our Baba is one of these, who incarnated for the welfare of the devotees. Supreme in knowledge and surrounded with divine luster, he loved all beings equally. He was unattached. Foes and friends, kings and paupers were the same to him. Hear his powers. For the sake of devotees, he spent his stock of merits and was ever alert to help them. But the devotees could never approach him unless he meant to receive them. If their turn did not come, Baba did not remember them and his leelas could not reach their ears. Then how could they think of seeing him? Some men desired to see Baba but they did not get any opportunity to have his darshan until his mahasamadhi. There are many people whose desire for Baba's darshan was not satisfied. If these people, believing in him, listen to his leelas their search for darshan will, to a great extent, be satisfied by the leelas. If some people went there by sheer luck and had Baba's darshan, were they able to stay there longer? No. No one could go there of their own accord, and no one could stay there long even if they so wished. They could stay there as long as Baba permitted them to stay, and had to leave when Baba asked them to do so. Everything depended on Baba's will.

Sent Home Immediately

Once Kaka Mahajani went to Shirdi from Mumbai. He wanted to stay there for one week and enjoy the Gokul Ashtami festival. As soon as he had Baba's darshan, Baba asked him, "When are you returning home?" He was rather surprised at this question, but he had to give an answer. He said that he would go home when Baba ordered him to do so. Then Baba said, "Go tomorrow." Baba's word was law and had to be obeyed. So, Mahajani left Shirdi immediately. When he arrived in his office in Mumbai, he found that his employer was anxiously waiting for him. His manager had suddenly fallen ill and Mahajani's presence was absolutely necessary. He had sent a letter to Kakasaheb in Shirdi, which was redirected to him in Mumbai.

REQUIRED TO STAY LONGER

Now listen to an opposite story. Once Bhausaheb Dhumal, a lawyer, was going to Niphad for a case. On the way he came to Shirdi, had Baba's darshan and wanted to proceed to Niphad immediately. But Baba did not permit him to do so. He made him stay in Shirdi for more than a week. In the meantime, the magistrate at Niphad suffered intense pain in his abdomen so the case was adjourned. Mr. Dhumal was then allowed to go and attend to his case. It went on for some months and was tried by four magistrates. Ultimately, Mr. Dhumal won the case and his client was acquitted.

PERMISSION TO STAY AWAY

Nanasaheb Nimonkar, Honorary Magistrate, was staying in Shirdi with his wife. The couple spent most of their time in the masjid serving Baba. It so happened that their son fell ill in Belapur and the mother decided, with Baba's consent, to go to Belapur to see her son and relatives. She wanted to stay for a few days but her husband asked her to return the next day. The lady was in a fix and did not know what to do, but her God, Sai Baba, came to her help. While leaving Shirdi she went to Baba, who was standing in front of Sathe's wada with Nanasaheb and others. She prostrated at his feet and asked his permission to go. Baba said to her, "Go. Go quickly. Be calm and without worry. Stay comfortably at Belapur for four days. See all your relatives and then return to Shirdi." How opportune were Baba's words! Her husband's proposal was overruled by Baba's decree.

BABA APPEARS AS THE LATE GURU OF MOOLAY SHASTRI

An orthodox agnihotri Brahmin from Nasik named Moolay Shastri, who had studied the six *Shastras* and was well versed in astrology and palmistry, once came to Shirdi to see Bapusaheb Buti, the famous millionaire of Nagpur. After seeing him, he and others went to see Baba in the masjid. Baba bought various fruits and other things from vendors with his own money and distributed them all to those present in the masjid. Baba used to press the mango on all sides so skillfully that when a person received it from Baba and sucked it, he got all the pulp at once in his mouth and could throw away the stone and the skin with ease. The plantains were peeled by Baba and distributed to the devotees while the skins were retained by Baba.

Moolay Shastri wanted to examine Baba's palm and requested him to extend his hand. Baba ignored his request and instead gave him four plantains. Then they all returned to the wada where Moolay Shastri bathed, dressed in sacred clothes, and started his practice of *agnihotra* (fire worship).

Then when Baba started for Lendi as usual he said, "Get some *geru* (red dye). Today we shall put on saffron colored cloth." None understood what Baba meant. When Baba returned, preparations for the noon Aarati were being made. Bapusaheb Jog asked Moolay Shastri whether he would accompany him for the Aarati. He replied that he would see Baba later in the afternoon. Very soon Baba sat on his seat and was worshipped by the devotees and Aarati commenced. Then Baba said, "Get some dakshina from the new Brahmin from Nasik."

Buti went to get the dakshina. But when he gave Baba's message, Moolay Shastri was very perplexed. He thought, 'I am a pure agnihotri Brahmin, why should I pay dakshina? Baba may be a great saint but I am not his dependent.' But as a great saint like Baba was asking for dakshina through a millionaire like Buti, he could not refuse. So leaving his routine unfinished, he started with Buti to the masjid. Thinking himself holy and sacred, and the masjid otherwise, he remained at a distance, joined his hands and threw flowers at Baba from afar. Then all of a sudden, he wasn't seeing Baba on the seat, he was seeing his late guru Gholap Swami!

He was wonderstruck. Could this be a dream? No, it was not; as he was wide awake. But how could his late guru be there? He was speechless for some time. He pinched himself and thought again, but could not reconcile the fact that his late guru was in the masjid. Ultimately, leaving aside doubt, he went up and fell at his guru's feet and then got up and stood there with folded hands. Other people sang Baba's Aarati, while Moolay Shastri chanted his guru's name. Then casting off all pride of caste and ideas about sacredness, he fell flat at his guru's feet and closed his eyes. When he got up and opened his eyes, he saw Baba asking for dakshina. Seeing Baba's blissful form and his inconceivable power, Moolay Shastri forgot himself. He was extremely happy; his eyes were filled with tears of joy. He again saluted Baba and gave the dakshina. He said that his doubt was removed and that he saw his own guru. On seeing this wonderful leela, everyone, including Moolay Shastri, was much moved, and they realized the meaning of Baba's words, "Bring geru, we shall wear a saffron colored cloth." Such is Baba's wonderful leela.

⚜

BABA IS RAMA

Once a Revenue Collector came to Shirdi with a doctor friend of his. The doctor said that his deity was Rama and that he would not bow before a Muslim, and so was unwilling to go to Shirdi. The Revenue Collector replied that nobody would press or ask him to bow, so he should just come and give him the pleasure of his company. They came to Shirdi and went to the masjid for Baba's darshan. All were wonderstruck to see the doctor going ahead and pranamming to Baba. They asked him how he forgot his resolve and bowed before a Muslim. The doctor replied that he saw his beloved deity Rama on the seat and so prostrated before him. Then as he was saying this, he saw Baba there again. He said, "Is this a dream? How could he be a Muslim? He is a great *yoga sampanna* (full of yoga) avatar."

Next day, he made a vow and began to fast. He left the masjid, resolving not to go there until Baba blessed him. Three days passed. On the fourth day, a close friend of his turned up and together they went to the masjid for Baba's darshan. After the salutation, Baba asked the doctor whether anybody had gone to call him to make him come. Hearing this vital question, the doctor was moved. The same night he was blessed by Baba and in his sleep experienced bliss supreme. Then he left for his town, where he experienced the same state for two weeks. And so, his devotion to Baba increased many fold.

The moral of these stories is this: we should have firm faith in our guru and no one else.

Pranams to Sri Sai

Peace Be to All

CHAPTER THIRTEEN

BABA'S CURES

"If you always say, 'Sai, Sai' I shall take you over the seven seas.
Believe in these words and you will certainly benefit."

Baba's words were always concise, deep, efficient, well balanced and full of meaning. He was ever content and never cared for anything. He said:

Though I have become a fakir, have no house or wife, have left all cares and stayed in one place, the inevitable *Maya* (illusion) teases me often. Even if I forget myself, I cannot forget her. She always envelops me. If this Maya of the Lord teases even Brahma, then what to speak of a poor fakir like me? Those who take refuge in the Lord will be freed from her clutches with his grace.

Baba spoke about the power of Maya in such terms. Lord Sri Krishna said to Uddhava in the *Bhagavad Gita* that the saints are his living forms. For the welfare of his devotee, Baba said the following:

Those who are fortunate and whose demerits have vanished, take to my worship. If you always say, 'Sai, Sai' I shall take you over the seven seas. Believe in these words and you will certainly benefit. I do not need any other worship, either eight-fold or sixteen-fold. I reside where there is total devotion.

Now read what Baba, the friend of those who surrender to him, did for their welfare.

⚜

BABA CURES A DESPERATE MAN

In 1909, Bhimaji Patil suffered from a severe and chronic chest disease, which ultimately developed into tuberculosis. He tried all sorts of remedies but to no effect. Losing all hope, he prayed to God, "Oh Lord Narayana, help me now." It is a well-known fact that when our circumstances are good we do not remember God, but when calamities and adversities overtake us, we are reminded of Him. So Bhimaji finally turned to God.

It occurred to him that he should consult Nanasaheb, a great devotee of Baba, in this respect. So he wrote a letter to him giving all the details of his malady and asked for his opinion. In reply, Nanasaheb wrote to him that there was only one remedy left and that was to seek the help of Baba's feet. Relying on Nanasaheb's advice, he made preparations to go to Shirdi.

He was brought there, taken to the masjid, and placed before Baba. Nanasaheb and Shama were present. Baba pointed out that the disease was due to previous bad karma and he was not inclined to interfere. But the patient cried out in despair that he was helpless and sought refuge in him, as he was his last hope, and prayed for mercy. Then Baba's heart melted:

Stay, cast off your anxiety. Your sufferings have come to an end. However oppressed and troubled one may be, as soon as he steps into the masjid, he is on the pathway to happiness. The fakir here is very kind. He will cure the disease and protect all with love and kindness.

The patient had been vomiting blood every five minutes, but now there was no vomiting in Baba's presence. From the time that Baba uttered the words of hope and mercy, the malady took a favorable turn.

Baba asked him to stay in Bhimabai's house, which was not a convenient or healthy place. But Baba's order had to be obeyed. While he was staying there, Baba cured him through two dreams. In the first dream, he saw himself as a boy suffering the severe pain of a flogging, which he received for not reciting his 'Swami (Baba) poetry' lesson before his class master. In the second dream, someone caused him intense pain and torture by rolling a stone up and down over his chest. In this way, through the pain suffered in dream, his cure was complete and he went home. After that, he came to Shirdi often, gratefully remembering what Baba did for him and prostrating before him. Baba also did not expect anything from devotees but grateful remembrance, unchanging faith and devotion. People in Maharashtra always celebrate Satya Narayana puja in their homes every two or four weeks. But Bhimaji Patil started a new Sai Satyavrata puja in his house when he returned to his village.

Baba's Cure for Malaria

Another devotee of Baba, Bala Shimpi, suffered much from a malignant type of malaria. He tried all sorts of medicines and concoctions but in vain, as the fever did not decrease even in the slightest. So he ran to Shirdi and fell at Baba's feet. In this case, Baba gave him a strange recipe, "Give a black dog some morsels of rice mixed with curds in front of the Lakshmi temple." Bala did not know how to execute this recipe but as soon as he went home, he found rice and curds. After mixing them together, he brought the mixture near the Lakshmi temple. There he found a black dog waving its tail. He placed the curds and rice before the dog. The dog ate it, and, strangely, Bala became healed of his malaria.

Baba's Recipe for Cholera

Bapusaheb Buti once suffered from dysentery and vomiting. His cupboard was full of drugs and medicines but none of them had any effect. Bapusaheb became very weak on account of purging and vomiting and was not able to go to the masjid for Baba's darshan. Then Baba sent for him and made him sit before him and said, "Now take care. You should not purge anymore." Then, waving his index finger at him, "The vomiting must also stop." Look at the force of Baba's words. Both the maladies disappeared and Bapusaheb Buti felt well.

On another occasion, Bapusaheb had an attack of cholera and suffered from severe thirst. The doctor tried all sorts of remedies but could give him no relief. Then he went to Baba and consulted him as to what to drink that would allay his thirst and cure the disease. Baba prescribed an infusion of almonds, walnuts and pistachio boiled in sugared milk. Any other doctor would consider this a fatal aggravation of the disease, but by strict obedience to Baba's order, the infusion was administered and the disease was cured.

⚜

Baba's Intention Cures Ear Pain

A Swami from Alandi wishing to have Baba's darshan came to Shirdi. He suffered from a severe pain in his ear that prevented him from getting sleep. His ear had been operated on, but it had no effect. The pain was severe and he did not know what to do. As he was leaving Shirdi, he came to take Baba's leave. When Shama requested Baba do something for the pain in the Swami's ear, Baba comforted him saying, "*Allah accha karega* (God will do good)." The Swami then returned to Poona and after a week sent a letter to Shirdi stating that the pain in his ear had subsided. But since some swelling was still there, he went to Mumbai for an operation. But on examining the ear, the surgeon said that no operation was necessary. Such was the wonderful effect of Baba's words.

⚜

Unusual Cure for Diarrhea

One time, Kaka Mahajani suffered from diarrhea. In order that there was no break in his service to Baba, Mahajani kept a pot with water in a corner of the masjid. Whenever there was a call, he would go out. As Baba knew everything, Mahajani did not inform him of his disease, thinking that Baba would cure it soon on his own.

Baba gave permission for the construction of the pavement in front of the masjid, but when the actual work began, Baba got wild and shouted loudly. Everybody ran away. As Mahajani was running away, Baba caught hold of him and made him sit. In the confusion that followed, somebody had left a small bag of groundnuts. Baba took a handful of groundnuts, rubbed them in his hands and blew away the skins. He gave the clean nuts to Mahajani and made him eat them. Scolding, cleaning the nuts, and making Mahajani eat them went on simultaneously. Baba himself ate some of them. Then, when the bag was finished, Baba asked him to fetch water as he felt thirsty. Mahajani brought him a pitcher full of water. Baba drank some water and made Mahajani drink it also. Then Baba said, "Now your diarrhea has stopped and you may attend to the work on the pavement." In the meantime, those who had run away returned and started to work again, including Mahajani, whose motions had now stopped. Are groundnuts a medicine for diarrhea? According to current medical opinion, groundnuts would aggravate the disease, not cure it. In this case, as in others, the true medicine was Baba's word.

RELIEF FROM A 14-YEAR STOMACH ACHE

A gentleman named Dattopant suffered from stomach aches for 14 years. No remedies gave him any relief. Then upon hearing of Baba's fame and his ability to cure diseases by sight, he ran to Shirdi and fell at Baba's feet. Baba looked at him kindly and gave him blessings. When Baba placed his hand on his head and he received Baba's udi and blessing, he felt relief. There was no further trouble with the malady.

ADDITIONAL MIRACLE CURES

At the end of this chapter, three cures are cited:

Shama suffered from hemorrhoids. Baba gave him a decoction of *sonamukhi* (senna pods). This relieved him. Then after two years, the trouble returned and Shama took the same remedy without consulting Baba. The result was that the disease became aggravated. Later on it was cured by Baba's grace.

Kaka Mahajani's elder brother, Gangadharpant, had suffered from stomach pain for many years. Hearing Baba's fame he came to Shirdi and requested Baba to cure him. Baba touched his belly and said, "God will cure." From that time there was no stomach pain and he was completely cured.

Nanasaheb also suffered from intense stomach pain. He was restless day and night. Doctors administered syringes, which produced no effect. Then he approached Baba, who told him to eat *burfi* (sweetmeat) mixed with ghee. This recipe gave him complete relief.

All these stories show that the real cure for disease was Baba's word and grace, not medicines or drugs.

Pranams to Sri Sai

Peace Be to All

CHAPTER FOURTEEN

In the last chapter, we described how Baba's word and grace cured many incurable diseases. Now we shall describe how Baba blessed Ruttonji Wadia with a child.

⚜

THE LIFE OF SAI BABA WAS NATURALLY SWEET

The life of this saint is naturally sweet in every aspect. His various habits, eating, walking and his natural sayings, are also sweet. His life is bliss incarnate. Baba gave his life as means for his devotees to remember him. He gave them various stories of duty and action which ultimately led them to true spirituality. His aim was that people should live happily in this world but they should be ever cautious to gain the true object of their life—self-realization. We get a human body as a result of merits in past births. It is worthwhile that with the body's aid, we should attain devotion and liberation in this life. So we should never be lazy, but always on the alert to gain the aim of life.

If you daily hear the leelas of Baba, you will always see him. Day and night you will remember him in your mind. When you absorb Baba in this way, your mind will lose its fickleness and if you continue in this manner it will finally merge in pure consciousness.

⚜

BABA RECEIVES DAKSHINA THROUGH OTHERS

Now let us come to the main story of this chapter. In Nanded, there lived a Parsi mill contractor and trader, Ruttonji Wadia. He had amassed a large amount of money and had acquired fields and lands. He had cattle, horses and carriages and was very prosperous. To all outward appearances he looked very happy and contented. But inwardly he was not so. Nature is such that no one in this world is completely happy and rich. Ruttonji was no exception to this.

He was liberal and charitable, gave food and clothing to the poor and helped all in various ways. The people took him to be a good and happy man. But, for a long time, Ruttonji was miserable because he didn't have a child. As singing kirtan without love or devotion, music without rhythmical accompaniments, a Brahmin without the sacred thread, proficiency in arts without common sense, pilgrimage without repentance, and ornamentation without a necklace are ugly and useless, so is the house of a householder without a son. Ruttonji always brooded on this matter and thought, "Will God ever be pleased to grant me a son?" He looked morose and had no relish for his food. Day and night he was enveloped with anxiety about whether he would ever be blessed with a son.

He had a great regard for Das Ganu. He saw him and opened his heart before him. Das Ganu advised him to go to Shirdi, to have Baba's darshan and fall at his feet seeking his blessing for a child. Ruttonji liked the idea and decided to go to Shirdi. After some days he went to Shirdi, had Baba's darshan and fell at his feet. Then opening a basket he took out a beautiful garland of flowers and placed it around Baba's neck, and offered him a basket of fruit. With great respect he sat near Baba and prayed to him saying, "Many people who find themselves in difficult situations come to you and you relieve them immediately. Hearing this, I have anxiously sought your feet. Please do not disappoint me."

Sai Baba asked him for Rs. 5 as dakshina, which Ruttonji was going to give. But Baba said that he had already received Rs. 3-14-0 from him and that he should only pay the balance. Hearing this, Ruttonji was rather puzzled. He could not make out what Baba meant. This was his first time in Shirdi. How was it that Baba said he had already received Rs. 3-14-0 from him? He could not solve the riddle. But he sat at Baba's feet and gave the balance of the dakshina as requested. He explained everything to Baba about why he had come and sought his help, and prayed for Baba to bless him with a son. Baba was moved and told him not to be worried; his bad days had ended. Baba then gave him udi, placed his hand on Ruttonji's head and blessed him, saying that Allah would satisfy his heart's desire.

Then after taking leave from Baba, Ruttonji returned to Nanded and told Das Ganu everything that took place in Shirdi. He said everything went well there. He had Baba's darshan and had received Baba's blessing and prasad but there was one thing that he could not understand. Baba said he had already received Rs. 3-14-0. "Please explain what Baba meant by this remark? I never went to Shirdi before. How could I give him the sum that Baba referred to?"

It was a puzzle for Das Ganu that he pondered over much for a long time. Some time later, it struck him that Ruttonji had received a Muslim saint, Moulisaheb, in his house some days earlier and had spent some money for his reception. Moulisaheb was a saint well known to the people of Nanded. When Ruttonji decided to go to Shirdi, Moulisaheb happened to come to Ruttonji's house. Ruttonji knew and loved him, so he gave a small party in his honor. Das Ganu got the list of expenses from Ruttonji for this reception. Everybody was wonderstruck to see that the expenses amounted to exactly Rs. 3-14-0, nothing more, nothing less. They all came to know that Baba was omniscient. Although he lived in Shirdi, he knew what happened outside and far away from Shirdi. In fact, he knew the past, present and future, and could identify himself heart and soul with anyone. In this particular instance, how could he know the reception given to Moulisaheb and the amount spent, unless he was one with him?

Ruttonji was satisfied with this explanation and his faith in Baba was confirmed and increased. In due time, he was blessed with a son and his joy knew no bounds. It is said that he had a dozen children in all, out of which four survived.

In another case, Baba told Rao Sathe after the death of his first wife to remarry and that he would have a son. Rao Sathe married a second time. The first two children by this wife were daughters and he felt very despondent. But the third child was a son. Baba's word proved true and he was satisfied.

⚜

PAYING DAKSHINA

In order to teach devotees the lesson of charity and to remove their attachment to money and so to purify their minds, Baba extracted dakshina from them. But there was this peculiarity: Baba said that he had to give back a hundred times more of what he received!

Now we shall close this chapter with a few remarks about dakshina. It is well known that Baba always asked for dakshina from people who went to see him. Somebody may ask a question, "If Baba was a fakir and perfectly detached, why should he ask for dakshina and care for money?" We now shall consider this question broadly.

For a long time, Baba did not accept anything. He stored burnt matches and filled his pocket with them. He never asked anything from anyone, whether a devotee or otherwise. If anyone placed a coin or two before him, he purchased oil or tobacco with it. He was fond of smoking. He always smoked a *bidi* (clove cigarette) and a *chillum* (pipe).

Then some people thought that they could not see saints empty handed, so they placed some copper coins before Baba. If a *pice* (coin of small value) was placed before Baba, he used to pocket it. If it was a two *pice* coin, it was returned immediately. After Baba's fame had spread far and wide, people began to flock in numbers, and then Baba began to ask dakshina from them. It is said in the *Shruti* (Veda) that puja to God is not complete unless a golden coin is offered. If a coin is necessary in the puja to God, why should it not be so in the puja of the saints also? Ultimately, the *Shastras* lay down that when one goes to see God, king, saint or guru, he should not go empty-handed. He should offer something, preferably money. In this connection, we should make note of the guidelines recommended by the *Upanishads*. The *Brihadaranyak Upanishad* says that the Lord Prajapati advised the gods, men and demons with one letter 'Da'. The Gods understood that they should practice *dama* (self-control). Men understood that they should practice *dana* (charity). The demons understood that they should practice *daya* (compassion).

To men, charity was recommended. The teacher in the *Taittiriya Upanishad* encourages his pupils to practice charity and other virtues. Regarding charity he says, "Give with faith, or even without it give with generosity. Give with modesty, with reverence and with compassion." In order to teach devotees the lesson of charity and to remove their attachment to money and so to purify their minds, Baba extracted dakshina from them. But there was this peculiarity: Baba said that he had to give back a hundred times more of what he received! There are many instances in which this happened. To quote an instance, the famous actor Ganpatrao Bodas wrote in his Marathi autobiography that since Baba pressed him over and over for dakshina, he emptied his moneybag before him. The result of this was that in later life he never lacked money, as it came to him abundantly. There were also secondary meanings of dakshina. In many cases, Baba did not want any monetary amount. To cite two instances:

One, Baba asked Rs.15 as dakshina from Professor G.G. Narke, who replied that he did not have even one coin. Baba said, "I know you have no money but you are reading the *Yoga Vashistha*. Give me dakshina from that." Giving dakshina in this case meant 'deriving lessons from the book and lodging them in the heart where Baba resides.'

Two, in the second case, Baba asked Mrs. Tarkhad to give Rs. 6 as dakshina. She felt pained, as she had nothing to give. Then her husband explained to her that Baba wanted these six inner enemies (desire, anger, greed, ego, jealousy, delusion) to be surrendered to him. Baba agreed with this explanation.

It is to be noted that although Baba collected a lot of money by dakshina, he would redistribute the whole amount the same day. The next morning he would become a poor fakir as usual. When Baba took his mahasamadhi, he had only a few rupees in his possession, after receiving thousands and thousands of rupees as dakshina for about ten years.

In short, Baba's main aim in taking dakshina from his devotees was to teach them the lessons of renunciation and purification.

MORE ON DAKSHINA

B.V. Deo of Thana, retired Revenue Collector, and a great devotee of Baba, wrote an article on the subject of dakshina in which he says, among other things, the following:

Baba did not ask dakshina from all. If some gave dakshina without being asked, he sometimes accepted it, and at other times he refused it. He asked it from certain devotees only. He never demanded it from those devotees who thought in their minds that Baba should ask for it, and only then would they pay it. If anybody offered it against his wish, he never touched it, and if they left it there, he asked them to take it away. He asked for either small or large amounts from devotees according to their wish, devotion and convenience. He asked it even from women and children. He didn't ask it from all the rich or from all the poor.

Baba never got angry with those from whom he asked dakshina but who did not give it. If any dakshina was sent through some friend who forgot to hand it over, Baba reminded him somehow and made him pay. On some occasions, Baba used to return a portion of the amount given as dakshina and ask the donor to guard it or keep it in his shrine for worship. This process benefited the donor immensely. If anyone offered more than Baba wanted, he returned the extra amount. Sometimes, Baba asked more dakshina from some than what they originally intended to give and, if they had no money, asked them borrow it from others. From some, he demanded dakshina three or four times a day.

Out of the amount collected as dakshina, Baba spent very little for his own sake except to buy chillum and fuel for his dhuni. All the rest, he distributed as charity in varying amounts to different people. All the articles of the Shirdi sansthan were brought by various rich devotees at the instance and suggestion of Radhakrishna Mai. Baba always used to get wild and scolded those who brought costly and rich articles. He said to Nanasaheb that all his property consisted of one *koupin* (waist cloth), one stray piece of cloth, one kafni and a *tumrel* (tinpot), and that people troubled him by bringing all these unnecessary, useless and costly articles.

Lust and wealth are the two main obstacles in the way of *Paramatma* (Supreme Reality). In Shirdi, Baba provided two institutions, dakshina and Radhakrishna Mai. Whenever men came to him, he demanded dakshina from them and then asked them to go to the 'school'—Radhakrishna Mai's house. If they stood these two tests well, and showed that they were free from attachment to woman and wealth, their progress in spirituality was rapid and assured by Baba's grace and blessings.

Mr. Deo has also quoted passages from the *Gita* and *Upanishads* showing that charity given in a holy place to a holy person is greatly conducive to the donor's welfare. What is more holy than Shirdi and its presiding deity Sai Baba?

Pranams to Sri Sai

Peace Be to All

CHAPTER FIFTEEN

The readers may remember that in Chapter Six mention was made about the Ramanavami Festival in Shirdi, how the festival originated, how in the early years it was difficult to get good singers for kirtan and how Baba permanently entrusted this function to Das Ganu. Now in this chapter we shall describe the manner in which Das Ganu was performing kirtan.

❦

DAS GANU CHANGES HIS CLOTHES

Generally, kirtan singers wear elaborate dress. They put on a headdress or turban, a long flowing coat with a shirt inside, an *uparane* (short cloth) on the shoulders and the usual long *dhotar* (cloth) from the waist below. Dressed in this fashion, Das Ganu once went to bow to Baba. Baba asked, "Well, bridegroom! Where are you going dressed so beautifully?"

"To perform a kirtan."

Baba said, "Why do you want all this paraphernalia, coat, uparane and turban and all that before me? Why wear them on the body?" Das Ganu immediately took them off and placed them at Baba's feet. From that time on, Das Ganu never wore these things while singing kirtan. He was always bare from waist up with a pair of chiplis in his hand and a garland around his neck. This is not the traditional practice by kirtan singers, but this is the best and purest method. The sage Narada, from whom kirtan originated, wore nothing on his trunk and head. He carried a *vina* (one stringed instrument) in his hand and wandered from place to place, everywhere singing the glory of the Lord.

⚜

Sugarless Tea and a Pilgrimage to Shirdi

Wherever you go over the wide world, I am with you. My abode is in your heart and I am within you. Always worship me, who is seated in your heart, as well as in the hearts of all beings. Blessed and fortunate, indeed, is he who knows me this way.

Initially, Baba was known in Poona and Ahmednagar Districts, but Nanasaheb's personal talks, and Das Ganu's splendid kirtans, spread Baba's fame to Mumbai. In fact, it was Das Ganu—may God bless him—who, by his beautiful and outstanding kirtans, made Baba available to so many people there.

Audiences who come to hear kirtans have different tastes. Some like the erudition of the kirtan leader. Some like his gestures, some his singing, some his wit and humor, some his dissertation on *Vedanta*, and some like his stories and so on. There are very few, who by hearing kirtan, get faith and devotion or love for God or the saints. The effect of hearing Das Ganu's kirtans on the minds of an audience, however, was electric. We give an instance of it here:

Das Ganu was once performing kirtan, singing the glory of Sai Baba in the Koupineshwar temple in Thana. Mr. Cholkar, a poor man serving in the civil courts in Thana, was among the audience. He listened to Das Ganu's kirtan most attentively and was very moved. There and then he mentally bowed and vowed to Baba, "Baba, I am a poor man, unable to support my family. If, by your grace, I pass the departmental examination and get a permanent post, I shall go to Shirdi, fall at your feet and distribute sugar candy in your name."

Mr. Cholkar did pass the examination and did get the permanent post. Now it remained for him to fulfill his vow, the sooner the better. Mr. Cholkar was a poor man with a large family to support. He could not afford to pay for the expenses of a Shirdi trip. As is well said, one can easily cross over Nahne ghat or even the Sahyadri Range, but it is very difficult for a poor man to cross the threshold of his own house.

As Mr. Cholkar was anxious to fulfill his vow as early as possible, he resolved to economize, cut down his expenses and save money. He determined not to use sugar in his diet and began to take his tea without it. After he was able to save some money in this way, he came to Shirdi. He had Baba's darshan, fell at his feet, offered a coconut, and distributed it with a clear conscience along with the sugar candy as per his vow. He told Baba that he was very happy with his darshan and that his desires were fulfilled that day.

Mr. Cholkar was in the masjid with his host, Bapusaheb Jog. When the host and the guest both got up and were about to leave the masjid, Baba said to Jog, "Give him cups of tea, fully saturated with sugar." Hearing these significant words, Mr. Cholkar was moved and wonderstruck, his eyes filled with tears and he fell at Baba's feet again. Jog was curious about this direction to give tea to his guest. Baba wanted to create faith and devotion in Mr. Cholkar's mind. He hinted about the sugar candy as per Mr. Cholkar's vow and that he knew full well Mr. Cholkar's secret determination not to use sugar in his diet. Baba said:

If you spread your palms with devotion before me, I am immediately with you, day and night. Though my body is physically here, still I know what you do, beyond the seven seas. Wherever you go over the wide world, I am with you. My abode is in your heart and I am within you. Always worship me, who is seated in your heart, as well as in the hearts of all beings. Blessed and fortunate, indeed, is he who knows me this way.

What a beautiful and important lesson Baba imparted to Mr. Cholkar.

TWO LIZARDS REUNITE IN SHIRDI

Now we close this chapter with a story of two little lizards. Once Baba was sitting in the masjid with a devotee sitting in front of him, when a lizard tick ticked. Out of curiosity, the devotee asked Baba whether this tick ticking of the lizard signified anything. Was it a good sign or a bad omen? Baba said that the lizard was overjoyed as her sister from Aurangabad was coming to see her. The devotee sat silent, not understanding the meaning of Baba's words.

Immediately, a gentleman from Aurangabad came on horseback to see Baba. He wanted to proceed farther but his horse would not go as it was hungry. He took a bag from his shoulders to bring out the grains and dashed it on the ground to remove the dirt. A lizard came out from the bag and in the presence of all, climbed up the wall. Baba asked the devotee who asked about the lizard to notice well. The lizard went strutting to her sister at once. Both sisters, meeting each other after a long time, kissed, embraced each other and whirled around and danced with love! Where is Shirdi and where is Aurangabad? How could the man on horseback come from Aurangabad to Shirdi with the lizard? And how should Baba make the prophecy of the meeting of the two sisters? All this is really very wonderful and proves the omniscience, the all-knowing nature, of Baba.

Whoever respectfully reads this chapter or studies it daily, will have all his miseries removed by the grace of the sadguru Sai Baba.

Pranams to Sri Sai

Peace Be to All

CHAPTERS SIXTEEN & SEVENTEEN

THE RICH GENTLEMAN WHO WANTED
BRAHMA JNANA QUICKLY

The last chapter described how Mr. Cholkar's vow of a small offering was completed and accepted. In that story, Sai Baba showed that he would happily accept anything, no matter how small, when it was offered with love and devotion. But if the same thing was offered with pride and conceit, he would reject it. He, being full of *satchitananda* (existence, consciousness and bliss), did not care for outward formalities but if an offering was made in a humble spirit, it was eagerly welcomed and accepted with pleasure. In fact, there is no person more generous and compassionate than a sadguru like Sai Baba. He cannot even be compared to the *Chintamani* jewel (the philosopher's stone which satisfies desires), the *Kalpataru* (the celestial tree which fulfills our desires) or the *Kamadhenu* (the celestial cow which gives what we desire), for they only give us what we desire. But the sadguru gives us the most precious thing, which is inconceivable and inscrutable—Reality. Now let us hear how Baba handled a rich man who came and implored Baba to give him *Brahma Jnana* (self-realization).

There was a rich gentleman who had amassed a large quantity of wealth, houses, fields and lands and had many servants and dependents. When Baba's fame reached his ears, he said to a friend that as he was not in want of anything he would go to Shirdi and ask Baba to give him Brahma Jnana, which would certainly make him happier. His friend tried to discourage him, saying, "It is not easy to know Brahman, especially for an avaricious man like you who is always engrossed in wealth, wife and children. Who will satisfy you in your search of Brahma Jnana if you won't even give one coin in charity?"

Not minding his friend's advice, the fellow engaged a tanga and went to Shirdi. He went to the masjid and when he saw Baba fell at his feet, saying, "Baba, hearing that you show Brahman to all who come here without delay, I have come all the way from my distant place. I am much fatigued by the journey and if I get the Brahman from you, my troubles will be well paid and rewarded."

Baba replied:

Oh my dear friend, do not be anxious. I shall immediately show you Brahman. All my dealings are in cash and never on credit. So many people come to me and ask for wealth, health, power, honor, position, cure of diseases and other temporal matters. Rare is the person who comes to me and asks for Brahma Jnana. There is no lack of people asking for worldly things, people interested in spiritual matters are very rare. I think it a lucky and auspicious moment when people like you come and press me for Brahma Jnana. So with pleasure, I will show you Brahman, with all that accompanies it and with all its complications.

Saying this, Baba started to show him Brahman. He had him sit there and engaged him in some talk which made him forget his question for the time being. Then he called a boy and told him to go to Nandu Marwari and borrow five rupees from him. The boy left and returned immediately saying that Nandu was not there and his house was locked. Then Baba asked him to go to Bala, the grocer, and get a loan of five rupees from him. This time the boy was also unsuccessful. This effort was repeated two or three more times with the same result.

Baba was, as we know, the living Brahma incarnate. Some may ask, "Why did he want the paltry sum of five rupees, and why did he try hard to get it on loan?" Really he did not want that sum at all. He must have fully known that Nandu and Bala would not be at home, and he seems to have adopted this procedure as a test for the seeker of Brahman. That gentleman had a bundle of currency notes in his pocket. If he were really earnest, he would not have sat quietly and been a mere onlooker when Baba was frantically trying to get the paltry sum of five rupees. He knew that Baba would keep his word and repay the debt and that the sum wanted was insignificant, still he could not make up his mind and advance the sum. Such a man wanted the greatest thing in the world from Baba, Brahma Jnana! Any other person who really loved Baba would have given five rupees at once, instead of being a mere onlooker. This was not the case with this man. He advanced no money nor did he sit silently but instead began to become impatient, as he was in a haste to return. So he implored Baba, saying, "Oh Baba, please show me soon."

Baba replied:

Oh my dear friend. Did you not understand the process that I went through, sitting here, to enable you to see Brahman? It is, in short, this—to see Brahman one has to surrender five things:

1. Five pranas (vital forces)
2. Five senses (five of action and five of perception)
3. Mind
4. Intellect
5. Ego

This path of Brahma Jnana or self-realization is as hard to tread as the edge of a razor.

Baba then gave a long discourse on the subject, the meaning of which is given below.

QUALIFICATIONS FOR BRAHMA JNANA OR SELF-REALIZATION

The knowledge of the Self is so subtle and mystic that no one can ever hope to attain it through his own individual effort. So the help of a teacher who has himself attained self-realization is absolutely necessary.

Everyone does not see or realize Brahma Jnana in their lifetime. To realize Brahma Jnana, certain qualifications are absolutely necessary:

Mumuksha. An intense desire for freedom. He who thinks that he is bound and should get free from bondage and works earnestly and resolutely to that end, and who does not care for any other thought, is qualified for spiritual life.

Virakti. A feeling of disgust with the things of this world and the next. Unless a man feels aversion with these things, and the rewards and honors which his action would bring in this world and the next, he has no right to enter into the spiritual realm.

Antarmukhata. Introversion. God has created our senses with a tendency to move outward and so man always looks outside himself and not inside. He who wants self-realization and immortal life must turn his gaze inwards, and look to his inner self.

Stop doing wrong. Unless a man has turned away from evil, stopped from doing wrong, and has gained self-control and unless his mind is at rest, he cannot gain self-realization, even by means of knowledge.

Right conduct. Unless a man leads a life of truth, spiritual practice, self-control and insight, he cannot get God-realization.

Prefer shreyas, the good, to preyas, the pleasant. There are two things, the good and the pleasant. The good deals with spiritual affairs, and the pleasant with mundane matters. Both of these approach man. He has to think and choose one of them. The wise man prefers the good over the pleasant; but the unwise, because of greed and attachment, chooses the pleasant over the good.

Control of the mind and the senses. The body is the chariot and the Self is its master. Intellect is the charioteer and the mind is the reins. The senses are the horses and sense objects their paths. He who has no understanding and whose mind is unrestrained, whose senses are uncontrollable like the vicious horses of a charioteer, does not reach his destination of self-realization and goes through the round of births and deaths. He who has understanding and whose mind is restrained, his senses being under control, like the good horse of a charioteer, reaches that place, the state of self-realization, and is not born again. The man, who has understanding as his charioteer (guide) and is able to rein his mind, reaches the end of the journey, which is the supreme abode of the all-pervading Lord.

Purification of the mind. Unless a man successfully fulfills the duties of his station in life with detachment, his mind will not be purified and, unless his mind is purified, he cannot attain self-realization. It is only in the purified mind that *viveka* (discrimination between the real and unreal) and *vairagya* (detachment from the unreal) crop up and lead to self-realization. Unless egoism is dropped, greed ended, and the mind made desireless (pure), self-realization is not possible. The idea that 'I am the body' is a great delusion, and attachment to this idea is the cause of bondage. Leave off this idea and attachment if you want self-realization.

The necessity of a guru. The knowledge of the Self is so subtle and mystic that no one can ever hope to attain it through his own individual effort. So the help of a teacher who has himself attained self-realization is absolutely necessary. What others cannot give with great labor and pain can be easily gained with the help of such a teacher. For he has walked on the path himself and can easily take the disciple, step by step, on the ladder of spiritual progress.

Lastly, the Lord's grace is the most essential thing. When the Lord is pleased with someone, he gives him *viveka* (discrimination) and *vairagya* (detachment) and takes him safely beyond the ocean of mundane existence. "The Self cannot be gained by the study of *Vedas*, nor by intellect, nor by much learning. He whom the Self chooses, gains it. To him, the Self reveals its nature," says the *Katha Upanishad.*

After the dissertation was over, Baba turned to the gentleman and said, "Well Sir, Brahman is in your pocket in the form of fifty times five rupees. Please take that out."

The gentleman took out a bundle of currency notes from his pocket and to his great surprise found on counting them that there were 25 notes of 10 rupees each. Seeing the omniscience of Baba, he was moved and fell at Baba's feet to receive his blessings. Then Baba said to him:

Roll up your bundle of Brahman (currency notes). Unless you completely get rid of your greed, you will not get the real Brahman. How can a person with a mind engrossed in wealth, children and desires expect to know Brahman without removing his attachment to them? The illusion of attachment or the love for money is a deep eddy of pain full of crocodiles in the form of conceit and jealousy.

Only he who is without desire can cross this whirlpool. Greed and Brahman are poles apart; they are eternally opposed to each other. Where there is greed, there is no room for meditation on Brahman. How can a greedy man get detachment and liberation? For a greedy man, there is no peace, nor contentment or certainty. If there is even a little trace of greed in the mind, all the *sadhanas* (spiritual practices) are of no use.

Even the knowledge of a well-read man who is not free from the desire of the fruit or reward of his actions is useless and can't help him achieve self-realization. The teachings of a guru are of no use to a man who is full of egoism and who always thinks about sense objects. Purification of mind is absolutely necessary. Without it, all our spiritual endeavors are nothing but useless show and pomp. It is better for one to take only what he can digest and assimilate. My treasury is full, and I can give anyone whatever he wants, but I have to see whether he is qualified to receive what I can give. If you listen to me carefully, you will certainly benefit. Sitting in this masjid, I never speak any untruth.

When a guest is invited to a house, all the members of the household and other friends and relations that happen to be present are entertained along with the guest. So all those who were present in the masjid at this time could partake of the spiritual feast that was served by Baba for the rich gentleman. After getting Baba's blessings, one and all, including the gentleman, left the place quite happy and contented.

SPECIAL QUALITIES OF BABA

There are many saints who leaving their houses, stay in the forest, caves or hermitages and remain in solitude to achieve liberation for themselves. They do not care for other people and are always self-absorbed. Sai Baba was not such a type. He had no home, no wife, no children, nor any relations, near or distant. Still, he lived in the world. He begged his bread from four or five houses, always lived at the foot of the neem tree, carried on worldly dealings, and taught people how to act and behave in this world. Rare are the sadhus and saints who, after attaining God-realization, strive for the welfare of the people.

Sai Baba was the foremost of these, and therefore, says Hemadpant, "Blessed is the country, blessed is the family, and blessed are the virtuous parents where this extraordinary, transcendent, precious and pure jewel Sai Baba was born."

Pranams to Sri Sai

Peace Be to All

CHAPTERS EIGHTEEN & NINETEEN

How Hemadpant Was Accepted and Blessed

In the last two chapters, Hemadpant described how a rich gentleman aspiring for quick Brahma Jnana was treated by Baba. Now in these two chapters, he describes how Hemadpant himself was accepted and blessed by Baba, how Baba encouraged good thoughts and brought them to fruition, and gave his teachings regarding self-improvement, gossip and remuneration for labor.

⚜

Sai Baba Imparts Spiritual Instructions

It is a well-known fact that the sadguru looks first to the qualifications of his disciples, then gives them suitable instructions and leads them on towards the goal of self-realization. In this respect, some say that what the sadguru teaches or instructs should not be divulged to others.

They think that their instructions become useless if they are published. This view is not correct. The sadguru is like a monsoon cloud. He pours down profusely, widely scattering his nectar-like teachings. These we should enjoy and assimilate to our heart's content and then serve others with them, without any reserve. This rule should apply not only to what he teaches in our waking state, but to the visions he gives us in our dreams. One example of this is when Budhakowshik Rishi composed his celebrated *Ramraksha Stotra*, which he had seen in his dream.

Like a loving mother forcing bitter but wholesome medicines down the throats of her children for the sake of their health, Sai Baba imparted spiritual instructions to his devotees. His method was not veiled or secret, but quite open. The devotees who followed his instructions reached their aim. Sadgurus like Sai Baba open the eyes of our intellect and show us the divine beauty of the Self, and fulfill our tender longings of devotion. When this is done, our desire for sense objects vanishes. The twin fruits of *viveka* (discrimination) and *vairagya* (detachment) come to our hands and knowledge sprouts up even in sleep. All this we get when we come in contact with saints, serve them and secure their love. The Lord, who fulfills the desires of His devotees, comes to our aid, removes our troubles and sufferings, and makes us happy. This progress or development is entirely due to the help of the sadguru, who is regarded as the Lord Himself. And so we should always follow the sadguru, hear his stories, fall at his feet and serve him. Now we come to our main story.

⚜

BABA GIVES INSTRUCTIONS DURING SLEEP

There was a gentleman named Mr. Sathe who had attained some renown many years before during the Crowford Regime. He suffered severe losses in trade. Other adverse circumstances gave him much trouble and made him sad and dejected. Being restless, he thought of leaving home to go to a distant place. Man does not generally think of God except when difficulties and calamities overtake him, then he turns to God and prays for relief. If his evil actions have come to an end, God arranges his meeting with a saint who gives him proper directions regarding his welfare. Mr. Sathe had a similar experience.

His friends advised him to go to Shirdi, where so many people were flocking to get Sai Baba's darshan to receive peace of mind and fulfillment of their desires. He liked the idea and at once went to Shirdi in 1917. Seeing Baba's form, which was like eternal Brahman, self-luminous, spotless and pure, his mind lost its restlessness and became calm and composed. He thought that it was the accumulation of merits from his former births that brought him to the holy feet of Baba. He was a man of strong will. He at once started to make a *parayana* (study) of the *Guru Charitra.*

When the *saptaha* (seven days of reading) the *Guru Charitra* was finished, Baba gave him a vision that night. It was to this effect: Baba, with the *Guru Charitra* in his hand, was explaining its contents to Mr. Sathe, who was sitting in front and listening carefully. When he woke up, he remembered the dream and felt very happy. He thought that it was extremely kind of Baba who awakens souls like his that are snoring in ignorance and makes them taste the nectar of *Guru Charitra.* Next day, he informed Kakasaheb of this vision and requested him to consult Baba regarding its meaning or significance, and whether one *saptah* (week-long) reading was sufficient or whether he should begin again.

When a suitable opportunity arrived, Kakasaheb asked Baba, "Deva, what do you suggest to Mr. Sathe from this vision? Should he stop or continue the saptah? He is a simple devotee. His desire should be fulfilled and the vision explained to him, and he should be blessed."

Baba replied, "He should make one more saptah of the book. If the work is studied carefully, the devotee will become pure and will benefit. The Lord will be pleased and will rescue him from the bondage of the mundane existence."

Hemadpant was present at this time and was shampooing Baba's legs. When he heard Baba's words, he thought, 'What! Mr. Sathe has read it only for a week and received a reward. I have been reading it for 40 years with no result! His seven-day stay here became fruitful while my seven-year stay goes for nothing. Like a chatak bird, I am ever waiting for the merciful cloud to pour its nectar on me and bless me with his instruction.' No sooner did this thought cross his mind, than Baba knew it then and there. It was the experience of his bhaktas that Baba read and understood all their thoughts, suppressed the evil thoughts and encouraged the good ones. Reading Hemadpant's mind, Baba at once asked him to get up, go to Shama, get Rs.15 from him as dakshina, sit and chitchat with him for a while and then return. Mercy dawned in Baba's mind so he issued this order. Who could disobey Baba's order?

Hemadpant immediately left the masjid and went to Shama's house. Shama had just bathed and was wearing a dhotar. He came out and asked

Hemadpant, "How is it that you are here now? It seems that you have come from the masjid. Why do you look restless and dejected? Why are you alone? Please sit and rest, I shall do my worship and return. In the meanwhile, please take some betel nuts and let us then have a pleasant chat."

After saying this, he went inside and Hemadpant sat alone in the front verandah. In the window, he saw a well-known Marathi book called *Nath Bhagwat* (dialogue between Krishna and his servant devotee Uddhava). This is saint Ekanath's commentary on the eleventh chapter of the *Bhagavad Gita*. At the recommendation of Sai Baba, every day Jog and Kakasaheb read *Jnaneshwari,* the *Bhagavad Gita* (dialogue between Krishna and his friend-devotee Arjuna) with Marathi commentary and also Ekanath's *Bhawartha Ramayana.*

When devotees came to Baba and asked him certain questions, he sometimes answered them in part and asked them to go and listen to the readings of these works, which are the main treatises of Bhagwat dharma. When the devotees went and listened, they received full and satisfactory replies to their questions. Hemadpant also used to read some portions of the *Nath Bhagwat* daily.

That day he did not complete the daily portion of his reading, but had left it unfinished in order to accompany some devotees who were going to the masjid. When he took the book from Shama's window and casually opened it, he found to his surprise that it opened to the part he had not completed. He thought that Baba very kindly sent him to Shama's house so he could complete his daily reading. So he went through the unfinished portion and completed it. As soon as this was over, Shama came out after completing his worship and the following conversation took place between them.

Hemadpant said, "I have come with a message from Baba. He has asked me to get Rs.15 as dakshina from you, sit with you for a while and have a pleasant chitchat, then return to the masjid with you."

Shama said with surprise, "I have no money to give. Take my 15 *namaskaras* (bows) in lieu of rupees as dakshina to Baba."

Hemadpant said, "All right, your namaskaras are accepted. Now let us have a chitchat. Tell me some stories and leelas of Baba, which will destroy our karmas."

Shama said, "Then sit here for a while. Wonderful is the sport of this God, Baba. You know it already. I am a village rustic while you are an enlightened citizen. You have seen many more leelas since your coming here. How can I describe them to you? Well, take these betel nuts and chunam leaves and eat while I go in and dress."

In a few minutes, Shama came out and sat and talked with Hemadpant. He said, "The leela of this God (Baba) is inscrutable. There is no end to his leelas. Who can see them? He sports with his leelas, still he is unaffected by them. What do we rustics know? Why does Baba not tell stories himself? Why does he send learned men like you to fools like me? His ways are inconceivable. I can only say that they are not human." With this preface Shama added, "I now remember a story, which I shall relate to you. I know of it personally. If a devotee is resolute and determined, so is Baba's immediate response. Sometimes Baba puts the devotees to the test, then gives them *upadesh* (mantra initiation).

As soon as Hemadpant heard the word upadesh, a flash of lightning crossed through his mind. He immediately remembered the story of Mr. Sathe's *Guru Charitra* reading and thought that Baba might have sent him to Shama in order to give peace to his restless mind. However, he curbed this feeling and began to listen to Shama's stories. They all showed how kind and affectionate Baba was to his devotees. Hemadpant began to feel joy while hearing them. Then Shama began to tell the following story.

⚜

RADHABAI DESHMUKH

"Make me the sole focus of your thoughts and actions and you will, no doubt, attain Paramatma (Supreme Reality). Look to me whole-heartedly, and I in turn will look at you."

There was an old woman by the name of Radhabai, who was the mother of Khashaba Deshmukh. Hearing of Baba's fame, she came to Shirdi. She had Baba's darshan and was much satisfied. She loved Baba immediately and resolved that she would accept Baba as her guru and receive upadesh from him. She knew nothing else. She was determined to fast unto death until Baba accepted her and gave her upadesh. She stayed in her lodging and did not take food or water for three days.

I was frightened by the ordeal of the old woman and interceded with Baba on her behalf. I said, "Deva, what is this you have started? You drag so many people here. You know that old lady. She is very obstinate and depends on you entirely. She has resolved to fast unto death if you don't accept and instruct her. If anything worse happens, people will blame you and say that Baba did not instruct her and consequently she met her death. So take some mercy on her, bless her and instruct her." On seeing her determination, Baba sent for her and changed her mind by addressing her like this:

Oh mother, why are you subjecting yourself to unnecessary tortures and hastening your death? You are really my mother and I am your child. Take pity on me and hear me through. I will tell you my own story, which if you listen carefully, will do you good.

I had a guru. He was a great saint and most merciful. I served him long, very long; still he would not blow any mantra into my ears. I had a keen desire never to leave him but to stay and serve him, and at all costs receive some instructions from him. But he had his own way. First, he had my head shaved and asked me for two *pice* (coin of small value) as dakshina. I gave them at once. If you say that my guru was perfect, why should he ask for money and how could he be called desireless? I reply simply that he never cared for coins. What had he to do with them? His two coins were (1) firm faith and (2) patience or cheerful endurance. I gave these two things to him and he was pleased.

I stayed with my guru for twelve years. He brought me up. There was no lack of food and clothing. He was full of love; no, he was love incarnate. How can I describe it? He loved me most. Rare is a guru like him. When I looked at him, he seemed as if he was in deep meditation, and we both were filled with bliss. Night and day, I gazed at him with no thought of hunger and thirst. Without him, I felt restless. I had no other object to meditate on, nor any other thing other than my guru to attend. He was my sole refuge. My mind was always fixed on him. This *Nishtha* (faith) is one coin. *Saburi* (patience or perseverance) is the other coin. I waited patiently and served my guru a long time. Saburi will ferry you across the sea of this mundane existence. Saburi is manliness in man, it removes all sins and afflictions, gets rid of calamities in various ways, casts aside all fear, and ultimately gives you success. Saburi is the mine of virtues, consort of good thought. *Nishtha* (faith) and *saburi* (patience) are like twin sisters, loving each other very intimately.

My guru never expected any other thing from me. He never neglected me, and protected me at all times. I lived with him but was sometimes away from him, still I never felt the want or absence of his love. He always protected me by his glance, just as the tortoise feeds her young ones by her loving looks, whether they are near her or away from her on the other side of the riverbank. Oh mother, my guru never taught me any mantra, then how shall I blow any mantra in your ear? Just remember that the guru's tortoise-like loving glance gives us happiness. Do not try to get mantra or upadesh from anybody. Make me the sole focus of your thoughts and actions and you will, no doubt, attain *Paramatma* (Supreme Reality). Look to me whole-heartedly, and I in turn will look at you. Sitting in this masjid, I speak the truth, nothing but the truth. No sadhanas, nor proficiency in the six *Shastras*, are necessary. Have faith and confidence in your guru. Believe fully that the guru is the sole actor or doer. Blessed is he who knows the greatness of his guru and thinks him to be *Hari*, *Hara* and *Brahma* (Trimurti) incarnate.

Instructed in this way, the old lady was convinced. She bowed to Baba and gave up her fast.

Hearing this story carefully and attentively, and marking its significance and appropriateness, Hemadpant was very happy. Seeing this wonderful leela of Baba, he was moved from top to toe, overflowing with joy and choked up, unable to utter a single word. Shama, on seeing him in this condition asked, "What is the matter with you, why are you silent? How many innumerable leelas of Baba can I describe!"

Just at that moment, the bell in the masjid began to ring, proclaiming that the noon worship and Aarati had begun. Shama and Hemadpant hurried to the masjid. Bapusaheb Jog had just started the worship. Women were up in the masjid and men were standing below in the open courtyard and all were singing the Aarati loudly in chorus to the accompaniment of drums. Shama went up, pulling Hemadpant with him. He sat to the right and Hemadpant in front of Baba.

On seeing them, Baba asked Hemadpant to give the dakshina brought from Shama. He replied that Shama gave namaskaras in lieu of rupees and that he was there in person. Baba said, "All right, now let me know whether you both had a chitchat, and if so, tell me all that you talked about." Not minding the sounds of the bell, the drum and the chorus songs, Hemadpant was eager to tell what they had talked about and started to narrate it. Baba was also anxious to hear, and so he leaned forward away from the bolster.

Hemadpant said everything they talked about was very pleasant and especially the story of the old lady was most wonderful. On hearing it, he thought that Baba's leela was inexplicable, and under the guise of that story Baba actually blessed him. Baba then said, "Wonderful is the story. How were you blessed? I would like to know everything in detail from you, so tell me."

Then Hemadpant related the story in full, which had made such a lasting impression on his mind. Hearing this Baba was very pleased and asked, "Did the story strike you and did you catch its significance?"

He replied, "Yes, Baba the restlessness of my mind has vanished and I have true peace and repose, and have come to know the true path."

Then Baba spoke:

My method is quite unique. Remember well this one story; it will be very useful. To get the knowledge (realization) of the Self, *dhyana* (meditation) is necessary. If you practice it continuously, the *vrittis* (thoughts) will be pacified. Being totally desireless, you should meditate on the Lord, who is in all creatures; when the mind is concentrated the goal will be achieved. Meditate always on my formless nature, which is knowledge, consciousness and bliss incarnate. If you cannot do this, meditate on my form from top to toe as you see here night and day. As you go on doing this, your thoughts will be concentrated on one point, then the distinction between the meditator, the act of meditation and what is meditated on will disappear, and the meditator will be one with consciousness and will be merged in Brahman. The mother tortoise is on one bank of the river and her young ones are on the other side. She gives neither milk nor warmth to them. Her mere glance gives them nutrition. The young ones do nothing but remember their mother. The tortoise's glance is a downpour of nectar to her young ones, the only source of sustenance and happiness. Similar is the relationship between the guru and disciple.

When Baba uttered these last words, the chorus of the Aarati songs stopped and all cried out loudly in one voice, "Victory to our sadguru Sai Maharaj, who is existence, consciousness and bliss!" Dear readers, let us imagine that we are standing among the crowd in the masjid and let us join them in this *Jaya Jayakar* (victory salutation).

After the Aarati ceremony was over, prasad was distributed. Bapusaheb Jog advanced as usual, and after saluting Baba, gave a handful of sugar candy in his hand. Baba put all of it into Hemadpant's hand and said to him, "If you take this story to heart and remember it well, your state will be as sweet as the sugar candy, all your desires will be fulfilled and you will be happy."

Hemadpant bowed before Baba and implored, "Do favor me like this, bless and protect me always."

Baba replied, "Hear this story, meditate on it and assimilate its spirit. Then you will always remember and meditate on the Lord, who will manifest Himself to you."

Dear readers! Hemadpant received prasad of sugar candy then. Now we get the prasad of the nectar of this story. Let us drink it to our heart's content, meditate on it, assimilate it, and be strong and happy by Baba's grace. Amen!

Towards the end of the 19th chapter, Hemadpant had dealt with some other matters which are given below.

BABA'S ADVICE REGARDING OUR BEHAVIOR

The following words of Baba are general and invaluable. If they are kept in mind and acted upon, they will always do you good.

Unless there is some relationship or connection, nobody goes anywhere. If any man or creature comes to you, do not discourteously drive them away, but receive and treat them well, with due respect. *Sri Hari* (God) will be certainly pleased if you give water to the thirsty, bread to the hungry, clothes to the naked, and your verandah to strangers for sitting and resting. If anybody wants any money from you, and you are not inclined to give it, do not give it but do not bark at him like a dog.

Let anybody speak hundreds of things against you; do not resent them by giving any bitter reply. If you always tolerate such things, you will certainly be happy. Let the world go upside down, you remain where you are. Standing or staying in your own place, look on calmly at the show of all things passing before you. Demolish the wall of difference that separates you from me, and then the road for our meeting will be clear and open. The sense of differentiation, 'I and you' is the barrier that keeps the disciple away from his master. Unless that is destroyed the state of union is not possible.

Allah Malik—God is the Sole Proprietor. No one else is our protector. His method of work is extraordinary, inestimable and inscrutable. His will be done and He will show us the way and satisfy our heart's desires. It is on account of *ranubhandah* (karma of a former relationship) that we have come together. Let us love and serve each other and be happy. He who attains the supreme goal of life is immortal and happy. All others merely exist.

ENCOURAGING GOOD THOUGHTS

It is interesting to note how Sai Baba encouraged good thoughts. You have to surrender yourself completely to him with love and devotion, and then you will see how he helps you in so many things. A saint said that when you have a good thought immediately after awakening from sleep, and if you develop this during the day, your intellect will expand and your mind will attain calmness. Hemadpant wanted to try this.

One Wednesday night before going to bed he thought, 'Tomorrow is Thursday, an auspicious day in a holy place, Shirdi. Let me pass the whole day in remembering and chanting the *Rama nama* (name of God).' Then he slept. The next morning when he got up he remembered the name of Rama without any effort and was much pleased. Then, after finishing his morning duties he went to Baba with flowers. When he left Dixit's wada and was passing Buti's wada (presently the Samadhi mandir) he heard a beautiful song sung by Aurangabadkar to Baba in the masjid. The song was *Guru kripanjan payo mere bhai* by Ekanath. In it he says that he received collyrium (eye wash) in the form of the guru's grace, which opened his vision and made him see Rama, inside and out, in sleep, dream and waking state, everywhere. There were so many songs. Why did Aurangabadkar choose this particular song? Is this not a curious coincidence arranged by Baba to encourage Hemadpant's determination to sing the name Rama unceasingly during the day?

All saints stress the importance of uttering Rama's name to fulfill the ambitions of devotees and protect and save them from all calamities.

VARIETY OF BABA'S INSTRUCTIONS & SLANDERER ADMONISHED

"Meditate always on my formless nature, which is knowledge, consciousness and bliss incarnate. If you cannot do this, meditate on my form from top to toe as you see here night and day."

Sai Baba required no special place, nor any special time, to give instructions. He gave them freely whenever an occasion demanded. Once it so happened that a devotee of Baba reviled another behind his back. While leaving aside merits, he dwelt on the faults of his brother and spoke so sarcastically that the hearers were disgusted. Generally, we can see that people have a tendency to scandalize others unnecessarily bringing about hatred and ill will. Saints see scandal in another light. They say that there are various ways of cleansing or removing dirt, by means of earth, water and soap, but a gossipmonger has a way of his own. He removes the dirt (faults) of others by his tongue; so in a way he obliges the person whom he reviles and for this he is to be thanked.

Sai Baba had his own method of correcting the gossipmonger. He knew through his omniscience what the slanderer had done. At noon, when he met him near Lendi, Baba pointed out a pig that was eating filth near the fence and said:

Behold how the pig is gorging dung with relish. Your conduct is similar. You go on reviling your own brethren to your heart's content. After performing many deeds of merit, you are born a man. If you act like this, will Shirdi help you in any way?

Needless to say, the devotee took the lesson to heart and went away.

In this way, Baba went on giving instructions whenever necessary. If these are accepted in our minds and acted upon, the spiritual goal is not far off. There is a proverb that says, "If my Lord is there, He will feed me on my cot." This proverb is true in respect of food and clothing, but if anyone trusts this and sits quietly doing nothing in spiritual matters, he will be ruined. One has to exert himself to his utmost to attain self-realization. The more he endeavors, the better for him.

Baba said that he was omnipresent, occupying land, air, country, world, light and heaven, and that he was not limited. To remove the misunderstanding of those who thought that Baba was only his body, three cubits and a half in length, he incarnated in this form so that if any devotee meditated on him day and night with complete self-surrender, he experienced complete union with him, like sweetness and sugar, waves and sea, eye and its sight. He who wants to end the cycle of births and deaths should lead a virtuous life, with his mind calm and composed. He should always engage in good actions, should do his duties and surrender heart and soul to him. Then he need not be afraid of anything. He who trusts Baba entirely, hears and talks of his leelas and does not think of anything else is sure to attain self-realization.

Baba asked many to remember his name and surrender to him. But to those who wanted to know who they were ('Who am I' inquiry), he advised *shravanam* (study) and *dhyana* (meditation). To some, he advised remembering God's name, to others hearing his leelas, to some worship of his feet, to others reading and studying *Adhyatma Ramayana, Jnaneshwari* and other sacred scriptures. Some he made sit near his feet, some he sent to Khandoba's temple, some he advised the repetition of the thousand names of Vishnu, and some the study of *Chhandogya Upanishad* and *Gita*. There was no limit nor restriction to his instructions. To some, he gave them in person, to others by visions in dreams. To one addicted to drink, he appeared in his dream, sat on his chest pressing down, and only released him after the person promised not to touch liquor anymore. To some, he explained some mantras like *Guru Brahma* in dreams. To some devotees who were practicing Hatha Yoga, he sent word that they should leave off Hatha Yoga practices, sit quietly and wait (saburi). It is impossible to describe all his ways and methods.

In ordinary worldly dealings, he set examples by his actions, one of which is given below.

REMUNERATION FOR LABOR

One day at noon, Baba came near Radhakrishna Mai's house and said, "Bring me a ladder." Some men brought it and set it against a house as directed by Baba. He climbed up on the roof of Vaman Gondkar's house, passed over the roof of Radhakrishna Mai's house, then got down from the other corner. What aim Baba had, no one knew. At the time, Radhakrishna Mai was shivering with malaria. It may be to drive off the fever that Baba went there. Immediately after getting down, Baba paid Rs.2 to the people who brought the ladder. Somebody asked Baba why he paid so much for this. He replied that no one should take the labor of others. The worker should be paid his dues promptly and liberally.

Pranams to Sri Sai

Peace Be to All

CHAPTER TWENTY

I n this chapter, Hemadpant describes how Kakasaheb's maidservant solved Das Ganu's problem.

⚜

THE KINDNESS OF BABA

Sai was originally formless. He assumed a form for the sake of devotees. With the help of the actress, Maya, he played the part of the actor in this big drama of the universe. Let us remember and visualize Sri Sai. Let us go to Shirdi and carefully see the programs following the noon Aarati. After the Aarati was over, Baba used to come out of the masjid and standing on its edge, distribute *udi* (sacred ash) to the devotees with very kind and loving looks. The devotees got up with equal fervor, clasped his feet, and standing and staring at him, enjoyed the shower of udi. Baba passed handfuls of udi into the palms of the devotees and used it to mark their foreheads with his own fingers. The love he bore for them was boundless. He addressed the devotees as follows, "Oh

Bhau, go to take your lunch. You, Anna, go to your lodgings. You, Bapu, go enjoy your meals." In this way, he approached each of the devotees then sent them home. Even now, you can enjoy these sights if you bring your imagination into play. You can visualize and appreciate them. Now bringing Baba before our mental vision, let us meditate on him, from his feet upwards to his face, prostrating before him humbly, lovingly and respectfully.

⚜

A BRIEF EXPLANATION OF THE ISHAVASYA UPANISHAD

Das Ganu started to write a Marathi commentary on the *Ishavasya Upanishad*. Let us first give a brief idea of this *Upanishad* before proceeding further. It is called a *Mantropanishad*, as it is embodied in the mantras of the *Vedic Samhita*. It constitutes the last or the 40th chapter of the *Vajasaneyi Samhita* (*Yajur Veda*), therefore it is called *Vajasaneyi Samhitopanishad*. Being embodied in *Vedic Samhitas*, it is regarded as superior to all other *Upanishads*, which occur in the *Brahmanas* and *Aranyakas* (explanatory treatises on mantras and rituals). Not only this, other *Upanishads* are considered to be commentaries on the truths mentioned briefly in the *Ishavasya Upanishad*. For instance, the biggest of the *Upanishads*, the *Brihadaranyaka Upanishad*, is considered by Pandit Satwalekar to be a running commentary on the *Ishavasya Upanishad*.

Professor R.D. Ranade says, "The *Ishopanishad* (Ishavasya Upanishad) is quite a small *Upanishad*, yet it contains many hints that show extraordinarily piercing insight. Within the short range of 18 verses, it gives a valuable mystical description of the *Atman*, the universal soul, a description of the ideal sage, whose mind stands unruffled by temptations and sorrows. It gives an outline of the doctrine of karma yoga, and finally an understanding of the claims of knowledge and work. The most valuable idea that lies at the root of the *Upanishad* is that of a logical synthesis between the two opposites of knowledge and work. According to the *Upanishad*, a higher synthesis of both knowledge and work is required." In another place he says, "The poetry of the *Ishopanishad* is a mixture of the moral, mystical and metaphysical."

From the brief description given above about this *Upanishad*, anyone can see how difficult it is to translate this *Upanishad* into a common vernacular and describe its exact meaning succinctly. Das Ganu translated it in *Marathi ovi metre*, verse by verse, but as he did not comprehend the real essence of the *Upanishad*, he was not satisfied with his translation. In order to clarify his doubts and questions, he consulted some learned men regarding the difficulties he was having with meanings in text. Although they discussed these issues at great length, they did not resolve his doubts, nor give any rational and satisfactory explanations, so Das Ganu was restless and uneasy.

⚜

BABA'S GRACE MAKES UNDERSTANDING THE ISHAVASYA UPANISHAD POSSIBLE

Baba passed handfuls of udi into the palms of the devotees and used it to mark their foreheads with his own fingers. The love he bore for them was boundless.

As we have seen, this *Upanishad* is the quintessence of the *Vedas*. It is the science of self-realization, it is the weapon that can rip the bondage of life and death to pieces and make us free. Therefore, Das Ganu thought, only he who has attained self-realization can give him the true interpretation of the *Upanishad*. When nobody could satisfy Das Ganu, he resolved to consult Sai Baba about this. When he had an opportunity to go to Shirdi, he prostrated before Baba and told him of his difficulties with the *Ishavasya Upanishad*. He asked Baba to give the correct explanation. Baba blessed him and said, "You need not be anxious, there is no difficulty in this matter. Kakasaheb's maidservant will solve your doubts at Vile Parle on your way home."

The people who were present and heard this thought that Baba was joking and said, "How could an illiterate maidservant solve the difficulties of this mystic nature?" But Das Ganu thought otherwise. He was sure that whatever Baba spoke must come true. Baba's word was the decree of the Almighty.

❧

HAPPINESS DEPENDS ON OUR ATTITUDE

Fully believing in Baba's words, he left Shirdi and went to Vile Parle, a suburb of Mumbai, and stayed with Kakasaheb. The next day, when Das Ganu was enjoying his morning nap, he heard a poor girl singing a beautiful song in clear and melodious tones. The subject matter of the song was a crimson colored sari, how nice it was, how fine its embroidery was, and how beautiful its ends and borders were. He liked the song so much that he went out to look at the young girl singing it. It was Kakasaheb's maidservant. The girl was cleaning vessels and had only a torn rag on her body. On seeing her impoverished condition and her jovial temperament, Das Ganu felt pity for her.

The next day, when Rao Bahadur gave Das Ganu a pair of dhotars, he asked him to also give a sari to the poor little girl. Bahadur then bought a good sari and presented it to her. Like a starving person getting good food to eat, her joy knew no bounds. The next day she wore the new sari and in great joy and merriment whirled and danced around and played fugadi with other girls, outshining them all. But then the following day, she kept the new sari in a box at home and wore the old and torn rag again, but still she looked as happy as on the previous day.

On seeing this, Das Ganu's pity was transformed into admiration. He thought the girl, being poor, had to wear torn rags. But now with her new sari in reserve, she put the old rags back on again but walked around showing no trace of sorrow or unhappiness. He realized then that all our feelings of pain and pleasure depend upon the attitude of our mind. On thinking deeply over this incident, he realized that a man should enjoy whatever God has bestowed on him with the firm conviction that God controls everything, from the front, back and all sides, and that whatever is bestowed on him by God must be for his own good. In this particular case, the impoverished condition of the poor girl, her torn rags and the new sari, the donor, the recipient, and the donation were all parts of God and pervaded by Him. Das Ganu received a practical demonstration of the lesson of the *Upanishad*—the lesson of contentment with one's own lot and the belief that whatever happens is ordained by God and is ultimately good for us.

⚜

BABA'S UNIQUE WAY OF TEACHING

From the above incident, the reader can see that Baba's method was unique and varied. Though Baba never left Shirdi, he sent some to Machchindraga, some to Kolhapur or Sholapur, to practice sadhanas. To some he appeared in his usual form, to some he appeared in waking or dreaming states, day or night, and satisfied their desires. It is impossible to describe all the methods that Baba used in imparting instructions to his bhaktas. In this particular case, he sent Das Ganu to Vile Parle where his problem was solved through the maidservant. To those who say that it was not necessary to send Das Ganu away and that Baba could have personally taught him, we say that Baba followed the right or best course. How else could Das Ganu have learned a great lesson that the poor maidservant and her sari were pervaded by the Lord. Now we will close the chapter with another beautiful extract about this *Upanishad.*

⚜

REALIZE THE ONENESS OF ALL THINGS

One of the main features of the *Ishavasya Upanishad* is the ethical advice it offers. It is interesting to note that the ethics of the *Upanishad* are definitely based upon the metaphysical position advanced in it. The very opening words of the *Upanishad* tell us that God pervades everything. As a corollary from this metaphysical position, the ethical advice it offers is that a man should enjoy whatever God bestows on him in the firm belief that as God pervades everything, whatever God bestows on him must be good. It naturally follows that the *Upanishad* should forbid us from coveting another man's property. In fact, we are appropriately taught a lesson of contentment with one's own lot in the belief that whatever happens is divinely ordained and is therefore good for us.

Another moral advice is that man must be in a mood of always accepting His will while doing actions, especially the karmas spoken of in the *Shastras*. Inactivity, according to this *Upanishad*, would be the canker of the soul. It is only when a man spends his lifetime doing actions in this manner that he can hope to attain the ideal of *naishkarmya* (actionless). Finally, the text goes on to say that a man who sees all beings in the Self and sees the Self as existing in all beings - how can such a man suffer infatuation? What ground would such a man have for grief? Hatred, infatuation, and grief proceed from our not being able to see the Atman in all things. But a man who realizes the oneness of all things, for whom everything has become the Self, must, by this very fact, cease to be affected by human weaknesses.

Pranams to Sri Sai

Peace Be to All

CHAPTER TWENTY-ONE

I n this chapter, Hemadpant relates three very interesting stories, which if very carefully read and grasped, will lead readers onto the spiritual path.

⚜

OUR PAST MERITS ENABLE US TO SEEK THE COMPANY OF SAINTS

It is a general rule that it is our good luck, in the form of the accumulation of merits from past births that enables us to seek the company of saints and profit from it. To illustrate this rule, Hemadpant gives his own example. He was a Resident Magistrate of Bandra, a suburb of Mumbai, for many years. A famous Muslim saint named Pir Moulan lived there and many Hindus, Parsis and others who followed different religions used to go to have his darshan. His priest, Inus, pressed Hemadpant over and over to go see him, but for some reason or other he was never able to.

After many years, his turn finally came to be in the company of a saint. He was called to Shirdi, where he was permanently enlisted in Sai Baba's court.

Unfortunate people do not get this contact of saints. It is only the fortunate ones that do.

⚜

INSTITUTIONS OF SAINTS

There has been the institution of saints in this world from time immemorial. Various saints incarnate themselves in various places to carry out the missions given to them. Although they work in different places, they are one. They work in unison under the common authority of the Almighty and know full well what the other is doing, supplementing the other's work where necessary. An instance illustrating this is given below.

⚜

MR. THAKUR MEETS BABA

Mr. Thakur was a clerk in the Revenue Department. He once came to a town named Vadgaum, along with a survey party. There he saw a Kanarese saint named Appa, and bowed before him. The saint was explaining to an audience a portion of the book, *Vichar Sagar of Nischaldas*, a standard work on *Vedanta*. As Thakur was taking to leave, the saint said to him, "You should study this book, and if you do your desires will be fulfilled. In the future when you go to the north to do your duties, you will come across a great saint. By your good luck he will show you your future path, give peace to your mind and make you happy."

Then he was transferred to Junnar, which could be reached only by crossing Nhane Ghat. This Ghat was very steep and impassible, and no other conveyance other than a buffalo was of use in crossing it. This meant he now had to take a buffalo ride through the Ghat, which inconvenienced and pained him much. Later, he was transferred to Kalyan on a higher post, and there he became acquainted with Nanasaheb. He heard much about Sai Baba from him and wished to see Baba. The next day, Nanasaheb had to go to Shirdi. He invited Thakur to accompany him. Thakur could not go as he had to go to the Thana court for a civil case.

So Nanasaheb went alone. Thakur went to Thana but the case was postponed. He regretted not accompanying Nanasaheb, so he then left for Shirdi himself. When he arrived, he found that Nanasaheb had left the previous day. Some of his other friends whom he met there took him to Baba. He saw Baba, fell at his feet, and was overjoyed. His eyes were full of tears of joy and his hair stood on end.

After some time, the omniscient Baba said to him, "The path to this place is not as easy as the teaching of the Kanarese saint Appa or even as the buffalo ride in the Nhane Ghat. On this spiritual path you have to give your best effort as it is very difficult." When Thakur heard these significant signs, which no one else knew, he was overwhelmed with joy. He came to know that the words of the Kanarese saint had become true. Then joining both hands and placing his head on Baba's feet, he prayed that he should be accepted and blessed. Then Baba said, "What Appa told you was right, but these things have to be practiced and lived. Mere reading won't do. You have to think and experience what you read; otherwise it is of no use. Mere book learning, without the grace of the guru and self-realization is of no benefit." The theoretical portion from the work *Vichar Sagar* was read by Thakur, but the practical way was shown to him in Shirdi. Another story given below will bring out this truth more powerfully.

ASKING FOR PEACE OF MIND

A gentleman from Poona, Anantrao Patankar, wished to see Baba. He came to Shirdi and had Baba's darshan. His eyes were satisfied and he was much pleased. He fell at Baba's feet and after performing proper worship said to Baba, "I have read a lot, studied the *Vedas, Vedanta, Upanishads* and heard all the *Puranas*, but as I still do not have peace of mind I think that all my reading was useless. Simple ignorant devout people are better off than I am. Unless the mind becomes calm, all book learning is of no use. I have heard from many people that you easily give peace of mind to so many people by your mere glance and word. I have come here, please take pity on me and bless me."

PARABLE OF THE NINE BALLS OF STOOL—
NINE TYPES OF DEVOTION

Then Baba told him the following parable. Baba said, "Once a merchant came here. Before him a mare passed nine balls of stool. The merchant, intent on his search, spread the end of his dhotar and gathered all the nine balls into it and so gained concentration (peace) of mind."

Patankar could not make out the meaning of this story so he asked Dadasaheb, "What does Baba mean by this?"

He replied, "I, too, do not know all that Baba says and means, but by his inspiration I can say what I've come to know. The mare is God's grace and the nine balls excreted are the nine forms of bhakti:

1. Shravana: hearing
2. Kirtana: singing
3. Smarana: remembering
4. Padasevana: worshipping God's feet
5. Archana: worship
6. Namaskara: bowing
7. Dasya: service
8. Sakhyatva: friendship
9. Atmanivedana: surrender of the self

"These are the nine types of bhakti. If any of these is faithfully followed, the Lord will be pleased and manifest Himself in the home of the devotee. All the sadhanas, *japa* (mantra repetition), *tapas* (austerities), yoga practice, and study and expounding of scriptures are quite useless unless they are accompanied by devotion. Knowledge of the *Vedas*, or fame as a great *jnani* (person of knowledge) or mere formal *bhajan* (devotional song) are of no avail. What is wanted is loving devotion. Consider yourself as the merchant or seeker of the truth, and be eager like him to collect or cultivate the nine types of devotion. Then you will attain stability and peace of mind."

Next day, when Patankar went to Baba, he was asked whether he had collected the nine balls of stool. Pantakar said that he, being a poor fellow, should first be graced by Baba then they could easily be collected. Baba blessed and comforted him, saying that he would attain peace and happiness. After hearing this, Patankar was overjoyed and happy.

⚜

NEVER SPEAK ILL OR CRITICIZE OTHERS

Sai Baba's greatness is unfathomable, and so are his wonderful leelas. His life is also such, for he is Parabrahman (God) incarnate.

We shall close this chapter with a short story showing Baba's omniscience and his use of it to correct people and set them on the right path. Once a solicitor from Pandharpur came to Shirdi and went to the masjid. On seeing Baba, he fell at his feet and without being asked, offered some dakshina then sat in a corner, eager to hear the talk that was going on. Baba turned his face towards him and said, "How cunning people are! They fall at my feet and offer dakshina but inwardly give abuses behind the back. Is this not wonderful?"

This remark fit the solicitor, though none understood it. The solicitor grasped it but kept silent. When they returned to the wada, the solicitor said to Kakasaheb, "What Baba said was perfectly right. The dart was aimed at me. It was a hint to me that I should not indulge in reviling or scandalizing others. When the sub-judge of Pandharpur came and stayed here to improve his health a discussion about his situation took place in the bar room at Pandharpur. The discussion was about whether the ailments the sub-judge suffered from were ever likely to be cured without medicines. Also, whether it was proper for an educated man like the sub-judge to turn to such methods as going to Sai Baba. The sub-judge was criticized, as was Sai Baba. I also took some part in this affair. Now Sai Baba showed the impropriety of my conduct. This is not a rebuke to me, but a favor, an advice that I should not indulge in any slander of others and not interfere unnecessarily in other's affairs."

Shirdi is more than 100 miles from Pandharpur. Still Baba through his omniscience knew what had transpired there in the bar room. The intervening places—rivers, jungles, and mountains—were not a block to his all-perceiving sight. He could see or read the hearts of all. There was nothing secret or veiled from him. Everything, far or near, was as clear to him as broad daylight. Whether a man be far or near, he cannot avoid the all-pervading gaze of Sai

Baba. From this incident, the solicitor took the lesson that he should never speak ill of others nor unnecessarily criticize them. This evil tendency was completely washed and he was set on the right path.

Though the story refers to a solicitor, it is applicable to all. All should take this lesson to heart and profit from it.

Sai Baba's greatness is unfathomable, and so are his wonderful leelas. His life is also such, for he is *Parabrahman* (God) incarnate.

Pranams to Sri Sai

Peace Be to All

CHAPTER TWENTY-TWO

BABA CONSTANTLY CHANGED HIS WAY

How to meditate on Baba? No one has been able to fathom the Nature or the form of the Almighty. Even the *Vedas* and the thousand-tongued *Shesha* (holy cobra) are not able to describe it fully. But devotees cannot help but know and look at the form of the Lord, for they know that his feet are the only means of their happiness. They know no other method of attaining the supreme goal of life except by meditating on his holy feet. Hemadpant suggests an easy way of devotion and meditation on Baba:

As the dark fortnight of every month gradually decreases so does the moonlight, and finally on the new moon night we do not see the moon at all, nor do we get her light. So when the bright fortnight begins, people are very anxious to see the moon. On the first day, the moon is not seen and on the second day she emerges as a thin crescent.

Then people are asked to see the moon through an opening between the two branches of a tree. While concentrating eagerly through this aperture, to their great delight they begin to see the distant small crescent of the moon as it comes into sight. Following this clue, let us try to see Baba's light. Look at

Baba's posture, how fine it is! He is sitting with his legs folded, the right leg held across the left knee. The fingers of his left hand are spread on the right foot. On the right toe are spread his two fingers, the index and middle one. By this posture Baba means to say that if you want to see my light, be egoless and most humble and meditate on my toe through the opening between the two branches, index and middle finger, and then you will be able to see my light. This is the easiest means of attaining devotion.

Now let us turn for a moment to Baba's life. Shirdi had become a place of pilgrimage on account of Baba staying there. People from all quarters began to flock there, and both the rich and the poor were benefited in more ways than one in some form or other. Who can describe Baba's boundless love, his wonderful natural knowledge and his all-pervasiveness? Blessed is he who could experience any or all of these. Sometimes Baba observed long silence, which was, in a way his dissertation on Brahman. At other times he was consciousness and bliss incarnate, surrounded by his devotees. Sometimes he spoke in parables, and at other times indulged in wit and humor. At times, he was quite unambiguous and at times he seemed enraged. Sometimes he gave his teachings in a nutshell, at other times he argued at length. Many a time he was very plain. In this way, he gave varied instructions to many, according to their requirements. His life was inscrutable, beyond the view of our mind, beyond our intellect and speech. Our longing to see his face, to talk with him and hear his leelas, was never satisfied; still we were overflowing with joy. We can count the showers of rain, tie the wind in a leather bag, but who can measure his leelas? Now we will look at one aspect of them, how he anticipated and foresaw the calamities of his devotees and warded them off in time.

THE MASJID MAI SAVES AND PROTECTS

This masjid mai (Mother) is very merciful, She is the Mother of the simple devotees, whom She will save in calamities. Once a person sits on Her lap, all his troubles are over. He who rests in her shade gets bliss.

Balasaheb Mirikar was the Revenue Officer of Kopergaon. He was going on tour to Chitali. On the way, he came to Shirdi to see Sai Baba. When he went to the masjid and prostrated himself before Baba, the usual conversation regarding health and other matters commenced, but then Baba gave a warning, "Do you know our Dwarkamai?"

As Balasaheb did not understand, he kept quiet. Baba continued:

This is our Dwarkamai where you are sitting. She wards off all dangers and anxieties of the children who sit on her lap. This masjid *mai* (Mother) is very merciful, She is the Mother of the simple devotees, whom She will save in calamities. Once a person sits on Her lap, all his troubles are over. He who rests in her shade gets bliss.

Then Baba gave him udi, and placed his protecting hand on his head. When Balasaheb was about to depart, Baba said, "Do you know the serpent?" And then closing the left fist he brought it near the right elbow, and moving his left arm like the hood of a serpent, he said, "He is so terrible but what can he do to the children of Dwarkamai? When the Dwarkamai protects, what can the serpent do?"

All who were present were curious to know the meaning of this and but none had the courage to ask Baba about it. Then Balasaheb saluted Baba and left the masjid with Shama. Baba called Shama back and asked him to accompany Balasaheb and enjoy the Chitali trip. Shama came to Balasaheb and told him that he would go with him according to Baba's wish. Balasaheb replied that he needn't come, as it would be inconvenient. Shama returned to Baba and told him what Balasaheb had said to him. Baba said, "All right, do not go. We should mean well and do well. Whatever is destined to happen, will happen."

In the meanwhile, Balasaheb thought it over again and asked Shama to accompany him. Shama went to Baba again, then took leave and started in the tanga with Balasaheb. They reached Chitali at 9 p.m. and encamped in the Maruti temple. The office people had not come yet so they sat quietly in the temple, chit-chatting. Balasaheb was sitting on a mat reading a newspaper. His upper dhotar was spread across his waist and on a part of it a snake was sitting unobserved. It began to move with a rustling sound, which was heard by a worker. The worker brought a lantern and pointed to the snake crying, "Snake! Snake!" Balasaheb was frightened and began to quiver. Shama was amazed. Then he and the others moved without making a sound and took sticks and clubs in their hands. The snake crawled slowly from Balasaheb's waist and as it was moving away was immediately put to death. This calamity, which was prophesied by Baba, was averted and Balasaheb's love for Baba was deeply confirmed.

OVERCOMING FEAR

One day when a great astrologer named Nanasaheb Dengale was in Shirdi, he told Bapusaheb Buti, "Today is an inauspicious day for you, there is a danger to your life." This made Bapusaheb very anxious.

When he came to the masjid, Baba said to Bapusaheb, "What does this Nana say? He foretells death for you? Well, you need not be afraid. Tell him boldly, 'Let us see how death kills.'"

Then later in the evening, Bapusaheb went to relieve himself in the field when he saw a snake. His servant saw it and lifted a stone to strike at it. Bapusaheb asked him to get a big stick, but before the servant had returned with the stick, the snake moved away and disappeared. Bapusaheb remembered with joy Baba's words of fearlessness.

BABA SAVES AMIR FROM A SERPENT

Amir Shankar was a native of the village Korale. He belonged to the butcher caste. He suffered from rheumatism which caused him much pain. This reminded him to think of God, so he left his business and went to Shirdi, and prayed to Baba to relieve him of his malady. Baba stationed him in the Chavadi, which was then a damp and unhealthy place, unfit for such a patient. Any other place in the village of Shirdi, or even in the village of Korale, would have been better for Amir, but Baba's word was the deciding factor and the chief medicine. Baba did not allow him to come to the masjid, but put him in the Chavadi where he had one very great advantage. Baba passed by the Chavadi every morning and evening, and every alternate day Baba slept there. So Amir had contact with Baba very often.

Amir stayed there for nine months, but then somehow got disgusted with the Chavadi. So one night he stealthily left the place and went to Kopergaon and stayed in a *dharmashala* (pilgrim guest house) there. There he saw an old dying fakir who asked him for water. Amir brought it and gave it to him. As soon as he drank it, he passed away. Amir was now in a fix. He thought that if he went and informed the authorities, he would be held responsible for the death, as he was the first and only person who knew something about it. He repented his action of leaving Shirdi without Baba's permission and prayed to Baba. He was then determined to return to Shirdi. That same night he ran back, remembering and muttering Baba's name along the way. He reached Shirdi before daybreak and became free from anxiety. Then he lived in the Chavadi in perfect accordance with Baba's order and was cured.

At midnight one night, Baba cried out, "Oh Abdul, some devilish creature is dashing against the side of my bed." Abdul came with a lantern and examined Baba's bed but found nothing. Baba asked him to examine the whole place carefully, then began to strike the ground with his satka. Seeing this leela of Baba, Amir thought that Baba might have suspected some serpent had come there. Amir knew by his close and long contact with Baba the meaning of Baba's words and actions. Baba then saw something moving near Amir's cushion. He asked Abdul to bring the light. When he brought it, he saw the coil of a serpent there, moving its head up and down. The serpent was immediately beaten to death. Like this, Baba gave a timely warning and saved Amir.

⚜

HEMADPANT'S EXPERIENCES WITH A SERPENT AND A SCORPION

At Baba's recommendation, Kakasaheb read the two works of Sri Eknath Maharaj, *Bhagwat* and the *Ramayana*, daily. Hemadpant had the good fortune to be one of the audience members when the reading was going on. Once when the part of the *Ramayana* was read relating to Hanuman testing Rama's greatness according to his mother's instructions, all the listeners were spell bound, including Hemadpant. A big scorpion jumped and sat on his right shoulder, on his *uparani* (upper cloth). First it was not noticed, but as the Lord protects those who are intent on hearing his stories, Hemadpant casually cast a glance over his right shoulder and noticed it. It was dead silent and did not move at all. It seemed as if it was also enjoying the reading. Then by the Lord's grace, Hemadpant, without disturbing the audience, took the two ends of his dhotar, folded and brought them together, enclosing the scorpion within it. Then he went out and threw it in the garden.

On another occasion, some people were sitting in the upper floor of Kakasaheb's wada just before nightfall when a serpent crept through a hole in the window frame and sat coiled up. A light was brought. Although it was shocked at first, it sat still and only moved its head up and down. Then many people rushed there with sticks and cudgels, but as it sat in an awkward place, no blow could be dealt. But hearing the noises of men, the serpent went out hastily through the same hole. Then everyone was relieved.

⚜

BABA'S OPINION ON KILLING CREATURES

A devotee named Muktaram said it was good that the poor creature escaped. Hemadpant challenged him saying that it was better that serpents be killed. There was a hot discussion between them. Muktaram contended that serpents and such creatures should not be killed, while Hemadpant said they should be. As night came on, the discussion came to an end without any conclusion being made. The next day the question was referred to Baba, who gave his opinion:

God lives in all beings and creatures, whether they are serpents or scorpions. He is the great wirepuller of the world, and all beings, serpents, scorpions, all creatures, obey his command. Unless he wills it, nobody can do any harm to others. The world is completely dependent on Him; no one is independent. So we should take pity and love all creatures, stop fighting and killing, and be patient. The Lord is the protector of all.

Pranams to Sri Sai

Peace Be to All

CHAPTER TWENTY-THREE

ALLAH MALIK – GOD IS ONE – GOD IS THE SOLE PROPRIETOR

*He never said, "I am God," but said that he was a humble servant
and he always remembered him and uttered, "Allah Malik."
(God is One, God is the Sole Proprietor).*

In reality, the *jiva* (individual soul) transcends the three *gunas* (qualities)—
sattva (purity), *rajas* (activity) and *tamas* (inertia)—but being deluded by Maya
he forgets his nature. His true nature is *satchitananda*—existence,
consciousness and bliss. He thinks that he is the doer and enjoyer and so
entangles himself in endless miseries and does not know the way of
deliverance. The only way of deliverance is through loving devotion to the
guru's feet. The great player or actor, Baba, has delighted his devotees and
transformed them into his own nature.

We regard Baba as an incarnation of God for all the reasons already stated,
but he always said that he was an obedient servant of God. Though an
incarnation, he showed people the way to behave and carry out the duties of

their respective stations in life. He never emulated others in any way, nor asked others to have something done for him. For him, who saw the Lord in all movable and immovable things of this world, humility was most appropriate. He disregarded or disrespected none, for he saw God in all beings. He never said, "I am God," but said that he was a humble servant and he always remembered him and uttered, "Allah Malik." (God is One, God is the Sole Proprietor).

We do not know the different kinds of saints, how they behave, what they do, what they eat. We only know that through God's grace they manifest themselves in this world to liberate the ignorant and bound souls. If there is a store of merit in our account, we have a desire to listen to the stories and leelas of the saints, otherwise not. Let us now turn to the main stories of this chapter.

ONLY THOSE WHO CAN DIGEST ONION SHOULD EAT IT

Once a *sadhaka* (spiritual aspirant) of yoga came to Shirdi with Nanasaheb. He had studied all the works on yoga, including the *Patanjali Yoga Sutras*, but had no practical experience. He could not concentrate his mind and attain samadhi even for a short time. He thought that if Baba was pleased with him, he would show him the way to attain samadhi. With this aim he came to Shirdi. When he went to the masjid, he saw Baba eating bread with onion. On seeing this, a thought arose, 'How can this man eating stale bread with raw onion solve my difficulties and help me?'

Baba read his mind and said to Nanasaheb, "Oh Nana, he who has the power to digest onion, should eat it and nothing else." Hearing this remark, the yogi was wonderstruck and fell at Baba's feet with complete surrender. With a pure and open mind, he expressed his difficulties and received the solutions from Baba. He was satisfied and happy and left Shirdi with Baba's udi and blessings.

BABA'S WORDS SAVE SHAMA'S LIFE

Before Hemadpant begins the story, he says that the *jiva* (individual soul) can be compared to a parrot, as they are both bound, one in the body and the other in a cage. Both think that their bound state is good for them. It is only when by God's grace a helper, or guru, comes and opens their eyes and liberates them from bondage that their eyes are opened to a greater and larger life, compared to which their former limited life is nothing.

In the last chapter, it was shown how Baba anticipated the calamity that was to befall Balasaheb Mirikar and rescued him from it. Now let the readers hear a story grander than that. One time a poisonous snake bit Shama. His little finger was stung and the poison began to spread into the body. The pain was severe and Shama thought that he would die soon. His friends wanted to take him to the God Vitoba, where such cases were often sent, but Shama ran to the masjid, to his Vitoba—Baba.

When Baba saw him, he began to scold and abuse him. He became enraged and said, "Oh vile priest, do not climb up. Beware if you do so." Then he roared, "Go! Get away! Come down!" Seeing Baba red with rage, Shama was very confused and disappointed. He thought the masjid was his home and Baba was his sole refuge. If he was driven away like this, where could he go? He lost all hope for his life and kept silent. After some time, Baba returned to normal and became calm and Shama went up and sat near him.

Then Baba said, "Don't be afraid. Don't care one bit. The merciful fakir will save you. Go and sit quietly at home. Don't go out. Believe in me and remain fearless and have no anxiety." Then he was sent home. Immediately afterwards, Baba sent Tatya and Kakasaheb to him with the instructions that he should eat what he liked, should move around in the home, but in no case should he lie down and sleep. Needless to say, these instructions were acted upon and Shama got better in a short time.

The only thing to be remembered in this connection is this, the words of Baba (the five-syllable 'mantra,' "Go! Get away! Come down!") were not addressed to Shama, as it seemingly looked. They were a direct order to the snake and its poison not to rise up and circulate through Shama's body. Baba did not have to use any mantra, formula, charged rice, charged water, nothing. His words alone were most successful in saving Shama's life.

Anyone hearing this story and similar ones will develop firm faith in the feet of Sai Baba. The only way to cross the ocean of Maya is to always remember Baba's feet in our heart.

⚜

BABA SETS AN EXAMPLE

Once, cholera was raging in Shirdi. The residents were very frightened and stopped all communication with people outside the village. The leaders of the village assembled together and decided upon two ordinances as a remedy to check and put down the epidemic. The ordinances were that no fuel cart should be allowed to come in the village and no goat should be killed there. If anybody disobeyed these ordinances, they were to be fined by the village authorities.

As Baba knew that all this was mere superstition, he cared not two bits for the cholera ordinances. While the ordinances were in force, a fuel cart came and wanted to enter the village. Everybody knew that there was a lack of fuel in the village; still the people turned the fuel cart away. Baba came to know of this. He came to the spot and asked the cart man to take the fuel cart to the masjid. None dared to raise his voice against Baba's action. He wanted fuel for his dhuni so he purchased it. Like an *agnihotri* (one who worships fire) keeping his sacred fire alive throughout his life, Baba kept his *dhuni* (fire pit) ever burning all day and night. For this, he always stocked fuel. Baba's home, the masjid, was free and open to all. As it had no lock and key some poor people removed wood from there for their own use. Baba did not grumble about this. Baba knew that the Almighty pervaded the whole universe and so he never bore enmity or ill will toward anyone. Though perfectly detached, he behaved like an ordinary householder to set an example to the people.

GURU BHAKTI—FOLLOWING THE GURU'S COMMAND

Let us now see how the second cholera ordinance fared with Baba. While it was in force, someone brought a goat to the masjid. It was weak, old and about to die. At this time, the fakir Bade Baba was near. Sai Baba asked him to behead the goat with one stroke and offer it as an oblation. Bade Baba was much respected by Sai Baba. He always sat on the right hand of Sai Baba. Bade Baba first smoked the chillum, and then it was offered to Sai Baba and others. After the dishes were served, at the time of taking noon meals, Baba respectfully called Bade Baba and made him sit on his left side, and then all partook of food. Baba also paid him Rs.50 daily out of the amount collected as dakshina. Baba accompanied him a hundred paces whenever he left. Such was his position with Baba. But when Baba asked him to behead the goat, Bade Baba flatly refused, saying, "Why should it be killed for nothing?"

Then Baba asked Shama to kill it. Shama went to Radhakrishna Mai and brought a knife from her house and placed it before Baba. But after finding out the purpose for which the knife was taken, Radhakrishna Mai took it back. Shama then went to get another knife but did not return soon. Then came Kakasaheb's turn. He was 'good-as-gold' no doubt, but had to be tested. Baba asked him to get a knife and kill the goat. He went to Sathe's wada and returned with a knife. He was ready to kill it at Baba's bidding. He was born in a pure Brahmin family and had never known killing in his life. Though quite averse to doing any act of violence, he made himself bold to kill the goat. The people wondered when they saw that Bade Baba, a Muslim, was unwilling to kill the goat while this pure Brahmin was making preparations to do so. He tightened his dhotar and with a semicircular motion raised his hand with the knife and looked at Baba for the final signal.

Baba said, "What are you thinking of? Go on, strike." Then, when the hand was just about to come down, Baba said, "Stop, how cruel you are! Being a Brahmin, you are killing a goat?"

Kakasaheb obeyed, put the knife down and said to Baba, "Your nectar-like word is law to us, we do not know any other law. We remember you always, meditate on your form and obey you day and night. We do not know or consider whether it is right or wrong to kill, we do not want to reason or discuss things, but unspoken and timely obedience to guru's orders is our duty and dharma."

Then Baba told Kakasaheb that he would do the killing and offering himself. It was settled that the goat should be disposed of near where fakirs used to sit. While the goat was being removed to that place, it fell down dead on the way.

Hemadpant closes the chapter with a classification of disciples. He says that they are of three kinds:

1. *Ordinary disciples* are those who go on postponing the carrying out of the guru's orders making mistakes at every step.

2. *Average disciples* are those who carry out the orders of their masters to the letter, without any delay.

3. *Superior disciples* are those who guess what their gurus want and immediately carry it out and serve them without waiting for an order from them.

The disciples should have firm faith, backed up by intelligence, and if they add patience to this, their spiritual goal will not be distant. Control of breath, ingoing and outgoing, or Hatha Yoga or other difficult practices are not at all necessary. When the disciples develop the above-mentioned qualities, they become ready for further instructions and then the Master appears to lead them on their spiritual path to perfection.

In the next chapter, we will see Baba's interesting wit and humor.

Pranams to Sri Sai

Peace Be to All

CHAPTER TWENTY-FOUR

BHAKTAS ACCEPT BABA'S RIDICULE

To say that we shall state such and such in this or the next chapter is a sort of egoism. Unless we surrender our ego to the feet of our sadguru, we will not succeed in our undertaking. If we become egoless, then our success is assured.

By worshipping Baba we attain aims both worldly and spiritual, become fixed in our true nature, and attain peace and happiness. Therefore, those who want to gain their welfare should respectfully hear Baba's leelas or stories and meditate on them. If they do this, they will easily attain the aim of their life and get bliss.

Generally, everyone likes wit and humor, but they don't like jokes when they are at their own expense. Baba's method was peculiar. When accompanied with good gestures, it was interesting and instructive and people did not mind being held up to ridicule. Hemadpant gives his own instance below.

⚜

THE LESSON OF EATING ALONE

"Do you remember me before eating? Am I not always with you?
Do you offer me anything before you eat?"

In Shirdi, the bazaar was held every Sunday. People from the neighboring villages came, erected booths and stalls on the street and sold their wares and commodities. Every noon, the masjid was more or less crowded, but on Sunday, it was crowded to suffocation. On one such Sunday, Hemadpant sat in front of Baba shampooing his legs and muttering God's name. Shama was on Baba's left, Vamanrao to his right, Shriman Bapusaheb Buti and Kakasaheb and others were also present. Then Shama laughed and said to Hemadpant, "See that some grains seem to have stuck to the sleeve of your coat." So saying he touched the sleeve and found that there were some grains. Hemadpant straightened his left forearm to see what the matter was, when to the surprise of all, some grains of gram came rolling down and were picked up by the people who were sitting there.

This incident furnished the subject matter for a joke. Everybody present began to wonder and said something as to how the grains found their way into the sleeve of the coat and became lodged there. Hemadpant also could not guess how they found their way there. When no one could give a satisfactory explanation in this matter, and everyone was wondering about this mystery, Baba said, "This fellow has the bad habit of eating alone. Today is a bazaar day and he was here chewing grams. I know his habit and these grams are a proof of it. What is there to wonder about in this matter?"

Hemadpant said, "Baba, I never eat alone. Why do you thrust this bad habit on me? I didn't go to the bazaar today, so how could I buy grams and how could I eat them if I had not bought them? I never eat anything unless I share it with others present near me."

Baba said, "It is true that you give to persons who are present, but if none are nearby, what could you do? But do you remember me before eating? Am I not always with you? Do you offer me anything before you eat?"

ALWAYS OFFER TO THE GURU AND
OUR DEFECTS WILL DISAPPEAR

Let us mark and note carefully what Baba has taught us by this incident. He has advised us that Baba should be remembered first before the senses, mind and intellect enjoy their objects. If this is done, it is a way of offering it to him. The senses can never remain without their objects, but if those objects are first offered to the guru, the attachment for them will naturally vanish. In this way, all the *vrittis* (thoughts) of desire, anger, greed, etc. should first be offered and directed to the guru and if this practice is followed the Lord will help you in eradicating all the *vrittis* (thoughts). When before enjoyment of the objects, you think that Baba is close by, the question whether the object is fit to be enjoyed or not will at once arise. Then the object that is not fit to be enjoyed will be shunned and in this way our bad habits or vices will disappear and our character will improve. Then love for the guru will grow and pure knowledge will sprout up.

When this knowledge grows, the bondage of body-consciousness will snap and our intellect will be merged in pure consciousness. Then we shall get bliss and contentment. There is no difference between guru and God. He who sees any difference in them, sees God nowhere. So leaving aside all ideas of difference, we should regard the guru and God as one and if we serve our guru as stated above, God will certainly be pleased and purifying our minds, he will give us self-realization. To put the matter in a nutshell, we should not enjoy any object with our senses without first remembering our guru. When the mind is trained in this way, we will be always be reminded of Baba, and our meditation on Baba will grow quickly. The *saguna* (form) of Baba will always be before our eyes and then devotion, non-attachment, and liberation will all be ours. When Baba's form is fixed before our mental vision this way, we forget hunger, thirst and this worldly existence. The consciousness of worldly pleasures will disappear and our mind shall attain peace and happiness.

ALWAYS SHARE YOUR FOOD

When the above story was being narrated, Hemadpant was reminded of a similar story of Sudama, which illustrates the same principle. It is given here.

Sri Krishna and his elder brother, Balarama, were living with a fellow student named Sudama in the ashram of their guru, Sandipani. Once Krishna and Balarama were sent to the forest to get fuel. Sandipani's wife had sent Sudama to the forest with a quantity of grams for the three.

When Krishna met Sudama in the forest, he said to him, "Dada, I want water as I am thirsty."

Sudama replied, "No water should be drunk on an empty stomach, so it is better to wait a while." He did not say that he had the grams with him and did not offer them to him. As Krishna was tired, he lay down for rest on Sudama's lap and was snoring. When Krishna was asleep, Sudama took out the grams and began to eat.

Then Krishna suddenly asked, "Dada, what are you eating? What is that sound?"

Sudama replied, "What is there to eat? I am shivering with cold and my teeth are chattering. I can't even repeat *Vishnu Sahasranama* distinctly."

Hearing this, the omniscient Krishna said, "I just dreamed I saw a man eating things of another and when asked about this, he said, 'What dust should he eat?' meaning that he had nothing to eat. The other man said, 'Let it be so.' Dada, this is only a dream. I know that you wouldn't eat anything without me. Under the influence of the dream I asked you what you were eating."

If Sudama had known even a little of the omniscient Sri Krishna and his leelas, he would not have acted as he did. For this reason, he had to suffer for what he did. Though he was a friend of Sri Krishna he had to pass his later life in utter poverty. But when he later offered Krishna a handful of parched rice earned by his wife with her own labor, Krishna was pleased and gave him a golden city to enjoy. This story should be remembered by those who have the habit of eating things alone without sharing them with others.

The *Shruti* also emphasizes this lesson and asks us to offer things first to God and then enjoy them after he leaves them. Baba also taught us the same lesson in his humorous and inimitable way.

BABA USES HUMOR TO PACIFY A QUARREL

Hemadpant now describes another witty incident in which Baba played the role of a peacemaker. There was one devotee named Mr. Anna Chinchanikar. He was simple, rough and straightforward. He cared for no one, always spoke plainly and carried all dealings in cash. Though he looked outwardly harsh and uncompromising, he was good natured and guileless. So Baba loved him.

One noon, like others serving Baba in their own way, Anna was standing and shampooing the left arm of Baba, which rested on the railing. On the right side, an old widow named Mavsibai, whom Baba called mother, was serving Baba in her way. Mavsibai was an elderly woman of pure heart. She clasped the fingers of both her hands round the trunk of Baba and was at this time kneading Baba's abdomen. She did this so forcibly that Baba's back and abdomen became flat and Baba moved from side to side. Anna on the other side was steady, but Mavsibai's face moved up and down with her strokes. Once it happened that her face came very close to Anna's. Being of a witty disposition she remarked, "Oh, this Anna is a lewd fellow, he wants to kiss me. Even being so old with grey hair, he feels no shame in kissing me."

These words enraged Anna and he pulled up his sleeves and said, "You say that I am an old bad fellow. Am I a fool? It is you that have picked a quarrel with me." All the people present were enjoying the encounter between them.

Baba, who loved both of them equally and wanted to pacify them, managed the affair very skillfully. Lovingly he said, "Oh Anna, why are you unnecessarily raising this hue and cry? I do not understand what harm or impropriety is there when the mother is kissed?" Hearing these words of Baba, everyone laughed merrily and enjoyed Baba's wit to their heart's content.

❧

BABA ALLOWS BHAKTAS TO SERVE IN THEIR OWN WAY

Baba allowed his devotees to serve him in their own way and did not like anyone interfering in this. To cite an instance, on another occasion Mavsibai was kneading Baba's abdomen. Seeing the fury and force she used, all the other devotees felt nervous and anxious. They said, "Oh mother, be more considerate and moderate, otherwise you will break Baba's arteries and nerves." At this, Baba at once got up from his seat, dashed his satka on the ground. He became enraged and his eyes became red like a live charcoal. None dared to stand before or face Baba. Then he took hold of one end of the satka with both hands and pressed it in the hollow of his abdomen. He fixed the other end to the post and began to press his abdomen against it. The satka, which was about two or three feet in length, seemed to go completely into his abdomen and the people feared that it would be ruptured. The post was fixed and immovable and Baba moved closer and closer to it and clasped the post firmly. Every moment the rupture was expected. They were all dismayed and stood dumbstruck with wonder and fear and did not know what to do.

Baba suffered this ordeal for the sake of his bhakta. The other devotees only wanted to give a hint to Mavsibai to be moderate in her service and not cause any trouble or pain to Baba. This they did with good intention, but Baba did not accept even this. They were surprised to see that their well-intentioned effort had resulted in this catastrophe. They could do nothing but wait and see. Fortunately, Baba's rage soon cooled down. He left the satka and resumed his seat. From this time onward, the devotees took the lesson that they should not meddle with anybody but allow him to serve Baba as he chooses, as Baba was capable to gauge the merits and worth of the service rendered to him.

Pranams to Sri Sai

Peace Be to All

CHAPTER TWENTY-FIVE

THROUGH FIRM FAITH AND DEVOTION
WISHES ARE FULFILLED

We begin this chapter bowing with all our eight limbs to Sai Baba, who is an ocean of mercy, God incarnate, who is *Parabrahman* (Absolute) and the great *Yogeshwara* (Lord of Yoga). Victory to Baba, who is the crest-jewel of the saints, who is the home of all auspicious things, who is our *Atmaram* (dear self) and the able refuge of devotees. We prostrate ourselves before him who has attained the aim and end of life.

Baba is always full of mercy. What is wanted on our part is whole-hearted devotion to him. When a devotee has firm faith and devotion, his wishes are soon fulfilled. When the desire arose in the mind of Hemadpant to write the life and leelas of Baba, Baba immediately had it written by Hemadpant. When the order 'to keep memos' was given, Hemadpant was inspired and his intellect got strength and boldness to undertake and finish the work. He was not, he says, qualified to write the work, but the gracious blessings of Baba enabled him to complete the undertaking. So you have this *Satcharitra,* which is a *somakant* (jewel) from which nectar, in the form of Sai leelas, oozes out for the readers to drink to their hearts' content.

Whenever a devotee had complete and wholehearted devotion to Baba, all his calamities and dangers were warded off and his welfare attended to by Baba. The story of Damu Anna illustrates this.

❧

BE CONTENT WITH HALF A LOAF OF BREAD

The readers are aware that a mention of Damu Anna was made in the 6th chapter in regard to the celebration of the Ramanavami Festival in Shirdi. He went to Shirdi about the year 1897 when the Ramanavami celebration began and provided an ornamental flag for that occasion every year afterwards. He also fed the poor and the fakirs that came for the festival.

A friend of Damu's from Mumbai wrote him suggesting they should enter into a cotton speculation business, which would bring them about two lakhs rupees as profit. The broker wrote that the business was good and involved no risks and that the opportunity should not be lost. Damu's mind was wavering. He couldn't quickly decide whether to venture in the speculation. He thought about it, and as he was a devotee of Baba, wrote a detailed letter to Shama giving all the facts and requested him to consult Baba to get his advice. Shama received the letter the next day and at noon brought it to the masjid and placed it before Baba. Baba asked Shama what the matter was and what the letter was about. He replied that Damu wanted to consult him about something.

Then Baba said, "What does he write and what does he plan? It seems that he wants to catch the sky and that he is not content with what God has given him. Read his letter."

Shama replied, "The letter contains what you just said. Oh, Deva, you sit here calm and composed and agitate the devotees. When they get restless, you draw them here, some in person and others through letters. If you know the contents of the letter, why do you press me to read it?"

Baba said, "Oh Shama, read it please. I speak at random and who believes me."

Shama read the letter. Baba listened to it attentively and said, "Damu has gone mad. Write to him in reply that nothing is wanting in his house. Let him be content with the half loaf of bread that he has now and let him not bother himself about lakhs."

Shama sent the reply, which Damu was anxiously awaiting for. Reading it all his hopes and prospects about lakhs of rupees profit were dashed to the ground. He thought he made a mistake in consulting Baba. But as Shama had hinted in the reply, there was always much difference in seeing and hearing and that he should come to Shirdi and see Baba.

Damu thought it advisable to go to Shirdi and consult Baba personally about the affair. So he went to Shirdi and prostrated himself before Baba and sat shampooing his legs. He had no courage to ask Baba openly about the speculation. In his mind, he thought that it would be better if some share of the business be assigned to Baba. If Baba were to help him in this transaction, he would surrender some share of profits to him. Damu was thinking this secretly but nothing was veiled from Baba. Everything past, present and future was as clear to him as an amalaka fruit in hand. A child wants sweets, but its mother gives bitter pills. The sweets spoil its health, while the bitter pills improve it. So the mother, looking to the welfare of her infant, coaxes it and gives it bitter pills. Baba, kind mother as he was, knew the present and future prospects of his devotees, and reading Damu's mind spoke to him openly, "Bapu, I do not want to be entangled in such worldly things." Seeing Baba's disapproval, Damu dropped the enterprise.

Then Damu thought of trading in grain, rice, wheat and other commodities. Baba also read this thought and said to him, "You will be selling at seven *seers* (unit of weight) a rupee and buying at five *seers* a rupee." So this business was also given up. The rise in grain prices kept up for some time and Baba's prophecy seemed to be false, but a month or two later there was abundant rain everywhere and suddenly the prices fell. Those who stored grains suffered a severe loss. Damu was saved from this fate. Needless to say, the cotton speculation also collapsed with a severe loss to the investors. After seeing how Baba saved him from two severe losses in cotton and grain speculations, Damu's faith in Baba grew strong and he remained a true devotee long after Baba's passing.

MANGO MIRACLE

"Do not be anxious that I will be absent from you. You will hear my bones speaking and discussing your welfare. But remember me always, believe in me heart and soul and then you will be most benefited."

Once a parcel of about 300 mangoes was received in Shirdi. A Revenue Collector named Rale had sent the parcel to Sai Baba from Goa. When it was opened all the mangoes were found in good condition and were put in Shama's charge. Only four were kept aside and placed in a pot by Baba, who said, "These four fruits are for Damu, let them lie there."

Damu had two wives and no children. He consulted many astrologers and studied astrology himself to some extent. He believed that as there was an inauspicious planet in his horoscope, there was no prospect of a child for him in this life. But he had great faith in Baba. When he went to Shirdi to worship Baba, two hours after the arrival of the mango parcel, Baba said, "Though people are looking for the mangoes, they are Dammya's. He who they belong to should eat and die." On hearing these words, Damu was shocked at first, but Mhalsapati explained to him that death meant the death of the little self or ego, and to have it at Baba's feet was a blessing. So Damu said he would accept the fruits and eat them.

But Baba said to him. "Do not eat them yourself, but give them to your junior wife. This *amra leela* (miracle of four mangoes) will give her four sons and four daughters." This was done and in due course Baba's words turned true and not those of the astrologers.

Baba's speech established its worth and greatness while he was living in the flesh, but wonder of wonders it did the same even after his passing away. Baba said:

Believe me, though I pass away, my bones in my tomb will give you hope and confidence. Not only me, but my tomb will also be speaking, moving and communicating with those who surrender themselves wholeheartedly to me. Do not be anxious that I will be absent from you. You will hear my bones speaking and discussing your welfare. But remember me always, believe in me heart and soul and then you will be most benefited.

⚜

PRAYER FOR LIBERATION

Hemadpant closes this chapter with a prayer. "Oh Sai Sadguru, the wishfulfilling tree for devotees, let us never forget and lose sight of your feet. We have been troubled with the births and deaths of this *samsara* (worldly bondage). Now free us from this cycle of births and deaths. Restrain us from the outgoing of our senses to their objects, and introvert us and bring us face to face with the *Atma* (Self). As long as this outgoing tendency of the senses and the mind is not checked, there is no prospect of self-realization. Neither son, nor wife, nor friend will be of any use in the end. It is only you who will give us salvation and happiness. Destroy completely our tendency for gossip and other negative tendencies. Let our tongue get a passion for chanting your name. Drive out our thoughts, good or otherwise, and make us forget our bodies and houses and do away with our egoism. Make us always remember your name and forget all other things. Remove the restlessness of our mind and make it steady and calm. If you just hold on to us, the dark night of our ignorance will vanish and we shall live happily in your light. That you made us drink the nectar of your leelas and awakened us from our slumber is due to your grace and our store of merits in past births."

Note: In this connection, the following excerpt from Damu Anna's full statement mentioned above is very worthy to read.

Damu Anna said, "Once when I sat at Baba's feet along with many others, I had two questions in my mind. He gave answers to both."

Q: There are so many crowding around Baba. Do they all get benefit from you?

Baba said, "Look at the mango tree in blossom. If all the flowers brought fruit, what a splendid crop it would be. But do they? Most fall off from the wind, very few remain."

Q: If Baba were to pass away, how hopelessly adrift I would be and how am I to fare then?

To this, Baba answered that he would be with me when and wherever I thought of him. That promise he kept before 1918 and has been keeping it after 1918. He is still with me. He is still guiding me. Baba gave this answer about 1910-11, when brothers separated from me, my sister died, and there was a theft and police inquiry. All of these incidents upset me very much. When my sister died, my mind was much upset. I did not care for life and enjoyments. When I went to Baba, he calmed me with his instruction and made me eat a feast of *pooran poli* (sweets) at Appa Kulkarni's house and get sandalpaste there. There was a theft in my house. A friend of thirty year's stole my wife's jewelry box, including her auspicious nose ring. I wept before Baba's photo. The next day, the man returned the jewelry box and prayed for pardon.

Pranams to Sri Sai

Peace Be to All

CHAPTER TWENTY-SIX

THE SADGURU OPENS OUR EYES

All the things that we see in the universe are nothing but a play of Maya, the creative power of the Lord. These things do not really exist. What really exists is the Absolute. Just as we mistake a rope, garland, or a stick for a serpent on account of darkness, we always see the phenomena—things as they appear outwardly—and not that which underlies all the visible things. It is only the sadguru that opens the eyes of our understanding and enables us to see things in their true light and not as they appear. Let us, therefore, worship the sadguru and pray to him to give us the true vision, which is nothing but God vision, God realization.

* * *

INNER WORSHIP

Hemadpant has given us a novel form of worship. He says let us use hot water in the form of tears of joy to wash the sadguru's feet. Let us besmear his body with the sandalpaste of pure love. Let us cover his body with the cloth of true faith. Let us offer eight lotuses in the form of our eight *sattvic* (pure) emotions, and fruit in the form of our concentrated mind. Let us apply *bukka* (black powder) to his head in the form of devotion, tie the waistband of *bhakti* (devotion) and place our head on his toes.

After decorating the sadguru with jewelry in this way, let us offer our all to him and wave the feather fan of devotion to ward off heat. After such blissful worship, let us pray like this, "Introvert our mind, turn it inward. Give us discrimination between the real and the unreal and non-attachment for all worldly things and so enable us to attain self-realization. We surrender ourselves body and soul. Make our eyes yours so that we should never feel pleasure and pain. Control our body and mind as is your will and wish. Let our mind get rest at your feet."

Now let us turn to the stories of this chapter.

❧

STICK WITH ONE GURU

Once it so happened that a devotee by the name Pant, a disciple of another sadguru, had the good fortune of visiting Shirdi. He had no mind to go to Shirdi, but man proposes one way and God disposes the other. He was traveling in a railway train when he met some friends and relations bound for Shirdi. They all asked him to accompany them and he could not say no. They got off at Mumbai while Pant got off at Virar. There he received permission from his sadguru for the Shirdi trip, and after arranging for the expenses, left with the party for Shirdi.

They all reached the place in the morning and went to the masjid at about 11 a.m. Seeing the crowd of devotees assembled for Baba's worship they were all pleased but Pant suddenly had a fit and fell senseless. They were all frightened. Still, they tried their best to bring him to his senses. With Baba's grace and the pouring of pitchers of water over his head, he regained consciousness and sat upright as if he was just awakened from sleep. The omniscient Baba, knowing that he was a disciple of another guru, inspired fearlessness and confirmed his faith in his own guru by addressing him as follows, "Come what may, leave not, but stick to your support (guru) and remain ever steady, always at one with him." Pant at once knew the significance of this remark and was reminded of his sadguru. Throughout his life, he never forgot this kindness of Baba.

⚜

BABA CURES EPILEPSY

"The Lord will protect him who has faith and patience."

There was a gentleman by name Harish Chandra Pitale in Mumbai. He had a son who suffered from epilepsy. He tried many allopathic and ayurvedic doctors, but there was no cure. There remained only one remedy, taking refuge in the saints. It was stated in Chapter 15 that Das Ganu's incomparable and splendid kirtans spread Baba's fame in Mumbai. Mr. Pitale heard some of these kirtans in 1910 and learned from others that Baba, by his touch and mere glance, cured many incurable diseases. A desire then arose in his mind to see Baba.

Making all preparations and taking presents and fruit baskets, Mr. Pitale came to Shirdi with his wife and children. He went to the masjid with them and prostrated before Baba and placed his sick son on Baba's feet. No sooner had Baba seen the child than an unfavorable thing happened. Immediately the son's eyes revolved up and he fell down senseless. His mouth began to foam and his whole body began to perspire profusely. It seemed as if he was breathing his last. Seeing this, the parents became very nervous and overwrought. The boy had such fits very often, but this fit seemed to persist long. Tears began to flow ceaselessly from the mother's eyes and she began to wail. She cried like a person who being afraid of robbers, runs into a house that then collapses on her. Or like a cow fearing a tiger, running into the hands of a butcher, or like a traveler, tormented by the heat of the sun, taking refuge under a tree that then falls on her. Or like a devout person going for worship into a temple that collapses on him.

Baba comforted her, saying, "Do not wail like this. Wait a bit. Have patience. Take the boy to your lodging, he will come to his senses within half an hour." They did as directed by Baba and found that his words came true. As soon as he was taken into the wada, the boy recovered and the entire family, husband, wife and others were very delighted and all their doubts disappeared. Then Mr. Pitale came with his wife to see Baba, prostrated before him very humbly, and respectfully shampooed his legs and mentally thanked Baba for his help.

Baba smiled and said, "Are not all your thoughts, doubts and fears calmed down now? The Lord will protect him who has faith and patience." Mr. Pitale was a rich and well-to-do gentleman. He distributed sweets on a large scale and gave Baba excellent fruits and *pan* (betel leaves).

Mrs. Pitale was a very *sattvic* (pure) lady, simple, loving and faithful. She used to sit near the post staring at Baba with tears of joy flowing in her eyes. Seeing her amiable and loving nature, Baba was much pleased with her. Like Gods, saints are always dependent on their devotees who surrender and worship them with all their heart and soul. After passing some happy days in Baba's company, the Pitale family came to the masjid to take Baba's permission to depart. Baba gave them udi and blessings and called Mr. Pitale close and said, "Bapu, I have given you two rupees before, now I give you three rupees. Keep these in your shrine for worship and you will benefit." Mr. Pitale accepted these as prasad, prostrated again before Baba and prayed for his blessings. A thought arose in his mind. He couldn't understand what Baba meant when he said that he had given two rupees previously, as this was his first trip to Shirdi. He was curious to have this mystery solved, but Baba kept silent.

When Mr. Pitale returned to Mumbai, he narrated to his old mother all that happened in Shirdi and about the mystery of Baba giving him two rupees previously. The mother also did not understand the mystery. But, thinking seriously about it, she was reminded of a previous incident, which solved the mystery. She said to her son, "As you went to Baba with your son now, so did your father many years ago when he took you to Akkalkot for darshan of the Maharaj there. The Maharaj was also a siddha, a perfect yogi, omniscient and liberal. Your father was pure, devout and his worship was accepted. He then gave your father two rupees to keep in the shrine for worship. Your father worshipped them until his death but thereafter the worship was neglected and the rupees were lost. The memory of these two rupees was also lost until now. You are very fortunate. Akkalkot Maharaj has appeared to you in the form of Baba to remind you of your duties and worship and to ward off all dangers. Now from this time forward, leave off all doubts and bad thoughts, follow your ancestors and behave well. Go on worshipping the family gods and the rupees.

Take pride and see the value in the blessing of the saints. Baba has kindly revived the spirit of bhakti in you; cultivate it to your benefit."

Hearing his mother's remarks, Mr. Pitale was very much delighted. He came to know and was now convinced about Baba's all-pervasiveness and the importance of his darshan. From that time he became very careful about his behavior.

YOU MUST ENJOY THE FRUIT OF YOUR PAST ACTIONS

Gopal Ambadekar of Poona was a devotee of Baba. He served for ten years in the Abkari Department in the Thana District, from where he had to retire. He tried to get another job but did not succeed. He was overtaken by other calamities and his condition grew from bad to worse. He passed seven years in this condition, visiting Shirdi every year and placing his grievance before Baba. In 1916, his plight became worse and he decided to commit suicide in Shirdi. So he went there with his wife and stayed for two months. One night while sitting in a bullock cart in front of Dixit's wada, he resolved to end his life by throwing himself into a well close by.

He proposed one thing but Baba wished to do something else. A few paces from this place, there was a hotel and its proprietor, Mr. Sagun, a devotee of Baba, came out and approached him, "Did you ever read this book about Akkalkot Maharaja's life?" Ambadekar took the book and began to read it.

Casually, or we can say providentially, he came across the following story: During Akkalkot Maharaj's life, a devotee suffered much from an incurable disease and when he could no longer endure the agony and pain, and desperate to end his miseries, one night threw himself into a well. Immediately, the Maharaj came and took him out with his own hands then advised him, "You must enjoy the fruit—good or bad—of your past actions. If the enjoyment is incomplete, suicide won't help you. You have to take another birth and suffer again. So instead of killing yourself, why not suffer for some time and finish up your store of the fruit of your past deeds and be done with it once and for all?"

Reading this appropriate and timely story, Ambadekar was much surprised and moved. Had he not received Baba's hint through the story, he would have been no more. On seeing Baba's all-pervasiveness and benevolence, his faith in him was confirmed, and he became a staunch devotee. His father was a devotee of Akkalkot Maharaj and Baba wanted him to walk in his father's footsteps and continue his devotion to him. He then received Baba's blessings and his prospects began to improve. He studied astrology and gained proficiency in it and thereby improved his lot. He was able to earn sufficient money and passed his later life in ease and comfort.

Pranams to Sri Sai

Peace Be to All

CHAPTER TWENTY-SEVEN

When a man takes refuge at the feet of the sadguru, he gets the merit of bowing to the trinity—Brahma, Vishnu and Shiva— and also Parabrahman.

This chapter describes how Baba favored his devotees by giving them spiritual books that he had blessed. His touch consecrated them for *parayana* (reading regularly) and certain other matters.

⚜

VICTORY TO SRI SAI

When a man takes a plunge into the sea, he gets the merit of bathing in all the *tirthas* (holy waters) and sacred rivers. Similarly, when a man takes refuge at the feet of the sadguru, he gets the merit of bowing to the trinity—Brahma, Vishnu and Shiva—and also Parabrahman. Victory to Sri Sai, the wish-fulfilling tree and ocean of knowledge who gives us self-realization. Oh Sai, create in us a regard for your stories. Let the readers and audience devour them with the same relish with which the chatak bird drinks the water from the clouds and becomes happy.

While listening to your stories, let each person and their families have all the *sattvic* (pure) emotions—let their bodies perspire, let their eyes be full of tears, let their *prana* (life force) be steady, let their minds be composed, let their hair stand on end, let them cry, sob and shake, let their hostilities and their distinctions, great and small, vanish. If these things happen, that is a sign of the grace of the guru dawning upon them. When these emotions develop in you, the guru is most pleased and will certainly lead you on to the goal of self-realization. The best way to get free from the shackles of Maya is our complete and wholehearted surrender to Baba. The *Vedas* cannot take you across the ocean of Maya. It is only the sadguru who can do so and make you see the Lord in all creatures.

BABA BLESSES BOOKS

The various methods by which Baba imparted instructions have already been noted in previous chapters. Now we shall deal with one aspect of it. It was the habit of some devotees to take spiritual books to Baba that they wanted to study. They considered it blessed after Baba touched it and returned it back to them. They felt that Baba was with them through daily reading of such books.

Once, Kaka Mahajani came to Shirdi with a copy of *Ekanath Bhagwat*. Shama took the book to read it in the masjid. There Baba took it from him, touched it, and after turning some pages, gave it back to Shama and asked him to keep it with him. Shama said that it belonged to Mahajani and had to be returned to him. "No, no," Baba said. "As I have given it to you, better keep it with you for safe custody. It will be of use to you." In this way, many books were entrusted to Shama. After some days, Mahajani came again with another copy of the *Bhagwat* and gave it in Baba's hand. Then Baba gave it back as prasad and asked him to preserve it well and assured him that it would stand him in good stead. Mahajani accepted it with a pranam.

SHAMA STUDIES THE VISHNU SAHASRANAM

Shama was a very intimate devotee of Baba. Baba wanted to favor him in a particular way by giving him a copy of *Vishnu Sahasranam* as prasad. This was done in the following way. Once a *Ramadasi* (follower of Saint Ramadas) came to Shirdi and stayed for some time. His daily routine was to get up early in the morning, bathe, put on saffron-colored clothes, and besmear himself with sacred ashes. Then he would faithfully read the *Vishnu Sahasranam*, a book with a thousand names in praise of Vishnu, and *Adhyatma Ramayana*, an esoteric version of Rama's story. He read these books quite often.

After some days, Baba thought of favoring and initiating Shama with the *Vishnu Sahasranam*. He called the Ramadasi to him and said that he was suffering from intense stomach pain, and unless he took *senna pods* (a purgative), the pain would not stop. He asked him to please go to the bazaar and bring the drug. The Ramadasi closed his book and went to the bazaar. Then Baba descended from his seat, came to where Ramadasi had been reading and took the copy of *Vishnu Sahasranam*. Returning to his seat, he said to Shama:

Oh Shama, this book is very valuable and effective, so I present it to you. You read it. Once I suffered so intensely that my heart began to palpitate and my life was in danger. At that critical time, I hugged this book to my heart and then, Shama, what a relief it gave me! I thought that Allah Himself came down and saved me. So I give this to you. Read it slowly, little by little, read daily one name at least and it will do you good.

Shama replied that he did not want it, and that the owner, the Ramadasi, was an angry, obstinate, irritable fellow who would certainly pick a quarrel with him. Besides, being a simple villager, he could not clearly read the Sanskrit letters in the book. Shama wondered if Baba wanted to set him against the Ramadasi by this act of his. He had no idea what Baba truly had in mind for him.

Baba must have thought to tie this necklace of *Vishnu Sahasranam* around the neck of Shama, an intimate devotee even though a rustic, to save him from the miseries of worldly existence. The effectiveness of God's name is well known. It saves us from all sins and bad tendencies, frees us from the cycles of birth and death. There is no easier sadhana than this. It is the best purifier of our mind. It requires no paraphernalia and no restrictions. It is so easy and so effective. Baba wanted Shama to practice this sadhana even though Shama did not desire it. So Baba forced this on him. It is also reported that long ago, Eknath Maharaj similarly forced the *Vishnu Sahasranam* on a poor Brahmin neighbor and thus saved him. The reading and study of this *Vishnu Sahasranam* is a broad, open way of purifying the mind. This is why Baba thrust it on his Shama.

The Ramadasi returned soon with the senna pods. Anna Chinchanikar, who was then present and who wanted to play the part of Narada (the celestial rishi who was well-known for setting up quarrels between gods and demons and vice versa), informed him of what had happened. The Ramadasi at once flared up. He came down at once on Shama with all fury. He said that it was Shama who set Baba to send him away, under the pretext of a stomachache, to bring back the medicine, in order to take the book. He began to scold and abuse Shama and remarked that if the book was not returned, he would dash his head. Shama calmly remonstrated with him, but in vain. Then Baba spoke kindly to him as follows:

Oh Ramadasi, what is the matter with you? Why are you so turbulent? Is not Shama our boy? Why do you scold him unnecessarily? How is it that you are so quarrelsome? Can you not speak soft and sweet words? You read daily these sacred books and still your mind is agitated and your passions uncontrolled. What sort of a Ramadasi you are! You ought to be indifferent to all things. Is it not strange that you should covet this book so strongly? A true Ramadasi should have no *mamata* (attachment) but have *samata* (equality) towards all. You are now quarrelling with the boy Shama for a mere book. Go, take your seat, books can be had in plenty for money, but not men; think well and be considerate. What worth is your book? Shama had no concern with it. I took it up myself and gave it to him. You know it by heart. I thought Shama might read it and benefit thereby, and so I gave to it him.

How sweet were these words of Baba, soft, tender and nectar-like! Their effect was wonderful. The Ramadasi calmed down and said to Shama that he would take *Panchratni Gita* in return. Shama was much pleased and said, "Why one, I shall give ten copies in return."

So the matter was ultimately settled. The question for consideration is, "Why should the Ramadasi press for *Panchratni Gita*, a book that he never cared to know before, and why should he, who daily read religious books in the masjid in front of Baba, quarrel with Shama in Baba's presence?" We do not know how to divide the blame and whom to blame. We only say that, had this incident not happened, the importance of the subject, the efficacy of God's name and the study of *Vishnu Sahasranam* would not have been brought home to Shama. So we see that Baba's method of teaching and initiating was unique. In this case, Shama did gradually study the book and mastered its contents to such an extent that he was able to explain it to Professor G.G. Narke, M.A. of the College of Engineering, Poona, the son-in-law of Shriman Bapusaheb Buti and a devotee of Baba.

VITTHAL VISION

One day, while Kakasaheb Dixit was in meditation after his morning bath in his wada at Shirdi, he saw a vision of Vitthal. When he went to see Baba afterwards, Baba asked him, "Did Vitthal Patil come? Did you not see him? He is very elusive, hold him fast, otherwise he will give you the slip and run away." Then at noon a certain hawker came there with 20 or 25 pictures of Vitthal of Pandharpur for sale. Kakasaheb was surprised to see that the form of Vitthal he saw in his meditation exactly tallied with that in the picture, and he was also reminded of Baba's words. He therefore bought one picture most willingly and kept it in his shrine for worship.

GITA RAHASYA

Baba always loved those who studied *Brahma Vidya* (self-realization) and encouraged them. To give an instance, once Bapusaheb Jog received a post-parcel. It contained a copy of the *Gita Rahasya* by Lokamanya Tilak. Taking it under his arm, he came to the masjid and prostrated himself before Baba, where the parcel fell at Baba's feet. Baba inquired what it was. It was opened then and there, and the book was placed in Baba's hand. He turned some pages here and there for a few minutes, took out a rupee from his pocket, placed it on the book and handed the same with the rupee to Jog and said to him, "Read this completely and you will be benefited."

⚜

MR. AND MRS. KHAPARDE

Let us close this chapter with a description of the Khapardes. Once Dadasaheb Khaparde came with his family and lived in Shirdi for some months. (The diary of his stay has been published in English in the *Shri Sai Leela Magazine*, I Volume.) Dadasaheb was not an ordinary man. He was wealthy and the most famous advocate of Amaravati, and a member of the Council of State, Delhi. He was very intelligent and a very good speaker. Still he dared not open his mouth before Baba. Most devotees spoke and argued with Baba off and on, but only three, Khaparde, Noolkar and Buti, kept always silent. They were meek, modest, humble and good-natured. Dadasaheb, who was able to expound *Panchadashi* (a well-known Sanskrit treatise on the Advaita Philosophy by the famous Vidyaranya) to others, uttered no word when he came to the masjid before Baba. A man, however learned he may be even in the *Vedas,* fades away before one who has realized Brahman and becomes one with it. Learning cannot shine before self-realization.

Dadasaheb stayed for four months, but Mrs. Khaparde stayed for seven. Both were highly pleased with their Shirdi stay. Mrs. Khaparde was faithful and devout, and loved Baba deeply. Every noon she brought naivedya to the masjid, and after it was accepted by Baba, she used to return and take her meals. Seeing her steady and firm devotion, Baba wanted to exhibit it to others. One noon she brought a dish containing *sanza* (wheat-pudding), purees, rice, soup, and *kheer* (sweet rice) and other sundry articles to the masjid. Baba, who usually waited for hours, got up at once, went to his dining seat and removing the outer covering from the dish, began to partake of the things zealously. Shama then asked him, "Why this partiality? At times you throw away dishes of others and do not care to look at them, but this appeals to you earnestly. Why is the dish brought by this lady so sweet? This intrigues us."

Baba then explained, "This food is really extraordinary. In former birth this lady was a merchant's fat cow, yielding much milk. Then she disappeared and took birth in a gardener's family; then in a Kshatriya family, where she married a merchant. Then she was born in a Brahmin family. I have seen her after a very long time, let me take some sweet morsels of love from her dish." Saying this, Baba did full justice to her dish, washed his mouth and hands, belched as a mark of satisfaction, and resumed his seat. Then she made a bow and began to shampoo Baba's legs, and Baba began to talk with her and knead her arms which were shampooing his legs. On seeing this reciprocal service, Shama began to joke and said, "It is going on well. It is a wonderful sight to see God and his bhakta serving each other." After being pleased with her sincere service, Baba asked her in low and fascinating tone to chant *Rajaram, Rajaram* then and always, and said, "If you do this, your life's object will be gained, your mind will attain peace and you will be immensely benefited." To persons unfamiliar with spiritual matters, this might appear as a polite gesture, but really it was not so. It was a case of shaktipat, the transference of power from the guru to the disciple. How effective were Baba's words! In an instant, they pierced her heart and lodged there.

This case illustrates the nature of the relations that should subsist between the guru and the disciple. Both should love and serve each other as one. There is no distinction, nor any difference between them. Both are one, and one cannot live without the other. The disciple placing his head on the guru's feet is a physical or outward vision; really and internally they are both one and the same. Those who see any difference between them are yet unripe and not perfect.

Pranams to Sri Sai

Peace Be to All

CHAPTER TWENTY-EIGHT

SPARROWS DRAWN TO SHIRDI

Sai Baba is not finite or limited. He dwells in all beings, from ants to insects to Brahman. He pervades all. Baba was well versed in the knowledge of the *Vedas*, as well as in the science of self-realization. As he was proficient in both of these, he was fit to be a sadguru. Even though a person is learned, if they are unable to awaken the disciples and establish them in self-realization, they do not deserve to be called a sadguru. Generally, the father gives birth to the body and death invariably follows life. But the sadguru does away with both life and death, so he is more kind and merciful than anyone.

Baba often said whatever distance his devotee is, even if it is a thousand *kos* (unit of distance of about three miles or 4.8 km) away from him, he will be drawn to Shirdi like a sparrow with a thread tied to its feet. This chapter describes the story of three such sparrows.

❧

MAGNETIZED TO BABA

Lala Lakshmichand met Baba in 1910. In a dream he had a few months before Christmas, he saw an old man with a beard standing surrounded by his devotees. Some days later, he went to the house of his friend to hear the kirtans sung by Das Ganu. It was always the practice of Das Ganu to keep Baba's picture in front of the audience while singing. Lakshmichand was surprised to see that the features of the old man he saw in his dream were exactly like those in the picture. He came to the conclusion that the old man in his dream was Baba himself. The sight of this picture, Das Ganu's kirtan, and the life of the Saint Tukaram about which Das Ganu discoursed, all made a deep impression on his mind and he longed to go to Shirdi.

It is always the experience of devotees that God helps them in their search for a sadguru and in their spiritual endeavors. That very night, his friend Shankar Rao knocked at his door and asked him whether he would accompany him to Shirdi. His joy knew no bounds and he immediately decided to go to Shirdi. He borrowed Rs.15 from his cousin and after making preparations, left for Shirdi. In the train, he and his friend sang bhajans and talked about Baba with fellow passengers, four Muslims returning to their home near Shirdi, who told them that Baba was a great saint who had lived in Shirdi for many years.

When they reached Kopergaon, he wanted to buy some good guavas to offer to Baba, but he was so taken with the scenery and sights that he forgot to purchase them. When they were nearing Shirdi, he was reminded of the guavas. Just then, he saw an old woman with a guava basket on her head running after the tanga. The tanga stopped and he happily purchased some select fruits. The woman said, "Take all the rest and offer them to Baba on my behalf." The encounter with the woman reminding him to purchase the guavas, and her devotion to Baba, were a surprise to both friends. Lakshmichand wondered if the old woman might be some relation of Baba.

They drove on and came to Shirdi. Upon seeing the flags flying on top of the masjid, they saluted them. With puja materials in hand they went to the masjid and worshipped Baba with due formality. Lakshmichand was very moved and extremely happy to see Baba. He was completely enraptured by Baba's feet, as a bee to a sweet-smelling lotus. Then Baba spoke, "Cunning fellow, he sings bhajans on the way and then asks others. Why ask others? We should see everything with our own eyes. Where is the necessity to question others? Think for yourself whether your dream is true or not. Where was the necessity of taking a loan from a clerk for darshan? Is the heart's desire now satisfied?" Hearing these words, Lakshmichand was wonderstruck by Baba's omniscience. He was at a loss to know how Baba knew about all the things that had happened enroute from his house to Shirdi.

One thing to note here is that Baba never liked people to go into debt to have his darshan, celebrate any holiday, or make any pilgrimage.

SANZA

At noon, when Lakshmichand was sitting for meals he received some *sanza* (wheat pudding) prasad from a devotee. He was pleased to get it. The next day he expected it again but got nothing and was anxious, hoping to have it again. Then on the third day at the noon Aarati, Bapusaheb Jog asked Baba what naivedya he should bring. Baba told him to bring sanza. The devotees then brought two big potfuls of sanza. Lakshmichand was very hungry and also had some back pain. Baba said to him, "It is good that you are hungry, take some sanza and some medicine for the pain in your back." He was wonderstruck to see Baba read his mind again and speak his thoughts aloud. How omniscient Baba was!

EVIL EYE

One night during this time, he witnessed the procession to the Chavadi. Baba suffered a lot from cough. Lakshmichand thought that this suffering by Baba might be due to someone's evil eye. Next morning when he went to the masjid, Baba said to Shama, "I suffered last night from cough. Is it due to some evil eye? I think that somebody's evil eye has worked on me so I am suffering." In this case, Baba again spoke out loud what was passing through Lakshmichand's mind.

On seeing these proofs of Baba's omniscience and his kindness to bhaktas, he fell at Baba's feet and said, "I am much pleased by your darshan. Always be kind and merciful to me and protect me always. For me, there is no other God in this world except your feet. Let my mind be ever absorbed singing your bhajans and in your feet. Let your grace protect me from the miseries of the world and let me always chant your name and be happy."

After getting Baba's udi and blessing, he returned home with his friend much pleased and contented, singing of Baba's glory on the way. He remained a staunch devotee of Baba and always sent garlands of flowers, camphor and dakshina with anyone that he knew was bound for Shirdi.

A Lady from Burhanpore

Now let us turn to another sparrow—Baba's word meaning devotee. In a dream, a lady in Burhanpore saw Sai Baba coming to her door and begging *khichadi* (rice and dhal). On awakening, she saw no one was at her door. But she was happy with the vision and told it to her husband. He was employed in the Postal Department and when he was transferred, both husband and wife decided to go to Shirdi. After visiting Gomati Tirth on the way, they reached Shirdi and stayed for two months. Every day they went to the masjid, performed worship to Baba and passed their time happily. The couple had planned to offer Baba khichadi as naivedya but for the first 14 days, but for some reason or other, it could not be offered. The wife did not like this delay.

On the 15th day, she came to the masjid at noon with her khichadi. There she found that Baba and the others were already sitting for meals and the curtain was down. Nobody dared enter in when the curtain was let down, but the lady could not wait. She threw up the curtain with her hand and entered. Strange to say, that day Baba seemed hungry for khichadi and had wanted it first thing. When she came in with the dish, Baba was delighted and began to eat mouthful after mouthful of khichadi. On seeing Baba's earnestness, everyone was wonderstruck and those who heard the story of khichadi were convinced about the extraordinary love he had for his devotees.

THE BRAHMIN MEGHA

Now let us go to the third and bigger 'sparrow.' Megha was Sathe's simple and illiterate Brahmin cook. He was a devotee of Shiva and always chanted the five-syllabled mantra *Namah Shivaya*. He did not know the *Sandhya* (a Vedic worship), nor its chief mantra, the *Gayatri*. But because Sathe was interested in his welfare, he taught him the Sandhya and the Gayatri. Sathe told him that Sai Baba was the incarnation of Shiva and made him start for Shirdi. At the railway station, Megha learned that Sai Baba was a Muslim. His simple and orthodox mind was very disturbed at the prospect of bowing to a Muslim, so he prayed that his boss would not send him there. Sathe insisted, however, that he go then gave him a letter of introduction to his father-in-law, Dadasaheb Kelkar in Shirdi, to introduce him to Baba.

When he reached Shirdi and went to the masjid, Baba was very indignant and would not allow him to enter. "Kick out the rascal!" roared Baba, "You are a high caste Brahmin and I am a low Muslim. You will lose your caste by coming here. So get away." Hearing these words Megha began to tremble. He was wondering how Baba had come to know what was passing through his mind. He stayed for some days serving Baba in his own way but was still not convinced. Then he went home. After that, he went to Tryambakeshwara and stayed there for a year and a half. Then he returned to Shirdi again. This time, through Dadasaheb's intervention, he was allowed to enter the masjid and stay in Shirdi.

Sai Baba's help to Megha was not through any verbal instruction. He worked on Megha internally and he was considerably changed and benefited. Megha began to look upon Sai Baba as an incarnation of Shiva. In order to worship Shiva, bela leaves are required and Megha used to walk for miles and miles every day to bring them and worship his Shiva (Baba). His practice was to worship all the gods in the village and then come to the masjid where, after saluting Baba's seat, he worshipped Baba. After doing some service like shampooing his legs, he drank the water from Baba's feet. One day, it so happened that he came to the masjid without worshipping Khandoba, as the temple door was closed. Baba did not accept his worship and sent him back, saying that the door was now open. Megha went, found the door open and worshipped the deity, then returned to Baba as usual.

***

GANGES BATH

On one *Makara Sankranti* day, Megha wanted to besmear Baba's body with sandalpaste and bathe him with Ganges water. At first Baba was unwilling to undergo this but finally after many repeated requests he consented. Megha had to travel a distance of over 18 miles round trip in order get the sacred water from the Godavari River. He brought the water and made the preparations for the bath at noon and asked Baba to get ready for it. Then Baba asked to be freed from his bath saying that as a fakir he had nothing to gain from Ganges water. But Megha would not listen. He knew that Shiva is pleased with a bath of Ganges water and that he must give his Shiva (Baba) a bath on that auspicious day. Baba finally consented and came down and sat on a wooden board, stuck his head out and said, "Oh Megha, at least do this favor. The head is the most important organ of the body, so only pour water over that. It is equivalent to a full bath."

"All right," said Megha. Then when he lifted up the water pot and began pouring it on Baba's head he became so overwhelmed with love that he cried out, "Hari Gange!" and emptied the pot on Baba's whole body. He put the pot aside and looked at Baba and to his surprise and amazement found that only Baba's head was drenched and his body dry!

***

TRISULA AND SHIVA LINGAM

"I don't require a door to enter. I have no form, nor any extension. I live everywhere. I act as the wirepuller of all the actions of a man who trusts me and merges in me."

Megha worshipped Baba in two places, in person in the masjid and Baba's big picture in the wada. He did this for 12 months. To increase his devotion and strengthen his faith, Baba gave him a vision. Early one morning, Megha was lying awake on his bed with his eyes closed when he clearly saw Baba's form. Baba threw *akshata* (red rice grains) and said, "Megha, draw a *trishula* (Shiva's symbol)." Then Baba disappeared. Hearing Baba's words, he opened his eyes eagerly hoping to see Baba, but instead he saw only the rice grains spread here and there. He then went to the masjid to see Baba to tell him about his vision and ask permission to draw a trishula.

Baba said, "Did you not hear my words asking you to draw a trishula? It was not a vision but a direct order. My words are always pregnant with meaning and never hollow."

Megha said, "You woke me up but all the doors were closed, so I thought it was a vision."

Baba replied, "I don't require a door to enter. I have no form, nor any extension. I live everywhere. I act as the wirepuller of all the actions of a man who trusts me and merges in me."

Megha returned to the wada and drew a red trishula on the wall near Baba's picture. The next day, the Ramadasi devotee came and saluted Baba and offered him a Shiva Lingam. Megha turned up at the same time and Baba said to him, "See, Shankar (Shiva) has come. Worship Him now." Megha was pleasantly surprised to see the Shiva Lingam immediately following the drawing of the trishula.

At the same time, Kakasaheb was in the wada standing with a towel on his head after having taken his bath and was remembering Sai, when he saw a Shiva Lingam in his mental vision. While he was wondering about this, Megha came and showed him the Shiva Lingam that was presented to him by Baba. Kakasaheb was happy to find out that the Shiva Lingam was exactly the same as the one he had seen a few minutes before in his vision. A few days after the drawing of the trishula, Baba installed the Shiva Lingam near the big picture which Megha was worshipping. The worship of Shiva was dear to Megha. It was by arranging the drawing of the trisula and the installation of the Shiva Lingam that Baba strengthened his faith.

In 1912, after serving Baba continuously and doing regular worship and Araati every noon and evening for many years, Megha passed away. Baba passed his hands over his corpse and said, "This was a true devotee of mine." Baba ordered that the usual funeral dinner be provided to the Brahmins at his expense. This order was carried out by Kakasaheb.

Pranams to Sri Sai

Peace Be to All

CHAPTER TWENTY-NINE

BABA GIVES DARSHAN OF LORD RAMA

It was in the year 1916 that a party consisting of a man, his wife, daughter and sister-in-law started on a pilgrimage to the holy city of Benares. On the way, they heard there lived a great sage named Sai Baba in Shirdi who was calm, composed and very generous. Everyday he distributed money to his bhaktas and skillful people who demonstrated their skill. A lot of money in the form of dakshina was collected daily by Baba. From this, each day he gave one rupee to a three-year-old girl, Amani, and six rupees to her mother, Jamali. Sometimes he gave two, five, ten, and even 50 rupees to bhaktas as he pleased.

After hearing this, the party went to Shirdi. They sang very good bhajans but inwardly they craved money. Three of the party were full of avarice, but the chief lady was of a very different nature. She had regard and love for Baba. It so happened that when the noon Aarati was going on, Baba was much pleased with her faith and devotion. He gave her darshan of her beloved deity Rama. Baba appeared to her as Lord Rama while to all the others he was the usual Baba. On seeing her beloved deity, she was deeply moved. Tears began to flow from her eyes and she clapped her hands in joy. The people began to wonder at her joyful mood but were not able to guess its cause. Later in the afternoon, she disclosed everything to her husband. She told him how she saw Lord Rama in Sai Baba. He thought that as she was very simple and devout, her seeing Rama might be a hallucination of her mind. He discounted what she said, saying that it was not possible that she alone should see Rama while everyone else saw Sai Baba. She did not resent this remark, as she was fortunate enough to have Rama's darshan now and then when her mind was calm and composed and free from avarice.

BABA TEACHES IN DREAMS AND VISIONS

Things were going on like this when one night her husband had a wonderful vision in his dream. He was in a big city where the police had arrested him, tied his hands with a rope, and locked him up in a cage. As the police were tightening the grip, he saw Baba standing quietly outside, close to the cage. On seeing Baba so near, he said in a lamenting tone, "Hearing your fame, I came to your feet. How can a calamity happen to me when you are standing here in person?"

Baba said, "You must suffer the consequences of your action."

He said, "I have not done anything in this life that would bring such a misfortune on me."

Baba said, "If not in this life, you must have committed some sin in your past life."

He replied, "I do not know anything of my past life, but assuming that I did commit some sin then, why should it not be burned and destroyed in your presence, as dry grass before fire?"

"Do you have such faith?" Baba asked.

"Yes," he said.

Baba then asked him to close his eyes. No sooner did he shut his eyes than he heard the thumping sound of something falling down.

Opening his eyes, he saw that he was free and it was the police that had fallen down bleeding. Becoming very frightened, he looked at Baba who said, "Now you are really caught. The officers will come and arrest you."

Then the man begged, "There is no other savior except you. Save me no matter what!"

Baba asked him to close his eyes again. He did and when he opened them again he saw that he was free, out of the cage and Baba was by his side. He then fell at Baba's feet. Baba asked, "Is there any difference between this namaskar and your previous ones? Think well and reply."

He said, "There is a lot of difference. My former namaskaras were offered with the goal to get money from you, but the present namaskar is one offered to you as God. Besides, formerly I resented that you, being a Muslim, were spoiling us Hindus."

Baba asked, "Do you not believe in Muslim gods?"

He said, "No."

Baba said, "Do you not have a *panja* (hand emblem) in your house and do you not worship in a mosque during Moharum? Also, in your house there is a Muslim deity by the name Kadbibi, whom you worship and appease for marriages and other festivals? Is it not so?" He admitted all this. Then Baba said, "What more do you want?"

A desire then arose in his mind to have darshan of his guru, Ramdas. Baba then asked him to turn back and see. When he turned, there was Ramdas in front of him! No sooner did he begin to fall at his feet when Ramdas vanished.

Inquisitively he asked Baba, "You look old. Do you know your age?"

Baba exclaimed, "What! You say I am old? Just run a race with me and see!" Saying this, Baba began to run and the man followed. Baba disappeared in the dust raised by his footsteps while running. Then the man awakened.

After waking up, he began to think seriously about the dream vision. His mental attitude was completely changed and he realized the greatness of Baba. After this, his grasping and doubting tendencies disappeared and true devotion to Baba's feet sprang in his mind. The vision was a mere dream, but the questions and answers within it were most significant.

That morning, when everyone assembled in the masjid for Aarati, Baba gave him two rupees worth of sweetmeats as prasad and two rupees from his pocket, and blessed him. Baba made him stay for a few more days then gave him his blessing, saying, "Allah will give you plenty and He will do you all good." He did not get more money then but he received far better things— Baba's blessing, which stood him in good stead throughout his life. The party received plenty of money afterwards, their pilgrimage was successful and they did not have to suffer any trouble or inconvenience during their journey. They all returned home safe and sound, thinking of Baba's words and blessings and the bliss they experienced by his grace.

This story illustrates one of the methods that Baba followed and follows even now in some cases to improve and transform his devotees.

⚜

FAITH IN BABA IS MORE POWERFUL THAN ASTROLOGY

If we only hold on steadily to Baba with full faith and continue our endeavors, our efforts will ultimately be crowned with success.

The Tendulkar family lived in Bandra, a suburb of Mumbai. All the members of the family were devoted to Baba. Mrs. Savitribai Tendulkar published a book in Marathi called *Sri Sainath Bhajan Mala*, containing 800 *abhangas and padas* describing the leelas of Baba. It is a book worth reading by those interested in Baba. The son, Babu Tendulkar, was studying hard day and night for a medical examination. He consulted some astrologers and upon examining his horoscope, they told him that the stars were not favorable that year and he should appear for the examination the next year, when he would be certainly successful. This cast a gloom over him and made him very restless.

A few days afterwards his mother went to Shirdi and saw Baba. Among other things, she mentioned the gloomy and morose condition of her son who was to appear for the examination in a few days. Hearing this Baba said to her, "Tell your son to believe in me, to throw aside horoscopes and predictions of astrologers and palmists and go on with his studies. Let him appear for the examination with a calm mind. He is sure to pass this year. Ask him to trust in me and not to get disappointed."

The mother returned home and communicated Baba's message to her son. So he studied hard and in due course appeared for his examination. He did well on the written test but being overwhelmed by doubts, thought that he did not secure sufficient marks for passing. So he did not plan to appear for the oral examination. But the examiner was after him, sending word through a fellow student that he had passed the written examination and should appear for the oral. This encouraged the son to appear for the oral examination and he was successful in it also. He successfully passed the examinations that year by Baba's grace even though the stars were against him. It is to be noted here that doubts and difficulties surround us just to move us and strengthen our faith. We are tested as it were. If we only hold on steadily to Baba with full faith and continue our endeavors, our efforts will ultimately be crowned with success.

Mr. Tendulkar was serving in a foreign mercantile firm in Mumbai. As he grew old, he was not able to attend to his work properly so he had to take leave and rest. As he did not improve during the period of leave, a permanent extension of his leave—retirement from service—was inevitable. The chief manager of the firm decided to retire him on a pension, as he was an old and reliable servant. The question regarding the amount of pension to be given was under consideration. He was getting Rs.150 per month as salary and his pension, which was half the amount, would not be enough to meet the expenses of the family. They were all anxious about this matter. Fifteen days before the final settlement, Baba appeared to Mrs. Tendulkar in her dream and said, "I wish that Rs.100 should be paid as a pension. Will this satisfy you?"

She replied, "Baba, why ask me this? We fully trust in you." Even though Baba said Rs.100, they were given an additional ten rupees, for a total of Rs.110, as a special case. Such wonderful love and care Baba exhibited for his bhaktas.

⚜

A Devotee Responds to Baba's Appearance in a Dream

Captain Hate was a great devotee of Baba. Once Baba appeared to him in his dream and said, "Did you forget me?"

Captain Hate then immediately held Baba's feet and replied, "If a child forgets his mother, how can it be saved?" Then Captain Hate went into the garden and took out fresh walpapadi vegetables and arranged for *shidha* (ghee, wheat flour, dhal) and dakshina. As he was about to offer all this to Baba, he was awakened and came to know that it was all a dream. After this, he decided to send all these things to Baba in Shirdi.

Some days afterwards, he sent Rs.12 by money order to a friend with instructions that Rs.2 should be spent in buying shidha articles and walpapadi vegetables, which would then be offered to Baba with Rs.10 as dakshina. The friend went to Shirdi and purchased the things mentioned except that walpapadi was not available. In a short time, a woman turned up with a basket on her head, which curiously enough contained walpapadi vegetables. It was purchased and then all the things were offered to Baba on behalf of Captain Hate. Mr. Nimonkar prepared the offering of rice and walpapadi vegetables the next day and offered them to Baba. All the people were surprised to see that while Baba dined, he ate the walpapadi and did not touch rice and other things. Captain Hate's joy knew no bounds when he heard of this from his friend.

BABA GIVES A BLESSED RUPEE

Another time, Captain Hate wished that he could have a rupee coin in his house which had been blessed by Baba's touch. He came across a friend who was bound for Shirdi. Captain Hate sent his rupee with him to give to Baba. The friend went to Shirdi and after the usual salutation gave his own dakshina to Baba first, which Baba then pocketed. Then he gave Captain Hate's rupee, which Baba took in his hand and began to stare at. He held it in front, tossed it up with his right thumb and played with it. Then he said to the friend, "Return this to its owner with udi, tell him that I want nothing from him, and ask him to live in peace and contentment."

The friend returned to Captain Hate and handed over the rupee that Baba had blessed, and told him all that happened at Shirdi. Captain Hate was much pleased and realized that Baba always encouraged good thoughts, and when he wished for something intently, Baba fulfilled it.

BABA TAKES A DEVOTEE'S RUPEE

Now let the readers hear a different story. A gentleman named Vamanrao loved Baba very much. Once he brought a rupee that had been engraved on one side with the figures of Rama, Laxman and Sita. On the other side the figure of Maruti with folded hands was engraved. He offered it to Baba with a hope that he would bless it with his touch and return it to him with udi. But Baba immediately pocketed it. Then Shama spoke to Baba regarding Vamanrao's wish and asked Baba to return it. In the presence of Vamanrao, Baba said, "Why should it be returned to him? We should keep it ourselves. If he pays Rs.25 for it, then it will be returned." For the sake of that one rupee, Vamanrao gave Rs.25 and placed them before Baba.

Then Baba said, "The value of that rupee far exceeds Rs.25. Shama, take this rupee. Let us have it in our store. Keep this in your shrine and worship it." No one had the courage to ask Baba why he did this particular action. Only he knows what is best and most suitable to each and all.

Pranams to Sri Sai

Peace Be to All

CHAPTER THIRTY

DRAWN TO SHIRDI

In this chapter, the story of two more devotees who were drawn to Shirdi is narrated.

SAI – THE OCEAN OF MERCY

Whoever is overcome with calamities and remembers and prays 'Sai,' his mind will become calm and peaceful through Baba's grace.

Bow to the kind Sai who is the abode of mercy and who is affectionate towards his devotees. By his mere darshan, he does away with their fear in samsara and destroys their calamities. He was first *nirguna* (formless) but on account of the devotion of his bhaktas, was obliged to take a form. To give liberation—self-realization—to bhaktas is the mission of the saints and for Sai, the chief of them, that mission is inevitable. Those who take refuge in his feet have all their karmas destroyed and their progress is certain. Remembering his feet, Brahmins from holy places come to him, read scriptures and chant the *Gayatri* mantra in his presence. We who are weak and without any merit do not know what *bhakti* (devotion) is, but we know this much, that although all others may leave us, Sai won't forsake us. Those whom he favors get enormous strength, knowledge and the ability to discriminate between the unreal and the real.

Sai fully knows the desires of his devotees and fulfills them. They get what they want and are grateful. So we invoke him and pranam before him. Forgetting all our faults let him free us from all anxieties. Whoever is overcome with calamities and remembers and prays, 'Sai,' his mind will become calm and peaceful through Baba's grace.

Hemadpant says Sai, the ocean of mercy, favored him and the result of this is this present work, the *Sai Satcharitra*. Otherwise what qualifications did he have and how could he undertake such an enterprise? But as Sai took all the responsibility, Hemadpant felt no burden, nor any care about it. When the powerful light of knowledge was there to inspire his speech and pen, why should he entertain any doubt or feel any anxiety? Sai received his service in the form of this book, which is due to Hemadpant's accumulation of merits from past births. Hemadpant considered himself fortunate and blessed.

The following story is not a mere tale but pure nectar. He who drinks it will realize Sai's greatness and all pervasiveness. Those who want to argue and criticize should not listen to these stories. What is wanted here is not discussion but unlimited love and devotion. Learned, devoted and faithful believers, or those who consider themselves as servants of the saints, will like and appreciate these stories; others will take them to be fables. The fortunate devotees of Sai will find Sai leelas to be the *kalpataru* (wish-fulfilling tree). Drinking this nectar of the Sai leelas will give liberation to the ignorant *jivas* (individual souls), satisfaction to householders, and a sadhana to spiritual aspirants. Now to the story of this chapter.

You Must Be Called to See a Saint

There lived in Vani, Nasik District, a man named Kakaji Vaidya. He was the priest of the Saptashringi Temple to the Goddess. He was so overwhelmed by adverse circumstances and calamities that he lost his peace of mind and became extremely agitated. One evening, while suffering from these circumstances, he went into the temple of the Goddess and prayed to Her from the bottom of his heart, invoking Her aid to free him from anxiety. The Goddess was pleased with his devotion and that night appeared in his dream and said, "Go to Baba, then your mind will become calm and composed." Kakaji was anxious to know from Her who Baba was, but before he could get any explanation he was awakened.

He began to think who this Baba might be that the Goddess had asked him to go see. After reflecting on it, he resolved that this Baba might be *Tryambakeshwar* (Lord Shiva). So he went to the holy place, Tryambakeshwar, and stayed there for ten days. During that time, he bathed in the early morning, chanted the *Rudram*, did *abhishekam* (pouring water over lingam) and other religious practices. But still, even with all that, he was as restless as before. Then he returned to his place and again invoked the Goddess most sorrowfully. That night She appeared in his dream again and said, "Why did you go to Tryambakeshwar in vain? By Baba, I mean, Sri Sai Sainath."

For Kakaji, the question now was how and when to go to Shirdi to see Baba. If anyone earnestly wants to see a saint, not only the saint but God fulfills his wish as well. In fact, the saint and God are one and the same. There is no difference between them. If anyone thinks that he goes by himself to see a saint that is an empty boast. Unless the saint wills it, who is able to go and see him? Even one leaf in the tree won't move without his bidding. The more anxious a bhakta is to visit a saint, the more devoted and faithful he is, the more quickly and effectively his wish is satisfied to his heart's content. And, he who invites a person to visit also arranges everything for his reception, and so it happened with Kakaji.

SHAMA'S VOWS

When Kakaji was planning his visit to Shirdi a guest arrived at his house to take him to Shirdi. The guest was no other than Shama. We shall see how he came to Vani at this juncture.

When Shama was very young and severely ill his mother took a vow to the family deity, the Goddess at Saptashringi Temple, that if her son recovered she would bring him and dedicate him at Her feet. Years later, his mother suffered greatly from ringworms on her breasts. At that time, she made another vow to the Goddess that if she was healed she would offer Her two silver breasts. These two vows remained unfulfilled.

On her deathbed she called her son, Shama, and told him of her unfulfilled vows to the Goddess. Then after making him promise to fulfill these two vows, she breathed her last. After some time, Shama also forgot about the vows. Thirty years had passed when a famous astrologer had come to Shirdi. His predictions about Bapusaheb Buti and others had proven true. Then Shama's younger brother, Bapaji, consulted him and was told that his mother's vows, which his elder brother promised to fulfill at her deathbed, were not yet fulfilled. The Goddess was displeased with them and it was bringing troubles on them. Bapaji told this to his brother, Shama, who was then reminded of the unfulfilled vows. Thinking that any further delay would be dangerous, he called a goldsmith and got a pair of silver breasts prepared.

Then he went to the masjid, prostrated himself before Baba and placing the two silver breasts before him, requested him to accept them and free him from the vows to the Goddess. Baba insisted that he go to the Saptashringi Temple himself and offer them personally at the feet of the Goddess.

After taking Baba's permission and udi, he left for Vani and searching for the priest, came to Kakaji's house. Kakaji had been very anxious to visit Baba and Shama had now come to see him at the same time. What a wonderful coincidence! Kakaji asked Shama who he was and from where he had come. On learning that he had just come from Shirdi, he immediately embraced him. He was overpowered with love! They talked about Sai leelas together. Then after fulfilling Shama's vows to the Goddess, both started for Shirdi.

On reaching Shirdi, Kakaji went to the masjid and fell at Baba's feet. His eyes were wet with tears and his mind became calm. As predicted in the vision of the Goddess, no sooner did he see Baba than his mind lost all its restlessness and became calm and composed. Kakaji began to think, 'What a wonderful power this is! Baba spoke nothing, there was no question and answer, no blessing said, just his mere darshan was so beneficial to happiness that the restlessness of my mind disappeared and the consciousness of joy overwhelmed me. This is what is called the greatness of darshan.' His vision was fixed on Sai's feet and he could not utter a word. Hearing Baba's leelas, his joy knew no bounds. He surrendered himself completely to Baba, forgot his anxiety and cares and experienced pure happiness. He lived happily there for twelve days, then returned home after taking Baba's leave, udi and blessings.

⚜

BABA GIVES INSTRUCTIONS IN A DREAM

It is said that a dream that we receive in the early hours of the morning generally comes true in the waking state. This may be so. But regarding Baba's dreams there is no restriction of time. To cite such an instance:

One afternoon Baba told Kakasaheb to go to Rahata and bring Khushalchand to Shirdi, as he had not seen him in a long time. Immediately Kakasaheb took a tanga and went to Rahata to give him Baba's message. When Khushalchand heard the message, he was surprised, as during his afternoon nap Baba had appeared in his dream and asked him to come to Shirdi immediately. He had been anxious to go but as he had no horse of his own, he sent his son to inform Baba. When his son was just outside the village border there was Kakasaheb's tanga, which Baba had sent specially to bring him! So they both went to Shirdi in the tanga. Khushalchand saw Baba and everyone was happy. Khushalchand was very moved to see this leela of Baba.

BABA APPEARS IN A DREAM AND INVITES TO SHIRDI

Once a Punjabi Brahmin from Mumbai named Ramalal had a dream in which Baba appeared and asked him to come to Shirdi. Baba appeared to him as a saint but he did not know where to find him. He thought that he should go and see him but as he didn't know his address, he didn't know what to do. But he who calls for an interview makes the necessary arrangements for it. The same happened in this case. That afternoon when he was strolling in the streets, he saw a picture of Baba in a shop. The features of the saint that he had seen in the dream were exactly like those in the picture. After making inquiries, he came to know that the picture was of Sai Baba of Shirdi. Soon after, he went to Shirdi and stayed there until his death.

In this way, Baba brought his devotees to Shirdi for darshan and satisfied their wants, material as well as spiritual.

Pranams to Sri Sai

Peace Be to All

CHAPTER THIRTY-ONE

ALWAYS REMEMBER GOD

T he last wish or thought that a man has at the hour of death determines his future course. Sri Krishna said in the *Gita*, "He who remembers me in his last moments comes to me, and he who meditates on other things goes to what he looks for." We cannot be certain that we will be thinking a particular good thought at our last moment. More often than not, we are likely to be frightened and terrified by different causes. This is why constant practice is necessary to enable us to fix our mind on a desired good thought in any moment. All saints recommend that we always remember God and always chant His name so that we may not be confused when the time of departure comes. For their part, devotees surrender themselves completely to the saints, fully believing that the all-knowing saints will guide and help them in their last moments. A few such cases are noted here.

A SANNYASI BREATHES HIS LAST

"Wealth and prosperity are transient and the body is subject to decay and death. Knowing this, do your duty, leaving all attachment to the things of this world and next. He who does this and surrenders himself to the feet of Hari (Lord) will become free from all troubles and attain bliss."

A *sannyasi* (renunciate) named Vijayananda started on a pilgrimage to *Manasarovar* (Mt. Kailash). En route, hearing of Baba's fame, he stopped at Shirdi. There he met Somadevaji Swami and inquired about the Manasarovar trip. The Swami told him Manasarovar was 500 miles above Gangotri and described the difficulties of the journey; plenty of snow, the change of dialect every 50 kos, and the apprehensiveness of the Bhutanese, which causes problems for pilgrims on the way. Hearing this, the sannyasi was dejected and cancelled the trip.

When he went to Baba and prostrated himself before him, Baba became enraged, "Drive out this useless sannyasi. His company is of no use." The sannyasi did not know Baba's nature. He felt uncomfortable but sat watching what was going on. In the morning, the masjid was overcrowded. Baba was being worshipped in various ways. Some were washing his feet, some taking the *tirth* (holy water) from his toe and drinking it heartily and some touching their eyes with it. Some were applying sandalpaste and other scents to his body. All were doing these things forgetting the distinction of caste and creed. Though Baba had become enraged with him, he was filled with affection for Baba and did not want to leave the masjid.

After staying in Shirdi for two days, he got a letter from Madras stating that his mother was very ill. He was very dejected and wanted to be by his mother's side, but could not leave without Baba's permission. So he went to Baba with the letter in hand and asked for his permission to return home. The omniscient Baba, knowing the future, said to him:

If you so loved your mother, why did you take sannyasa? Partiality or attachment is not becoming to ochre garb (orange renunciate robes). Go and sit quietly at your lodging and wait with patience for a few days. In the wada, there are many robbers. Bolt your doors, be very vigilant or the thieves will carry everything out. Wealth and prosperity are transient and the body is subject to decay and death. Knowing this, do your duty, leaving all attachment to the things of this world and next. He who does this and surrenders himself to the feet of *Hari* (Lord) will become free from all troubles and attain bliss. The Lord runs and helps him who remembers and meditates on Him with love and affection. Your store of past merits is considerable, so you have come here. Now listen to what I say and realize the end of your life. Be desireless and tomorrow begin the study of the *Bhagwat*. Do three *sapthas* (three readings during three weeks) conscientiously. The Lord will be pleased with you and destroy your sorrows, your illusions will vanish and you will get peace.

Seeing that his end was approaching, Baba prescribed that remedy and made him read *Rama Vijaya*, which pleases the God of death. Next morning after bathing and other purifying rites, he started to read *Bhagwat* in a secluded part of the Lendi garden. He completed two readings and felt very exhausted afterwards. He returned to the wada and stayed in his lodging for two days, and on the third day he breathed his last on fakir Bade Baba's lap. Baba asked the people to preserve the body for a day for a reason, as the police later came making inquiries. They then gave permission for the disposal of the body. It was buried in a proper place with due rites. In this way Baba helped the sannyasi and insured his liberation.

BABA APPEARS TO A DEVOTEE FAR AWAY FROM SHIRDI

There was a householder devotee of Baba named Balaram Mankar. When his wife passed away, he became dejected. He entrusted his household to his son, left his home and came to Shirdi and lived with Baba. Baba was pleased with his devotion and wanted to give a good turn to his life. He did so in the following way. Baba gave him Rs.12 and asked him to go and live in Macchindragad. At first, Balaram was unwilling to go and be away from Baba. But Baba convinced him that he was giving the best course for him and asked him to practice meditation three times a day on the *gad* (mount).

Believing in Baba's words, Balaram came to the gad. He was very pleased with the surroundings, the serenity, the pure water and healthy air. He began to practice the meditations tirelessly as Baba recommended. After some days he had a revelation. Generally, bhaktas get revelation in their samadhi or trance states, but in Balaram's case he had it when he came down from his trance to his ordinary consciousness.

Baba appeared to him in person. Balaram saw Baba and asked Baba why he was sent there. Baba replied, "In Shirdi many thoughts and ideas began to rise in your mind. I sent you here to rest your unsteady mind. You thought that I was only in Shirdi with a body composed of the five elements and three and a half cubits in length. Now you see and can conclude for yourself if the person you see here now is the same you saw at Shirdi. It is for this reason that I sent you here."

Then after the period was over, Balaram left the gad and proceeded to his native place, Bandra. He wanted to travel by rail to Dadar but when he went to the booking office to get a ticket, he found it to be very crowded. He could not get his ticket. Soon a villager with a *langoti* (piece of cloth) on his waist and kambali on his shoulder turned up and said, "Where are you going?"

"To Dadar," replied Balaram.

The villager said, "Please take this ticket of mine. As I have some urgent business here, I have cancelled my Dadar trip."

Balaram was very glad to receive the ticket and was just taking money out from his pocket when the rustic disappeared in the crowd. Balaram tried to find him in the crowd but in vain. He waited for him until the train left the station but found no trace. This was the second revelation Balaram had in a strange form. Then after visiting his home, Balaram returned to Shirdi and remained there at Baba's feet, always following his commands and advice. In the end, he was very fortunate to leave this world in Baba's presence and with his blessings.

A RELUCTANT MAN REALIZES BABA IS GOD INCARNATE

Hemadpant gives no particulars regarding Tatyasaheb Noolkar except mentioning the fact that he died in Shirdi. A brief summary of his account is given here. Tatyasaheb was a Sub-Judge in Pandharpur in 1909, while Nanasaheb Chandorkar was the Revenue Collector there. They met often and exchanged conversation. Tatyasaheb did not believe in saints, while Nanasaheb loved them. Nanasaheb often told him about the leelas of Sai Baba and pressed him to go to Shirdi and see Baba. He finally agreed to go to Shirdi on two conditions, that he must have a Brahmin cook and must get good Nagpur oranges to present to Baba.

Both these conditions were providentially fulfilled. A Brahmin came to Nanasaheb for work, and was then sent to Tatyasaheb to cook. Then Tatyasaheb received a parcel of fruit from an unknown sender containing 100 beautiful Nagpur oranges. As his conditions were fulfilled, Tatyasaheb had to go to Shirdi.

At first, Baba was much enraged with him, but in time through his experiences, Tatyasaheb was convinced that Baba was God incarnate. He became so enamored with Baba that he stayed there until his death. As his end was approaching, sacred literature was read to him and at the last hour Baba's *pada tirth* (holy water from washing Baba's feet) was given to him for drinking. On hearing of his death, Baba said, "Oh, Tatyasaheb went ahead of us. He won't be reborn."

Baba Grieves Over the Death of a Devotee

The story of Megha was described in Chapter 28. When Megha died, all the villagers followed the funeral procession. Baba accompanied them and showered flowers on Megha's body. After the rituals were performed, tears flowed from Baba's eyes and he was overcome with grief and sorrow, like an ordinary mortal. After covering the body with flowers and crying like a close relative, Baba returned to the Dwarkamai.

Tiger Passes at Baba's Feet

Many saints have given liberation to men, but Baba's greatness is unique. Even a cruel animal like a tiger came to Baba's feet to be saved. This story will be narrated now.

Seven days before Baba passed away, a wonderful incident occurred. A country cart came and stopped in front of the masjid. A tiger was on the cart, fastened with iron chains, with its fierce face turned to the rear. It was suffering from some disease and in pain and agony. Its keepers, three dervishes, were taking it from place to place making money by exhibiting it. It was the means of their subsistence. They tried all sorts of remedies to cure the tiger from the malady it was suffering, but all was in vain. They heard of Baba's fame and came to him with the animal. With the chains in their hands, they got the tiger down from the cart and made it stand at the door.

Besides being disease-ridden, it was naturally fierce, so it was restless. The people began to look at it with fear and amazement. The dervishes went in and told Baba everything about the animal, and with his consent, brought it before him. As the tiger approached the steps, it was taken aback on seeing Baba's radiance and hung its head down. When both finally saw each other, the tiger got up on the step and looked at Baba with affection. Immediately it moved the tuft of its tail and dashed it three times against the ground, then fell down senseless.

On seeing it dead, the dervishes were at first very dejected and full of sorrow, but on further reflection they came to terms with it. They understood the tiger was diseased and nearing its end, and it was very meritorious for it to meet its death at the feet and in the presence of Baba. It had been in their debt and when the debt was paid off, it was free and met its end at Sai's feet.

When any creatures bow their heads down at a saint's feet and meet death, they are saved. Unless they have a good store of merit in their account, how else would it be possible to attain such a happy end?

Pranams to Sri Sai

Peace Be to All

CHAPTER THIRTY-TWO

BANYAN TREE ALLEGORY

In the beginning, Hemadpant describes *samsara* (worldly bondage) through an allegory of a banyan tree. In the words of the *Gita*, the banyan tree has roots above and branches below. Its branches are spread downwards and upwards and are nourished by the *gunas* (qualities). Its sprouts are the objects of the senses. Its roots, leading to actions, are extended downwards to this world of men. Its form cannot be known in this world, nor its end, nor its beginning, nor its support. Cutting the banyan tree of its strong roots with the sharp weapon of non-attachment, one should seek the path beyond, treading where there is no return.

For traversing this path, the help of a good guide is absolutely necessary. However learned a man may be, or however deep his study of sacred literature, he cannot go to his destination safely. If the guide is there to help him and show him the right way, he will avoid the pitfalls and the wild beasts on the journey and everything will go smoothly.

❦

THE QUEST FOR GOD

The following is a story that Baba gave of his own experience in this matter, which is really wonderful. It gives the reader faith, devotion and liberation.

Once four of us were studying religious scriptures and books, and being informed by doing this, began to discuss the nature of *Brahman* (Ultimate Reality). One of us said that we should raise the self by the Self and not depend on others. To this, the second replied that he who controls his mind is blessed. We should be free from thoughts and ideas as the world doesn't exist without these. The third said that the world is always changing and only the formless is eternal, so we should discriminate between the unreal and the real. And the fourth person (Baba) said bookish knowledge is worthless and added, "Let us do our prescribed duty and surrender our body, mind and life to the guru's feet. The guru is God and all pervading. To have this conviction, never-ending faith is necessary.

Discussing in this way, we four learned men began to ramble through the woods in search of God. Three of them wanted to make the search through their intellectual efforts alone.

On the way, a *vanjari* (merchant), one who trades grain on a bullock cart, met us and asked, "It is hot. Where and how far are you going?"

"To search the woods," we replied.

He inquired, "On what quest are you bound?"

We gave him an ambiguous and evasive reply. Seeing us rambling aimlessly, he was moved and said, "Without knowing the woods fully, you should not wander at random. If you want to walk through forests and jungles you should take a guide with you. Why do you exert yourselves unnecessarily in the noontime heat? You may not tell me your secret quest, but still you can sit down, eat bread, drink water, take rest and then go. Be always patient at heart."

Though he spoke so tenderly, we discarded his request and marched on. We thought we were self-contained men and needed no one's help. The woods were vast and without any trails, the trees grew so close and tall that the sun's rays could not penetrate them. So we lost our way and wandered here and there for a long time. Ultimately, through sheer good luck, we came back to the place where we started.

The merchant met us again and said, "Relying on your own cleverness, you missed your way. A guide is always necessary to show us the right way in small or great matters. And no quest can be successfully carried out on an empty stomach. Unless God wills it, no one meets us on the way. Do not discard offers of food; this food should not be pushed away. Offers of bread and food should be regarded as auspicious signs of success." After saying this, he again offered us food and asked us to be calm and patient.

Again my companions did not like this unsolicited hospitality and discarded his offer and left again. Without taking any food, the three of them continued on our journey—so obstinate were they. I was hungry and thirsty and I was moved by the merchant's extraordinary love. We thought ourselves very learned but were strangers to compassion and kindness. The merchant was an illiterate and unqualified fellow and belonged to a low caste. Still he had love in his heart and asked us to eat bread. He who loves others without ulterior motives is truly enlightened, so I realized that accepting his hospitality was the best beginning of knowledge. So very respectfully, I accepted the loaf of bread offered, ate it and drank water.

Then lo! At once, the guru stood before us. "What was the dispute about?" he asked and I told him everything that had happened.

Then he said, "Would you like to come with me? I will show you what you want. But only he who believes in what I say will be successful." The others did not agree to what he said and left him. But I bowed to him reverently and accepted his command.

Then he took me to a well, tied my feet with a rope and hung me from a nearby tree upside down by my feet! I was suspended three feet above the water, which I could not reach with my hands, nor could I drink with my mouth. After suspending me like this, he went away, and no one knew where. After four or five hours he returned, quickly removed me and asked how I fared. "In bliss supreme. How can a fool like me describe the joy I experienced?" I replied.

On hearing my answer, the guru was much pleased with me, drew me near him and stroking my head with his hand, kept me with him. He took care of me as tenderly as a mother bird cares for her young ones. He put me into his school. How beautiful it was! There I forgot my parents, all my attachment was snapped and I was liberated easily. I thought that I should embrace his neck and remain staring at him always. If his image were not fixed in my pupils, I would prefer to be blind. Such was the school! No one who entered it once could leave empty-handed. My guru became my all-in-all, my home and property, mother and father, everything. All my senses left their places and concentrated themselves in my eyes, and my gaze was centered on him. My guru was the sole object of my meditation and I was conscious of nothing else. While meditating on him, my mind and intellect were stunned and I had to keep quiet and bow to him in silence.

There are other schools where you see an altogether different scene. The disciples go there to seek knowledge and spend their money, time and labor, but ultimately they regret their time there. The guru boasts of his secret knowledge and straightforwardness. He makes a show of his sacredness and holiness, but he is not tender at heart. He speaks a lot and sings of his own glory. But his words do not touch the disciples' hearts and they are not convinced. So far as self-realization is concerned, he has none. How can such schools be of any use to the disciples and how can they benefit? The guru mentioned above was of a different type. By his grace, realization flashed upon me on its own, without effort or study. I did not have to seek anything. Everything became clear to me as broad daylight. Only the guru knows how topsy-turvy suspension, upside down by the feet, can give happiness!

Among the four, one was a ritualist who only knew how to observe or abstain from religious rites. The second was a *jnani* (person of knowledge) who was puffed up with pride of knowledge and the third was a *bhakti* (devotee) who surrendered himself completely to God, believing that God was the sole doer. When they were discussing and arguing, the question of God turned up and they, depending on their knowledge alone, went in search of Him. (Sai, who was discrimination and dispassion incarnate, was one of the four.)

Being himself *Brahman* (Ultimate Reality) incarnate, some may ask, "Why did he mix with the others and act foolishly?" He did this for attaining the good of the people, to set an example for them to follow. Though an incarnation himself, he respected a lowly merchant by accepting his food with the firm belief that 'food is Brahman'. He showed how those who rejected the merchant's hospitable offer suffered and how it was impossible to get *jnana* (knowledge) without a guru.

The *Shruti Taittiriya Upanishad* encourages us to honor and worship mother, father and guru, and to study the sacred scriptures. These are the means of purifying our minds and unless this purification is done, self-realization is not possible. Neither the senses, nor the mind and intellect, reach the Self. Modes of proof, such as perception and deduction will not help us in the matter. It is the grace of the guru that counts. The aims of our life such as *dharma* (duty), *artha* (wealth) and *kama* (desires) are attainable with our effort, but the fourth aim, *moksha* (liberation) can only be had with the help of the guru.

In the masjid reception area of Sri Sai, many personalities appear and play their part. Astrologers come and give their predictions. Princes, noblemen, ordinary men, poor men, sannyasis, yogis, songsters and others come for darshan. Even an untouchable comes and, making his salutation, says this Sai is the true parents who will do away with our rounds of births and deaths. So many others such as jugglers, artisans, the blind, the lame, *nathpanthis* (Shiva renunciates), dancers and other performers come and are given suitable reception. Biding his own time, the vanjari also appeared, and played the part assigned to him. Let us now go to the following story.

FASTING IS NOT ALLOWED

Baba never fasted, nor did he allow others to do so. As the mind of the person fasting is never at ease, then how could he attain his *Paramatma* (Absolute)? God is not attained on an empty stomach. First the soul has to be appeased. If there is no food and nutrition in the stomach, with what eyes should we see God, with what tongue should we describe his greatness, and with what ears should we hear the same? In short, when all our organs get proper nutrition and are sound, we can practice devotion and other sadhanas to attain God. Therefore, neither fasting nor overeating is good. Moderation in diet is wholesome both to the body and the mind.

Mrs. Gokhale came to Shirdi with an introductory letter to Dada Kelkar. She came to Baba with a determination to sit at Baba's feet observing a three-day fast. The previous day, Baba said to Dada that he would not allow his children to starve during the holy holidays and that if they starved, why was he there? Next day, when the woman sat at Baba's feet, Baba at once said to her, "Where is the necessity of fasting? Go to Dadabhat's house, prepare a dish of *puran polis* (sweets) and feed his children and yourself too."

The holy holidays were on. Mrs. Kelkar was on her menses and there was no one to cook in Dadabhat's house, so Baba's advice was very timely. Mrs. Gokhale went to Dadabhat's house and prepared the dish as directed and fed the others and herself. What a good story and how beautiful its import!

⚜

BABA'S MASTER

"My Master's treasury (spiritual wealth) is full; it is overflowing. I say, 'Dig out and take away this wealth in cartloads, the blessed son of a true mother should fill himself with this wealth."

Baba gave a story of his boyhood as follows:

When I was a youngster, I was in search of bread and went to Beedgaum where I got embroidery work. I worked hard, sparing no pains. The employer was very much pleased with me. Three other boys worked before me. The first got Rs.50, the second Rs.100, and the third Rs.150. I was given double the total of all these—Rs. 600.

After seeing my cleverness, the employer loved me, praised me and honored me with a full dress, a turban for the head and a robe for the body. I kept this dress intact without using it. I thought that what a man might give does not last long and is always imperfect. But what God gives, lasts to the end of time. No other gift from any man can be compared to his.

My master says, "Take, take," but everyone comes to me and says, "Give, give." Nobody listens carefully to the meaning of what I am saying. My Master's treasury (spiritual wealth) is full; it is overflowing. I say, "Dig out and take away this wealth in cartloads, the blessed son of a true mother should fill himself with this wealth." The skill of my fakir, the leela of my *Bhagawan* (Lord), the aptitude of my master is quite unique. What about me? The body will mix with earth, breath with air. This time won't come again. No matter where I go or where I sit, the hard Maya troubles me much; I always feel anxiety for my men. He who does any spiritual endeavor will reap its fruit and he who remembers my words will get inestimable happiness.

Pranams to Sri Sai

Peace Be to All

CHAPTER THIRTY-THREE

PRANAM TO THE SAINTS

L et us bow now before the great saints. Their merciful glances will destroy mountains of *karmas* (sins) and and do away with all the negative defects of our character. Even their casual talk is a teaching and confers imperishable happiness on us. Their minds do not know differences such as, "This is ours and that is yours." Such differentiation never arises in their minds. We can never repay our debt to them in this life or in many future lives.

THE SPIRITUAL IMPLICATIONS OF UDI – SACRED ASH

Dakshina taught us non-attachment from the unreal and udi taught us discrimination between the unreal and real.

It is well known that Baba took dakshina from all. Out of the amount collected, he spent a lot on charity and purchased wood with the balance. He used the wood for his dhuni, the sacred fire, which he kept ever burning. The ash from this fire was called udi and it was freely distributed to the devotees upon leaving Shirdi.

What was Baba teaching with this udi? Baba taught by his udi that all the visible phenomena in the universe are as transient as ash. Our bodies, composed of matter made of the five elements, will fall down after all their enjoyments are over and be reduced to ash. To remind the devotees that their bodies will be reduced to ash, Baba distributed udi. He also taught by the udi that Brahman was the only reality, the universe was ephemeral and that no one in this world, not son, father or wife, is really ours. We come in this world alone and we leave alone.

Although it has been found that udi cured many physical and mental maladies, Baba wanted to repeat into the devotee's ears the principle of discrimination between the real and unreal. Dakshina taught us non-attachment from the unreal and udi taught us discrimination between the unreal and real. Unless we have these two principles, it is not possible for us to cross over the sea of mundane existence. So Baba asked for and took dakshina, and as devotees left he gave udi as prasad, spreading some on their foreheads and placing his boon–conferring hand on their heads. When Baba was in a cheerful mood, he used to sing merrily. One such song was about udi. The message of this song was, "Oh, playful Rama, come, come, and bring with you sacks of udi." Baba used to sing in very clear and sweet tones.

So much for the spiritual effect of udi. It also has its material significance. It bestows health, prosperity, freedom from anxiety, and many other worldly gains. So the udi helps us to gain both goals, material and spiritual. We shall now begin with stories about the udi.

HEALING A SCORPION STING

Narayan Jani served under another devotee of Baba. Once he went to see Baba with his mother. Baba told the mother that her son should no longer serve under another but start an independent business. Some days after, the prophecy turned true. Narayan Jani left service and started a boarding house, 'Ananda Ashram,' that thrived well.

One time, Narayan Jani's friend was stung by a scorpion. The pain was severe and unbearable. In such cases, udi is most effective when applied at the point of the pain. Narayan searched for udi but found none. So he stood before Baba's picture and invoked Baba's aid. He chanted Baba's name and took out a pinch of ash from the incense stick burning in front of Baba's picture. Thinking of it as Baba's udi, he applied it to the sting. As soon as he moved his fingers away, his friend's pain vanished and both were moved and delighted.

CURING BUBONIC PLAGUE

Once a devotee learned that his daughter was down with bubonic plague. He had no udi with him, so he sent word to Nanasaheb Chandorkar to send some. Nanasaheb received the message while travelling with his wife. He had no udi with him either, so he picked up some dust from the road, meditated on Baba and imploring his help, then applied the dust to his wife's forehead.

When the devotee went to his daughter's house he was very happy to learn that after having suffered for three days, she had begun to improve the very moment Nanasaheb prayed for Baba's help.

THE JAMNER MIRACLE

Around 1904, Nanasaheb was Revenue Collector at Jamner, which was more than 100 miles away from Shirdi. His daughter Mainatai was pregnant and about to deliver. Her case was very serious and she had suffered labor pains for a few days. Nanasaheb tried all remedies but they proved in vain. Then he remembered Baba and invoked his aid.

At the same time in Shirdi, Bapugirbuva wanted to travel to his native home. Baba called him and told him to stop at Jamner on his way, take rest and give udi and the Aarati to Nanasaheb. He told Baba he only had two rupees, which was barely enough for the railway fare to Jalgaon. He didn't have enough to go the 30 miles farther to Jamner. Baba assured him that he need not worry, everything would be provided for. Baba asked Shama to write down the Aarati and gave the copy of it with udi to Bapugirbuva to deliver to Nanasaheb.

Relying on Baba's words, Bapugirbuva left Shirdi and reached Jalgaon at about 2:45 a.m. He had only two *annas* (coins) left and was in a difficult position. To his great relief he heard someone calling out, "Who is Bapugirbuva of Shirdi?" He went and told him he was Bapugirbuva. The attendant, professing to be sent by Nanasaheb, led him to an excellent tanga with two good horses. They both rode in the fast tanga and early in the morning came to a small brook. The horses drank from the brook and the attendant asked Bapugirbuva to partake of some food. On seeing the beard, moustache and the attire of the attendant, Bapugirbuva suspected he was Muslim and so was unwilling to partake in the refreshments. But the attendant made him feel at ease by saying he was Hindu, and that, in fact, Nanasaheb had sent the refreshments, so there should be no doubt about accepting them. Then both of them ate and started again.

They reached Jamner at dawn. Bapugirbuva descended the tanga to attend the call of nature. He returned within a few minutes but found there was no tanga, and no attendant. He was dumbfounded. So he went to the neighboring village and made inquiries and learned that Nanasaheb was at home. He went to Nanasaheb's house, announced himself, and gave him Baba's udi and Aarati.

At this time, Mainatai's delivery was most serious and all were in deep anxiety about her. Nanasaheb called out to his wife and asked her to give their daughter the udi mixed with water to drink, and to sing Baba's Aarati. He thought that Baba's help was most timely. Then in a few minutes, she delivered safely and the crisis passed. When Bapugirbuva thanked Nanasaheb for the attendant, the tanga and the refreshments, Nanasaheb was very surprised as he had not sent anything to the station and was not aware of any person coming from Shirdi!

The following are Bapugirbuva's own words on this story:

One day, Baba called me to him and gave me a packet of udi and a copy of his Aarati. At the time, I had to go to Khandesh but Baba directed me to go to Jamner and deliver the Aarati and udi to Nanasaheb. I told Baba that all I had was Rs.2, and asked him how that could take me by train from Kopergaon to Jalgaon and then by tanga to Jamner. Baba said, "God will give." That was Friday and I started at once. I reached Jalgaon at 2:45 a.m. At that time, plague regulations were enforced and I had much trouble about getting to Jamner. But then, the way to get to Jamner was revealed. At about 3 a.m, an attendant in boots, turban and well equipped with other details of good dress, came and took me to a tanga and drove me on. On the way, I took refreshments. We reached Jamner early in the morning and after I attended the call of nature, the tanga and its driver had disappeared.

VISION OF BABA

The bhakta Narayana Rao had the good fortune to see Baba twice while Baba was alive. Three years after Baba passed away, he wanted to go to Shirdi but was unable to. Within a year of Baba's mahasamadhi, he had fallen sick and continued to suffer much. All ordinary remedies gave him no relief. So he meditated on Baba day and night. One night he had a vision of Baba in his dream. Baba came to him through a cellar and comforted him saying, "Don't be anxious, you will be improving starting from tomorrow, and within a week you will be on your legs." Narayana Rao became perfectly well within the time Baba mentioned.

Now the point for consideration is this: Was Baba living because he had a body, and was he dead because he left it? No, Baba is ever alive, for he transcends both life and death. He who loves Baba wholeheartedly gets response from him at any time and at any place. He is always by our side, and will take any form and appear before the devoted bhakta and satisfy him.

LOOKING AT BABA'S PICTURE IS THE SAME AS SEEING HIM

In 1917, Appasaheb Kulkarni's chance came. He was transferred to Thana and began to worship Baba's picture. In real earnest he did the worship. He offered flowers, sandalpaste, and naivedya to Baba's picture daily, longing intently to see him. In this connection, it can be said that looking at Baba's picture is truly equivalent to seeing him in person. The following story illustrates this statement.

A saint from Bombay named Balabuva Sutar, who was called the modern Tukaram on account of his piety, devotion and bhajans, came to Shirdi for the first time in 1917. When he bowed before Baba, Baba said, "I have known this man for four years." Balabuva wondered how that could be, as it was his first trip to Shirdi. But thinking about it intently, he recalled that he had prostrated before Baba's portrait in Mumbai four years earlier. He was convinced about the significance of Baba's words and said to himself, 'How omniscient and all pervading are the saints and how kind they are to their devotees! I merely bowed to his photo, which was noticed by Baba, and in due time he made me realize that seeing his photo is equivalent to seeing him in person!'

To return to Appasaheb's story, while he was in Thana, Appasaheb had to go on tour to Bhivandi and was not expected to return for a week. On the third day of his absence, a fakir turned up to his house at noon. His features exactly resembled those of Baba's photo. Mrs. Kulkarni and the children all asked him whether he was Sai Baba of Shirdi. He said, no, that he was an obedient servant of Baba and came there at his order to inquire after the health of the family. Then he asked for dakshina. The lady gave him one rupee. He gave her a small packet of udi and asked her to keep this in the shrine along with the photo for worship. Then he left the house and went away. Now hear the wonderful leela of Sai.

Appasaheb could not proceed with his tour as his horse fell sick. He returned home that afternoon and learned from his wife about the fakir's visit. His mind was disturbed that he didn't receive darshan of the fakir and he didn't like that only one rupee was paid as dakshina. He said that had he been present, he would have offered not less than ten rupees. He immediately started in search of the fakir in the masjid and other places, and did not take any food. His search was in vain, so he returned home and ate. The reader may remember here Baba's statement in Chapter 32 that a search for God should not be made on empty stomach. Appasaheb got a lesson about this here.

After eating, he went out for a walk with a friend, Mr. Chitre. After going some distance, they saw a man approaching them rapidly. Appasaheb thought he must be the fakir that had come to his house at noon, as his features were the same as those of Baba in the photo. The fakir immediately put out his hand and asked for dakshina. Appasaheb gave him a rupee. The fakir demanded again, then again, and so Appasaheb gave him two more. Still he was not satisfied. Then he borrowed Rs.3 from Mr. Chitre and gave them to the fakir. He still wanted more. Then Appasaheb asked him to accompany him to his home.

When they all returned to his home, Appasaheb gave the fakir three rupees, in all he had given nine. The fakir still looked unsatisfied and demanded more. Appasaheb told him that he had ten rupees to give. The fakir asked for these ten rupees, and then returned the nine rupees and went away. These nine had been blessed by Baba's touch. The figure nine is significant. It may also be noted here that Baba gave nine rupees to Laxmibai at his last moment. They represent the nine types of devotion (Chapter 21).

Appasaheb examined the udi packet and found it also contained some flower petals and rice. Some time afterward, he received a strand of Baba's hair when he saw him in Shirdi. He put it in a talisman along with the udi packet, which he then always wore on his arm.

Appasaheb later realized the power of the udi. Though he was very clever he was only paid forty rupees as salary. After he secured Baba's photo and udi, he received many times more than that per month and also acquired much power and influence. Along with these worldly benefits, his spiritual progress was also rapid. So those who are fortunate enough to get Baba's udi should, after a bath, apply it on the forehead and drink a little of it mixed with water as holy *tirth* (water).

ONE MORE RUPEE—SAINTS WORK IN UNISON

In 1917, Haribhau Karnik came to Shirdi on Guru Purnima day and worshipped Baba with every formality. He offered clothes and dakshina and after taking Baba's leave, descended the steps of the masjid. As he was leaving, he had a thought that he should offer one more rupee to Baba. Just as he was turning to go back up the stairs, Shama informed him that as he had already received Baba's leave, he should go and not return. So he started home.

On his way, he entered the Kalarama temple for darshan. The saint, Narsing Maharaj, was in the temple with his bhaktas. The saint walked over to Haribhau, caught his wrist, and said, "Give me my one rupee." Karnik was surprised. He paid the rupee most willingly and thought that through this saint, Baba received the rupee that he had intended to give. This story illustrates the fact that all saints are one and shows how they work in unison.

Pranams to Sri Sai

Peace Be to All

CHAPTER THIRTY-FOUR

T his chapter continues the subject of the 'Greatness of Udi' and describes cases in which the application of udi was most efficacious.

A DOCTOR'S NEPHEW CURED WITH UDI

"Those who take refuge in this masjid shall never suffer anything in this life until the end of time."

There lived a qualified and degree-holding doctor, whose young nephew suffered from an incurable tubercular bone abscess. The doctor and his brothers, along with other medical practitioners, tried all sorts of remedies including an operation. There was no relief and no end to the little boy's suffering. Friends and relations advised the boy's parents to seek divine aid and recommended they try Baba, who was known to cure such incurable cases by his mere glance.

So the parents went to Shirdi. They prostrated to Baba, placed the boy before him and pleaded humbly and respectfully, imploring him to save their son. The merciful Baba comforted them, saying:

Those who take refuge in this masjid shall never suffer anything in this life until the end of time. Be carefree now. Apply udi on the abscess and within one week he will recover. Believe in God. This is no masjid, but Dwarkamai. He who steps here will soon get health and happiness and his sufferings will come to an end.

The boy was made to sit before Baba, who moved his hands on the affected part and cast his loving glances on him. The patient was pleased, and with the application of udi he began to recover. Then after some days, he fully recovered. The parents left Shirdi with their son, thanking Baba for the cure, which resulted from the udi and Baba's gracious looks.

After hearing this, the doctor, the uncle of the boy, became wonderstruck and desired to see Baba while he was on his way to Mumbai for some business. But on his journey somebody spoke against Baba and poisoned his ears. He dropped the idea of visiting Shirdi and went directly to his destination. He wanted to spend the rest of his leave in Alibag, but for three successive nights while in Mumbai he heard a voice crying out, "Still you disbelieve me?" The doctor changed his mind and resolved to go to Shirdi.

The doctor had to attend to a case of infectious fever, which showed no signs of abatement. So he thought his Shirdi trip would be postponed. However, he proposed a test in his mind and said, 'If the patient gets well today, I start for Shirdi tomorrow.' The wonder is that exactly at the time he made his proposal, the fever began to abate and the temperature became normal. Then he went to Shirdi, took Baba's darshan and prostrated himself before him. Baba gave him such experiences that he became his devotee. He stayed there for four days and returned home with Baba's udi and blessings. Within two weeks he was promoted and transferred to Bijapur. His nephew's case gave him opportunity to see Baba, and his visit engendered in him a never-failing love for the saint's feet.

A PLEA FOR KARMIC DEFERMENT

Dr. Pillay was an intimate bhakta of Baba. He was much liked by Baba, who always called him *Bhau* (brother). Baba talked with him off and on and consulted him in all matters, and always wanted him at his side. Once Pillay suffered very badly from guinea worms. He said to Kakasaheb Dixit, "The pain is most excruciating and unbearable. I prefer death to it. I know this pain is for repaying past karma, but go to Baba and tell him to stop the pain and transfer the working of my past karma to ten of my future births."

Kakasaheb went and told Baba his request. Baba was moved by his request and said to Kakasaheb, "Tell him to be fearless. Why should he suffer for ten births? In ten days he can work out the sufferings and consequences of his past karma. While I am here to give him temporal and spiritual welfare, why should he pray for death? Bring him here on somebody's back and let us work and finish his sufferings once and for all."

The doctor was brought and seated on Baba's right side, where he always sat. Baba gave him his bolster and said:

Lie calmly here and be at ease. The true remedy is that the result of past actions has to be suffered and overcome. Our karma is the cause of our happiness and sorrow, therefore, put up with whatever comes to you. God is the sole dispenser and protector; always think of Him. He will take care of you. Surrender completely to his feet with body, mind, wealth and speech, and then see what he does.

Dr. Pillay replied that Nanasaheb had put a bandage over the leg, but still he found no relief. "Nana is a fool," replied Baba. "Take off that bandage or else you will die. Now a crow will come and peck you, and then you will recover."

While this conversation was going on Abdul, who always cleaned the masjid and trimmed the lamps, turned up. While he was attending to his work, his foot accidentally stepped upon the stretched leg of Dr. Pillay. The leg was already swollen and when Abdul's foot stepped and pressed against it, all seven guinea worms were squeezed out at once!

The pain was unbearable and Dr. Pillay cried out loudly. After some time, he calmed down and began to sing and cry alternately. Then Pillay asked when the crow was coming to peck. Baba said, "Did you not see the crow? He won't come again. Abdul was the crow. Now go and rest yourself in the wada and soon you will recover."

By application of udi and drinking it with water, and without taking any other treatment or medicine, the disease was completely cured in ten days as assured by Baba.

ANOTHER UDI MIRACLE CURES BUBONIC PLAGUE

Shama's younger brother Bapaji was staying near Sawool well. Once his wife was attacked with bubonic plague. She had high fever and two buboes in her groin. Bapaji rushed to Shama at Shirdi and asked him to come and help. Shama was frightened, but according to his custom, he went to Baba, prostrated before him, invoked his aid, and requested him to cure the case. He also asked his permission to go to his brother's house. Then Baba said, "Don't go there at this late hour. Send her udi. Why care for the fever and buboes? God is our father and master. She will be all right easily. Do not go now, but go there in the morning and return immediately."

Shama had full faith in Baba's udi. It was sent with Bapaji and applied to the buboes and some was mixed with water and given to the patient to drink. No sooner was it taken, than perspiration set in profusely, the fever abated and the patient had a good sleep.

Next morning, Bapaji was surprised to see his wife was fine and refreshed and had no fever and no buboes. When Shama went he was surprised to see her at the hearth preparing tea.

On questioning his brother, he learned that Baba's udi cured her completely in one night. Then Shama realized the significance of Baba's words. "Go there in the morning and return immediately." After taking tea, Shama returned. After paying respects to Baba, he said, "Deva, what is this play of yours? You first raise a storm and make us restless and then calm it down and ease us."

Baba replied:

Mysterious is the path of action. Though I do nothing, they hold me responsible for the actions that take place on account of destiny. I am only their witness. The Lord is the sole doer and inspirer. He is also most merciful. Neither am I God, nor Lord. I am His obedient servant and remember Him often. He who casts aside his egoism, thanks Him and who trusts Him entirely, will have his shackles removed and will obtain liberation.

UDI CURES CONVULSIONS

Now read the experience of an Iranian gentleman. His young daughter had fits every hour. When the convulsions came she lost her power of speech, her limbs contracted and she fell down senseless. No remedy gave her any relief. A friend recommended Baba's udi to her father and asked him to get it from Kakasaheb. The Iranian gentleman got the udi, mixed it with water, and gave it to his daughter daily for drinking. In the beginning, the convulsions came every seven hours and after a few days the daughter recovered completely.

UDI CURES BLADDER STONES

An old gentleman was suffering from a stone in his bladder. Such stones are generally removed by surgical operations, which people recommended him to undergo. He was old and weak, lacked strength of mind and could not think of submitting himself to surgical treatment. His suffering soon ended in another way.

The City Officer of his town happened to go there at that time. He was a devotee of Baba and always had a stock of udi with him. On the recommendation of friends, the ill gentleman's son got some udi and gave it to his old father to drink. Within five minutes the udi was assimilated, the stone dissolved and passed through his urine, and the old man was soon relieved.

UDI HELPS A WOMAN DELIVER SAFELY

A woman in Mumbai always suffered terrible pain during her deliveries. She was very much frightened each time she became pregnant and did not know what to do. Sri Rama Maruti, who was a devotee of Baba, advised her husband to take her to Shirdi for a painless delivery. When she became pregnant next, both husband and wife went to Shirdi and stayed there for some months, worshipping Baba and receiving all the benefits of his company.

After some time, the hour of delivery came and as usual there was an obstruction in the passage from the womb. She began to suffer labor pains, and not knowing what to do, she began to pray to Baba for relief. In the meantime, some neighboring women turned up and after invoking Baba's aid, gave her udi mixture to drink. In five minutes, the woman delivered safely and painlessly. The baby was stillborn according to its fate. But the mother, who was freed from anxiety and pain, thanked Baba for the safe delivery and remained ever grateful to him.

Pranams to Sri Sai

Peace Be to All

CHAPTER THIRTY-FIVE

TESTED AND NOT FOUND WANTING

This chapter also continues the subject of the importance of udi and gives two cases in which Baba was tested and not found wanting.

❧

A MATTER OF FORM

In spiritual matters or endeavors, sectarianism is the greatest obstacle to our progress. Those who believe God is without form say that to believe God is with form is an illusion and saints are only human beings. Then why should they bend their heads before them and offer dakshina? People belonging to other sects will also raise objections and say, "Why should I bow and offer allegiance to other saints, leaving my own sadguru?"

Similar objections regarding Sai Baba were heard before and are heard even now. Some said that when they went to Shirdi, Baba asked for dakshina from them; is it good that saints should collect money in this fashion? If they do so, where is their sainthood? But there are many instances where men went to Shirdi to ridicule, but instead remained there and prayed. Two such instances are given below.

❧

FORGETTING RESOLUTIONS

A friend of Kaka Mahajani was a worshipper of God without form and was averse to idolatry. Out of curiosity, he agreed to go to Shirdi with Mahajani on two conditions: that he would neither bow to Baba nor pay him any dakshina. Mahajani agreed to these conditions and they both went to Shirdi.

As soon as they put their feet on the steps of the masjid, Baba, looking at the friend from a little distance, addressed him with sweet words, "Oh, welcome, Sir." The tone that uttered these words was very peculiar. It exactly resembled the tone of the friend's father. It reminded him of his departed father and sent a thrill of joy through his body. What an enchanting power the tone had! Being surprised, the friend said, "This is no doubt the voice of my father." Then at once he went up and placed his head on Baba's feet, forgetting his resolution.

Baba asked for dakshina twice, once in the morning and again at noon as they took leave, but he asked it from Mahajani only and not from the friend. The friend whispered to Mahajani, "Baba asked for dakshina from you twice. I am with you, why does he omit me?"

"You ask Baba himself," was Mahajani's reply. Baba then asked Mahajani what his friend was whispering.

The friend asked Baba whether he should pay any dakshina. Baba replied, "You had no mind to pay, so you were not asked. But if you want to pay now you may." Then the friend paid Rs.17, the same amount that Mahajani paid. Baba addressed him with a few words of advice, "Do away with and destroy the sense of difference between us so that we can see and meet each other face to face."

Then Baba allowed them to depart even though the weather was cloudy and threatening. Baba assured them a safe journey and they both reached Mumbai safely. When the friend reached his home and opened the door and windows of his house, he found two sparrows fallen dead on the ground and one just flying out through a window. He thought that if he had left the windows open, two sparrows would have been saved. On rethinking this, he realized they had met their lot and that Baba had sent him back early to save the third sparrow.

⚜

SEEDLESS GRAPES

"Wealth should be the means to work out dharma."

Mahajani was the manager in a firm of a solicitor in Mumbai. Both the master (boss) and the manager were on intimate terms. Mr. Thakkar, the master, knew that Mahajani went to Shirdi often, staying there for some days and returning when Baba permitted him. Out of curiosity, and just to test Baba, Mr. Thakkar decided to go to Shirdi with Mahajani during the holidays. As Mahajani's return was uncertain, Mr. Thakkar took another man, an associate, with him. The three started together and Mahajani bought two bushels of grapes on the way to present to Baba.

They reached Shirdi in due time and went to the masjid for darshan. Babasaheb Tarkhad was there and Mr. Thakkar asked him why he came. "For darshan," Babasaheb replied. Mr. Thakkar asked if miracles took place there. Babasaheb said that to see miracles was not the objective, but the sincere intentions of devotees were satisfied here.

Mahajani prostrated himself before Baba and offered the grapes to him. Baba ordered them to be distributed and Mr. Thakkar received a few. He did not like grapes and was advised by his doctor not to eat them without washing and cleaning them. So he was in a fix. He did not like them, nor could he reject them. To keep up formalities, he put them into his mouth, but did not know what to do with the seeds. He could not spit them out on the floor of the masjid, so he pocketed them against his wish. In his mind, he questioned that if Baba was a saint, how could he be ignorant of his dislike for grapes and force them on him.

When this thought arose in his mind, Baba again gave him more grapes. He could not eat them, but held them in his hand. Then Baba asked him to eat them all. He obeyed Baba and found, to his surprise, that they were all seedless. He wanted to see miracles and here was one. He knew that Baba had read his thoughts, and according to his wish, converted grapes with seeds into seedless grapes. What a wonderful power!

Again to test Baba further he asked Babasaheb, "What kind of grapes did you get?" He replied, "The variety with seeds." Mr. Thakkar was even still more surprised to hear this. Then to confirm his growing faith, Mr. Thakkar thought that if Baba was a real saint, the grapes should be now given to Mahajani first. Reading this thought also, Baba ordered the distribution to be started with Mahajani. These proofs were sufficient for Mr. Thakkar.

Then Shama introduced Mr. Thakkar as Mahajani's master (boss), after which Baba said, "How could he be his master? He has a different kind of master altogether." Mahajani appreciated this reply. Forgetting his resolve, Mr. Thakkar pranammed to Baba and returned to the wada.

After the noon Aarati was over, they all went to the masjid to take Baba's leave. Shama spoke for them. Baba replied:

There was a fickle-minded gentleman. He had health and wealth and was free from both physical and mental afflictions, but he took on needless anxieties and burdens and wandered here and there losing his peace of mind. Sometimes he dropped his burdens and at other times carried them again. His mind knew no steadiness. Seeing his state, I took pity on him and said, now please keep your faith on any one point that you like. Why roam like this? Stick quietly to one place.

Mr. Thakkar knew at once that this was an exact description of him. He also wished that Mahajani should leave with him, but no one expected that Mahajani would be allowed to leave Shirdi so soon. Baba also read this thought in his mind, and permitted Mahajani to return with him. Mr. Thakkar had another proof of Baba's capacity to read another's mind. Baba asked Mahajani for Rs.15 as dakshina and received it. Then he said to Mahajani:

If I take one rupee as dakshina from anybody I have to return it to him. I never take anything free. I never ask any one indiscriminately. I only ask and take from him whom my guru points out. If anyone is formerly indebted to the fakir, money is received from him. The donor gives—sows his seeds—only to reap a rich harvest in the future. Wealth should be the means to work out dharma. If it is used for personal enjoyment, it is wasted. Unless you have given it before, you do not get it now. So the best way to receive is to give. Giving of dakshina develops *vairagya* (detachment) and so bhakti and jnana. Give one and receive tenfold.

On hearing these words, Mr. Thakkar gave Baba Rs.15, forgetting his resolve not to do so. He thought he did well in coming to Shirdi, as all his doubts were solved and he learned so much.

Baba's skill in handling such cases was unique. Though he did all those things, he was totally non-attached to them. Whether anybody saluted him or not, or whether anybody gave him dakshina or not, it was the same to him. He disrespected no one. He felt no pleasure because he was worshipped and no pain because he was disregarded. He transcended the pairs of opposites, pleasure and pain, etc.

UDI CURES INSOMNIA

A Kayastha Prabhu gentleman suffered from insomnia for a long time. As soon as he lay down to sleep, his departed father appeared to him in his dream and abused and scolded him severely. This broke his sleep and made him restless the whole night. Every night this went on and he did not know what to do. One day he consulted a devotee of Baba about this. He recommended udi as the only infallible remedy he knew. He gave him some udi and asked him to apply a little of it to his forehead before going to bed and keep the udi packet under the pillow. He tried this remedy and found to his great surprise and joy that he had a sound sleep, without disturbance of any kind. He continued the remedy and always remembered Baba. Then he got a picture of Baba, which he hung on the wall near his pillow, and started worshipping it daily, making offerings such as garlands and naivedya. In time, he got well and forgot his past trouble altogether.

EXCELLENT SERVICE

Balaji Newaskar was a great devotee of Baba. He rendered most excellent service without any desire for anything in return. Every day he swept and cleaned all the passages and streets in Shirdi that Baba walked during his daily routine. After him, this work was done equally well by Radhakrishna Mai, and after her by Abdula. When Balaji harvested his corn every year, he brought the whole yield of his crop and presented it to Baba. He left with whatever Baba gave him and maintained himself and his family with that. He followed this course for many years and after him, it was done by his son.

UDI AND THE MIRACLE OF PLENTY

After Balaji's death, his wife invited guests in honor of his death anniversary. But at dinnertime, it was found that three times the number of people invited had turned up. Mrs. Newaskar was in a fix. She thought that the food would not suffice for the people assembled and that if it fell short, the honor of the family would be at stake. Her mother-in-law comforted her by saying, "Don't be afraid, it is not our food but Baba's. Cover every vessel with cloth, put some udi in it, and serve without opening them. Baba will save us from disgrace." She did as she was advised and to their surprise and joy they found not only did the food suffice for all, but there was also plenty remaining after having served everyone. 'As one feels intently, so he realizes accordingly' was proven in this case.

BABA APPEARS AS A SERPENT

Once, Raghu Patil went to visit Balaji Patil. That evening he found a serpent had entered the cowshed and was hissing. All the cattle were afraid and began to move. The residents of the house were frightened but Balaji thought it was Baba who had appeared in his house as a serpent. Without being afraid in the least, he brought a cup of milk, placed it before the serpent and said, "Baba, why do you hiss and make noise? Do you want to frighten us? Take this cup of milk and drink it with a calm mind." Saying this, he sat close by unperturbed. The other members were frightened and did not know what to do. In a short time the serpent disappeared. Nobody knew where it went, and although a search was made it was not found in the cowshed.

Balaji had two wives and children, who sometimes went to Shirdi to take Baba's darshan. Baba gave them saris and clothes, which were given with his blessings.

Pranams to Sri Sai

Peace Be to All

CHAPTER THIRTY-SIX

Two Gentlemen from Goa

Once two gentlemen came from Goa to have Baba's darshan. They both prostrated before Baba, but Baba only asked one of them for Rs.15 dakshina, which was paid willingly. The other man voluntarily offered Rs. 35, but it was rejected by Baba to the astonishment of all.

Shama asked Baba, "What is this? Both came together, one's dakshina you accept, the other, though voluntarily offered, you refuse. Why this distinction?" Baba replied:

Shama, you know nothing. I take nothing from anybody. The *masjid mayi* (masjid Mother) calls for the debt, the donor pays it and becomes free. Have I any home, property or family to look after? I require nothing. I am ever free. Debt, enmity and murder have to be atoned for, there is no escape. Baba then continued the story in his characteristic way as follows:

The man was poor and made a vow to God that he would donate his first month's salary if he got a job. He got a job that paid Rs.15 per month. Then he steadily got promotions, from Rs.15 to 30, 60, 100, 200 and ultimately

Rs.700 per month. But in his prosperity, he forgot the vow he took. The force of his karma has driven him here and I asked that amount (Rs.15) from him as dakshina.

Baba then told another story: While wandering by the seaside I came to a huge mansion and sat on its verandah. The Brahmin owner gave me a good reception and fed me sumptuously. He showed me a neat and clean place near a cupboard for sleeping. While I was sound asleep, the man removed a slab to break the wall and entered. He scissored off my pocket and took all the money from it. When I woke up, I found that Rs. 30,000 was stolen. I was greatly distressed and sat weeping and moaning.

The money was in currency notes and I thought that the Brahmin had stolen it. I lost all interest in food and drink and sat on the verandah for two weeks bemoaning my loss. Then a passing fakir saw me crying, and made inquiries regarding the cause of my sorrow. I told him everything. He said, "If you act according to my instructions, you will recover your money. Go to a fakir—I shall give his whereabouts—and surrender yourself to him. He will get back your money. In the meanwhile, give up your favorite food until you recover your money." I followed the fakir's advice and got my money back.

I left the wada and went to the seashore to catch a steamer. I could not get into it, as it was crowded. But a good-natured attendant interceded for me and luckily I got in. The steamer brought me to another shore, where I caught a train and came to the Masjid mayi.

The story finished, Baba asked Shama to take the guests and arrange for their feeding. Shama took them home and fed them. During dinner, he mentioned to the guests that Baba's story was rather mysterious, as he had never gone to the seaside, never had any money, never traveled, never lost any money nor recovered it. He asked whether they understood its significance. The guests were deeply moved and shed tears. In choked voices, they said that Baba was omniscient, infinite, the One (Parabrahman), without a doubt. They said the story he gave was exactly their story and what he said had happened to them. How he knew this is a wonder of wonders! They said they would give all the details after the meal.

Then after they ate their meals, while chewing betel leaves, the guests began to tell their stories. The first one shared the following:

My native place is a hill station on the *ghats* (cremation grounds). I went from there to Goa to earn a living by securing a job. I took a vow to Lord

Datta that if I were hired for any service, I would offer him my first month's salary. By His grace I received an appointment that earned Rs.15 per month, and then I got promotions, as Baba described. I forgot all about my vow. Baba's story just reminded me of it and he recovered the Rs.15 from me. It is not dakshina as one may think, but payment of an old debt and fulfillment of a long-forgotten vow.

MONEY AND SPIRITUAL PROGRESS

Baba never, in fact, actually begged for any money, nor allowed his bhaktas to beg. He regarded money as a danger or bar to spiritual progress and did not allow his bhaktas to fall into its clutches. Mhalsapati is an instance on this point. He was very poor and could hardly make ends meet. Baba never allowed him to make any money, nor gave him anything from the dakshina amount. Once a kind and generous merchant named Hansaraj gave a large amount of money to Mhalsapati in Baba's presence, but Baba did not allow him to accept it.

PROOF OF BABA'S OMNISCIENCE

The second guest then began his tale:

My Brahmin cook served me faithfully for 35 years. Unfortunately, he fell into bad ways, his mind changed and he robbed me of my treasure. By removing a slab from the wall where my cupboard is fixed, he came in while we were asleep and carried away all of my accumulated wealth, Rs. 30,000 in currency notes. I don't know how Baba knew the exact amount. I sat crying day and night. My inquiries came to nothing. I spent two weeks in great anxiety.

One day as I sat on the verandah, sad and dejected, a passing fakir noted my condition and inquired of its cause. I told him all about it. He told me that a saint by the name 'Sai' lives in Shirdi. Make a vow to him and give up some food that you like best and say to him mentally, 'I have given up eating that food until I have your darshan.' Then I made the vow and gave up eating rice and thought, 'Baba, I will eat it after recovering my property and after having your darshan.'

Fifteen days passed. Of his own accord, the Brahmin came to me and returned my money and apologized saying, "I went mad and acted in this way. I now place my head on your feet, please forgive me." Thus everything ended well.

The fakir that helped me was never seen again. An intense desire to see Sai Baba, whom the fakir pointed out, arose in my mind. I thought that the fakir who had come all the way to my house was none other than Sai Baba. Would he, who helped me recover my lost money, ever covet Rs.35? On the contrary, without expecting anything from us, he always tries his best to lead us on the path of spiritual progress.

I was overjoyed when I recovered my stolen property and being ignorant, I forgot all about my vow. One night I saw Baba in my dream. This reminded me of my promised visit to Shirdi. I went to Goa and from there wanted to take a steamer to Mumbai. But when I came to the harbor, I found that the steamer was crowded and there was no space. The captain did not allow me on, but through the intervention of an attendant who was a stranger to me, I was allowed to get onto the steamer to Mumbai. From there, I caught the train and came here.

Surely I think that Baba is all pervading and all knowing. Who are we and where is our home? How fortunate are we that Baba got our money back and drew us here to him. Shirdi folks must be infinitely superior and more fortunate than us, for Baba has played, laughed, talked and lived with you for so many years. I think that your store of good merits must be infinite for it attracted Baba to Shirdi. Sai is our Datta. He ordered the vow. He gave me a seat on the steamer and brought me here, giving proof of his omniscience and omnipotence.

BABA GIVES THE BLESSING FOR A SON

The wife of Sakharam Aurangabadkar had no child for a long period of 27 years. She had made a number of vows to gods and goddesses but was not successful. She was almost hopeless. As a last attempt, she went to Shirdi with her stepson and stayed for two months serving Baba. Whenever she went to the masjid, she found it full and Baba surrounded by devotees. She wanted to see Baba alone, fall at his feet and open her heart and pray for a child, but didn't have any suitable opportunity

Finally, she requested Shama to intercede for her when Baba was alone. Shama said that Baba's reception was open. He would try on her behalf so the Lord might bless her. He asked her to sit ready with a coconut and incense sticks in the open courtyard at the time of Baba's meals. Then when he beckoned to her, she should come up.

One day after dinner, Shama was rubbing Baba's wet hands with a towel when he pinched Shama's cheek. Shama, feigning anger, said, "Deva, is it proper for you to pinch me like this? We don't want such a mischievous God who pinches us. We are your dependents, is this the fruit of our intimacy?"

Baba replied, "Oh Shama, during the 72 generations that you were with me, I never pinched you till now and now you resent my touching you."

Shama, "We want a God that will always love us and give us sweets to eat. We do not want any respect from you, or heaven, or anything else. Let our faith be on your feet and may we be ever wide awake."

Baba, "Yes, I have indeed come for that. I have been feeding and nursing you and have love and affection for you." Then Baba went up and took his seat.

Shama beckoned to Mrs. Aurangabadkar. She came up, bowed and presented the coconut and incense sticks. Baba shook the coconut, which was dry. The kernel within it rolled and made a noise. Baba said, "Shama, this is rolling, see what it says."

"The woman prays that a child might be similarly rolling and quickening in her womb. So give her the coconut with your blessings," Shama said.

"Will the coconut give her a child? How foolish people are to fancy such things!" Baba said.

Shama said, "I know the power of your word and blessing, your word will give her a string or series of children. You are wrangling and not giving real blessing."

Their parley went on for a while, Baba repeatedly ordering the breaking of the coconut, and Shama pleading for the gift of the unbroken fruit to the lady. Finally, Baba yielded and said, "She will have a child."

"When?" asked Shama.

"In 12 months," was Baba's reply. Then the coconut was broken into two parts. Baba and Shama ate one part and the other was given to Mrs. Aurangabadkar.

Then Shama turned to her and said, "Dear Madam, you are a witness to my words. If within 12 months you do not have any child, I will break a coconut against this Deva's head and drive him out of this masjid. If I fail in this, I will not call myself Madhava. You will soon realize what I say."

She delivered a son in one year's time and the son was brought to Baba in his fifth month. Both husband and wife prostrated themselves before Baba and the grateful father paid a sum of Rs.500, which was spent in constructing a shed for Baba's horse, Shyamakarna.

Pranams to Sri Sai

Peace Be to All

CHAPTER THIRTY-SEVEN

BLESSED BABA

B lessed is Sai's life and blessed is his daily routine. His ways and actions are indescribable. Sometimes he was intoxicated with *Brahmananda* (divine bliss), and at other times content with self-knowledge. At all times, even though doing many things, he remained unconcerned with them. At times he seemed quite actionless but he was not idle or dozing; he was always abiding in his own Self. Though he looked calm and still as a placid sea, he was deep and unfathomable. Who can describe his ineffable nature? He regarded men as brothers, and women as sisters and mothers. He was a perfect renunciate and had total self-control. May the knowledge we received in his company last long unto death. Let us ever serve him with wholehearted devotion. Let us see God in all beings and let us ever love his name.

CHAVADI PROCESSION

Men and women, rich and poor, all flocked together to witness this sight. Baba walked very slowly as bhaktas followed on both

*sides with love and devotion. With joy pervading the whole
atmosphere, the procession reached the Chavadi.*

Baba's dormitory already has been described. One day he would sleep in
the Dwarkamai and on the next in the Chavadi, a small building near the
Dwarkamai. This alternate sleeping between these buildings went on until
Baba's mahasamadhi. Starting December 10th, 1909, devotees began to offer
regular worship to Baba in the Chavadi. This we will now describe with his
grace.

On alternate evenings, when the time of retiring to the Chavadi came,
people flocked to the masjid and sang bhajans in the courtyard in front of
Baba for a few hours. Behind them was a beautiful small palanquin and to the
right a *tulsi vrindavan* (tulsi planter). Men and women sang bhajans and played
various musical instruments, the tal, chiplis, kartal, mridanga, khanjiri, vina and
ghol. Sai Baba was the magnet that drew all the devotees to him.

Outside in the open, some trimmed their torches, some decorated the
palanquin, and some stood with tall cane sticks in their hands and uttered cries
of victory to Baba. The corners of the masjid were decorated with garlands and
rows of oil burning lamps shed their light. Baba's horse, Shyamakarna, stood
fully decorated outside.

Then Tatya came with a party of men to Baba and asked him to be ready.
Baba sat quietly in his place until Tatya helped him get up by putting his arm
under Baba's arm. Tatya called Baba 'Mama' as their relationship was
extremely intimate. Baba wore the usual kafni, took his satka under his arm
and was ready to start after taking his chillum and placing a cloth over his
shoulder. Then Tatya threw a beautiful golden embroidered shawl over his
body. After this, Baba himself put a few wood sticks lying nearby into the
dhuni to keep it alive, extinguished the oil lamp burning near the dhuni with
his right hand, and then started for the Chavadi. All sorts of musical
instruments would then be heard and colored fireworks went off. Men and
women singing Baba's name started walking, some playing musical
instruments, some dancing with joy and some carrying flags and banners.

The bhaldars announced Baba's name as he walked down the steps of the
masjid. On both sides of Baba stood people who held *chavaris,* fly whiskers
with ornamental tassels, and others who fanned him. On the way, cloth was
spread on the ground for Baba to walk on while being supported by devotees'

hands. Tatya held his left hand while Mhalsapati held the right, and Bapusaheb Jog held the umbrella over his head. In this fashion Baba marched on to the Chavadi.

The fully decorated horse, Shyamakarna, led the way and behind him were all the carriers, waiters, musical players and the crowd of devotees. *Harinama* (name of the Lord) was chanted to the accompaniment of music and the skies were filled with the name of Sai. In this manner, the procession reached the corner and all the people that joined the party seemed well pleased and delighted. On coming to the corner, Baba stood facing the Chavadi and shone with a peculiar splendor. It seemed as if Baba's face shone like the dawn, or like the glory of the rising sun. Baba stood there with a concentrated mind, facing north, as if he was calling someone. Everyone played their instruments while Baba moved his right arm up and down for some time. Then Kakasaheb Dixit came forward with a silver plate containing flowers besmeared with *kum kum* (red powder) and gently threw them on Baba's body now and then. The musical instruments played their best during this part and Baba's face beamed with indescribable radiance and beauty, which everyone drank in to their hearts' content.

Words fail to describe the scene and splendor of this occasion. Sometimes Mhalsapati began to dance as if being possessed by some deity, and all were surprised to see that Baba's concentration was not in the least disturbed. With a lantern in his hand, Tatya walked on Baba's left side and Mhalsapati on the right, holding the hem of Baba's garment. What a beautiful procession and what an expression of devotion! Men and women, rich and poor, all flocked together to witness this sight. Baba walked very slowly as bhaktas followed on both sides with love and devotion. With joy pervading the whole atmosphere, the procession reached the Chavadi.

That scene and those days are gone now. Nobody can see them now or in the future. Still remembering and visualizing that scene can bring solace and comfort to our minds now.

The Chavadi was also fully decorated with a white ceiling, mirrors and many oil lamps. Tatya went ahead and on reaching it, spread an *asana* (seat) for Baba. Placing a bolster, he made Baba sit there and then put a good coat on. Then the devotees worshipped him in different ways. They put a crown with a tuft on his head, placed garlands of flowers and jewels round his neck, and marked his forehead with musk vertical lines and a dot, as Vaishnava devotees do. Then they gazed at Baba to their hearts' content. They changed his headdress now and then and held it above his head, fearing that Baba might throw it away. Baba knew their hearts and meekly submitted to all their ways without objection. With these decorations he looked wonderfully beautiful. Nanasaheb Nimonkar held the umbrella with its lovely pendants over Baba's head and Bapusaheb Jog washed Baba's feet in a silver dish and offered *arghya*, water offered to God. He besmeared Baba's arms with sandalpaste and offered him betel leaves. Baba sat on the asana supporting himself with the bolster, while Tatya and some stood near him and others fell at Baba's feet. Devotees on both sides waved fans.

Shama then prepared the chillum and handed it over to Tatya, who drew out a flame, then handed it to Baba. After Baba had his smoke, it was given to Mhalsapati and then passed around to all. Blessed was the inanimate chillum. It had first to undergo many ordeals of penance, such as being kneaded by potters, dried in the open sun and burned in fire, only then did it have the good fortune to be in Baba's hands and receive his kiss. After this function was over, devotees put garlands of flowers on his neck and gave him fragrant nosegays and flowers. Baba, who was dispassion and detachment incarnate, cared nothing for necklaces of jewels, garlands of flowers, or other decorations, but out of real love for his devotees, he allowed them to have their own way and to please themselves.

Finally, Bapusaheb Jog waved the Aarati tray to Baba while the musical instruments played. When the Aarati was over, the devotees returned home, one by one folding their hands to Baba and taking his leave. When Tatya, after offering the chillum, *attar* (scent) and rose water, stood to leave, Baba said lovingly to him, "Guard me properly. Go if you like, but return sometime at night and inquire after me." Replying in the affirmative, Tatya left the Chavadi and went home. Then Baba prepared his bed. He arranged 50 or 60 palm leaves one upon another, and after making his bed, went to rest.

We shall also now take rest and close this chapter with a request to the readers that they should remember Sai Baba and his Chavadi procession daily before they retire and go to bed.

Pranams to Sri Sai

Peace Be to All

CHAPTER THIRTY-EIGHT

Oh, blessed sadguru Sai, we bow to you, who has given happiness to the whole world, provided for the welfare of the devotees, and removed the afflictions of those who have take refuge in your holy feet. As the protector and savior of bhaktas who surrender themselves to you, you have incarnated in this world to bless and help the people. The liquid essence of the pure Self was poured into the mold of Brahman and out of this has come the crest jewel of saints, Sai. Sai is Atmaram Himself. He is the abode of perfect divine bliss. Having attained mastery of this life, and being detached and without desire, Sai makes his devotees free and desireless.

⚜

BABA'S COOKING POT

Other kinds of charity are imperfect, but anna dana (giving food) is the most meritorious.

Different sadhanas are prescribed in the scriptures for different ages. *Tapas* (austerities) is recommended for the Krita age, *jnana* (knowledge) for the Treta age, *yajna* (sacrifice) for the Dwarpara age, and *dana* (charity) for the Kali (present) age. Of all the charities, giving food is the best one. We are very disturbed when we do not get food at noon. Other beings feel the same way under these circumstances. Knowing this, he who gives food to the poor and hungry is the best donor or charitable person. The *Taittiriya Upanishad* says, "Food is Brahma. From food all creatures are born, and having been born, by food they live, then having departed, into food again they enter." When an uninvited guest comes to our door at noon, it is our duty to welcome him by giving him food. Other kinds of charities, like giving away wealth, property and clothes require some discrimination but in the matter of food no such consideration is necessary. Let anyone who comes to the door at noon be served immediately. If lame, crippled, blind or diseased indigents come, they should be fed first and then the able-bodied persons and relations afterwards. The merit of feeding the former is much greater than that of feeding the latter. Other kinds of charity are imperfect, but *anna dana* (giving food) is the most meritorious.

Now let us see how Baba prepared and distributed food. It has been stated in previous chapters that Baba required very little food for himself and that which he needed was obtained by begging from a few houses. However, when Baba distributed food to everyone, he made all the preparations from beginning to end by himself. He depended on no one and troubled none in this matter.

First, he would go to the bazaar and buy all the ingredients such as corn, flour and spices needed for cooking, paying cash. Then, in the open courtyard of the masjid he would build a big hearth and after lighting a fire underneath, he would place a cooking pot over it containing the proper measure of water. There were two cooking pots. The small one could hold enough food to provide for 50 people, and the large cooking pot could provide enough food for 100 people.

Sometimes Baba cooked *mitthe chaval* (sweet rice) and at other times *pulava* with meat. Frequently, when boiling soup he added small balls of thick or flat breads of wheat flour. He did all the grinding himself. Baba would also pound spices on a stone slab and put the thin pulverized spices into the cooking pot. He took great pains to make the dishes very tasty. He prepared *ambil* by boiling jawari flour in water and mixing it with buttermilk. He would then distribute this ambil along with the other food to everyone.

Baba had his own unusual method of checking to see if the food was properly cooked or not. He would roll up the sleeve of his kafni and put his bare arm directly into the boiling cauldron without the least fear and churn the whole mass from side to side and up and down. There was never any burn mark resulting from this method, nor did Baba ever show any fear or pain. When the cooking was over, Baba brought pots from the masjid and had them blessed by the *moulvi* (Muslim priest). First, Baba sent part of the food as prasad to Mhalsapati and Tatya, then he served the remaining contents with his own hand to all the poor and helpless people, allowing them to have their fill. Blessed and fortunate indeed are those people who received food prepared by Baba and who were served by him as well.

Some may have a doubt here and ask, "Did Baba distribute both vegetarian and non-vegetarian food as prasad to all his devotees?" The answer is simple. Those who were accustomed to eat non-vegetarian food were given such food from the cooking pot as prasad, while those who were not so accustomed were not allowed to touch it and were given vegetarian food. Baba never created any wish or desire in them to indulge in this food. There is a well-established principle that when a guru gives anything as prasad, the disciple who thinks and doubts whether it is acceptable or not experiences negative consequences. In order to see how a disciple had absorbed this principle, Baba sometimes gave tests.

For instance, on an Ekadashi day, Baba gave some rupees to Dada Kelkar and asked him to go in person to Koralha to buy some mutton. Dada Kelkar was an orthodox Brahmin and followed all orthodox practices in his life. He knew that offering wealth, grain and clothes to a sadguru was not enough because obedience and prompt compliance with his order was the real dakshina that pleased him most. In view of this, Dada Kelkar dressed and started out for Koralha to get the mutton. As he started to leave, Baba called him back and said, "Don't go yourself, but send someone else."

Dada Kelkar then sent his servant Pandu for the purpose. Then, seeing Dada Kelkar's servant starting to leave, Baba cancelled his request, asking Dada Kelkar to call him back. On another occasion, Baba asked Dada Kelkar to see if the salty *pulava* (mutton dish) was done. Dada Kelkar replied casually that it was. Baba then said to him, "Neither have you seen it with your eyes, nor tasted it with your tongue, so how can you say it was good? Just take the lid off the pot and have a look." Saying this, Baba caught Dada's arm and thrust it into the pot and added, "Take some out of this and put it in a dish. Let go of your orthodoxy without getting angry." When a wave of love rises in a mother's mind, she pinches her child and when he begins to cry, hugs him close to her bosom. Baba, in a true motherly way, pinched Dada in this way. Baba's ways were inscrutable, for in reality, he would never force his orthodox disciple to eat forbidden food and defile himself.

The cooking went on for some time until 1910, at which time it stopped. As stated previously, Das Ganu, through his kirtans, spread Baba's fame far and wide in the Mumbai area and people from that part of the country began to flock to Shirdi. Shirdi then became a holy place of pilgrimage. The devotees brought various articles and dishes of food to present and offer as naivedya. There was such an abundance of naivedya offered by them that fakirs and paupers could eat their fill and there was still some surplus left. Before stating how naivedya was distributed, we shall refer to Nanasaheb Chandorkar's story describing Baba's regard and respect for local shrines and deities.

DISRESPECT OF A SHRINE

People could only draw inferences or guess as to whether Sai Baba was a Brahmin or a Muslim. He actually belonged to no caste. No one knew definitely when he was born, what community he was from, or who his parents were. Then how could he be a Muslim or Brahmin? If he were a Muslim, why did he keep a dhuni fire ever burning in the masjid?

Why was there a *tulsi vrindavan* (tulsi planter)? Why did he allow the blowing of conches and ringing of bells and the playing of musical instruments? If he were a Muslim, how could he have allowed all the different forms of Hindu worship? Moreover, how could he have pierced ears and how could he have spent money from his pocket to repair Hindu temples? Furthermore, Baba never tolerated the slightest disrespect to Hindu shrines and deities.

Once Nanasaheb Chandorkar came to Shirdi with his brother-in-law, Mr. Biniwalle. They went to the masjid and sat before Baba and while they were conversing, Baba suddenly became angry with Nanasaheb and said, "You have been with me for such a long time. How could you behave like this?" At first, Nanasaheb did not understand what Baba meant so he humbly requested him to explain. Baba then asked him what he did when he arrived in Kopergaon and afterward, how he traveled to Shirdi from there. Nanasaheb at once realized his mistake. Nanasaheb's brother-in-law, Mr. Biniwalle, a Datta bhakta, usually worshipped at the shrine of Datta on the banks of the Godavari on his way to Shirdi, but this time Nanasaheb dissuaded his brother-in-law from going to the shrine so as to avoid delay, allowing them to continue directly on to Shirdi. Nanasaheb confessed all this to Baba and then went on to tell him that while bathing in the Godavari, a big thorn went into his foot and gave him quite a bit of trouble. Baba pointed out to Nanasaheb that the thorn was a slight punishment for his disregard of the Datta shrine and warned him to be more careful in the future. Now we revert to the description of the distribution of naivedya.

FEEDING THE DEVOTEES

After the Aarati was over and Baba had sent all the people away with udi and blessings, he went inside the masjid and sat behind a curtain with his back to the *nimbar* (niche) for meals. A row of bhaktas sat on each side of Baba. The bhaktas brought the naivedya dishes containing a variety of food such as puri, mande, polis, basundi, sanza and rice inside the masjid, where Baba had sat down to partake of his meal. They hoped to receive prasad from Baba that had been consecrated by his touch. All the dishes of food received were mixed together into one and placed before Baba. He offered it all to God and blessed it. Portions of it were then given to the devotees who were waiting outside and the rest was served inside to the two rows of bhaktas, with Baba seated at their center. Everyone ate as much as they wanted of the blessed food. Everyday Baba would ask Shama and Nanasaheb to serve the blessed food to all the people sitting inside the masjid and to look after their individual needs and comforts. They did this task very willingly and carefully, so every morsel of the food partaken provided nutrition and satisfaction. Such sweet and blessed food it was, ever auspicious and ever holy.

LAST CUP OF BUTTERMILK

Once when Hemadpant had just eaten his fill in the masjid, Baba offered him a cup of buttermilk. Its white appearance pleased him but he was afraid there would be no space inside his stomach for it. He did, however, take a sip, which proved very tasty. Seeing his faltering attitude, Baba said, "Drink it all. You won't get another such opportunity again." Hemadpant drank the entire cup of buttermilk and later found Baba's words were prophetic, as he passed away soon after.

Note: Now readers, we certainly have Hemadpant to thank because he not only drank the cup of buttermilk, but he has supplied us with an abundance of nectar in the form of Baba's leelas. Let us drink cups and cups of this nectar and be satisfied and happy.

Pranams to Sri Sai

Peace Be to All

CHAPTER THIRTY-NINE

BABA'S KNOWLEDGE OF SANSKRIT

This chapter discusses Baba's interpretation of a verse from the *Bhagavad Gita*. Some people did not believe that Baba knew Sanskrit, but given his interpretative teachings to Nanasaheb Chandorkar, Hemadpant refuted that objection in Chapter 50. As Chapter 50 deals with the same subject matter, it is incorporated into this chapter.

⚜

PRELIMINARY

Blessed is Shirdi and blessed is the Dwarkamai where Sri Sai lived and moved until he took mahasamadhi. Blessed are the people of Shirdi whom he helped and for whom he came such a long distance. Shirdi was a small village first, but it attained great importance on account of his contact and became a *tirtha*, holy place of pilgrimage. Equally blessed are the women of Shirdi; blessed is their complete and undivided faith in him. They sang the glories of

Baba while bathing, grinding, pounding corn and doing other household work. Blessed is their love, for they sang sweet songs which calm and pacify the minds of the singers and listeners.

BABA'S INTERPRETATION

The true devotee sees everything to be God.

Nobody believed that Baba knew Sanskrit. One day he surprised everyone by giving a good interpretation of a verse from the Bhagavad Gita to Nanasaheb. A brief account of this was written by B.V. Deo and published in Marathi in Sri Sai Leela magazine. Short accounts of this are also published in 'Sai Baba's Charters and Sayings' and in 'The Wondrous Saint Sai Baba,' both by B.V. Narsimha Dwami. B.V. Deo has also given an English version of this in his statement. As he received this account first hand from Nanasaheb, his version is below.

Nanasaheb was a good student of Vedanta. He had read the *Bhagavad Gita* with commentaries and prided himself on his knowledge. He imagined that Baba knew nothing of all this or of Sanskrit. So, one day Baba pricked this bubble. Those were the days before crowds flocked to Baba and Baba had solitary talks in the masjid with devotees.

Nanasaheb was sitting near Baba and massaging his legs and muttering to himself. Baba said, "Nana, what are you mumbling to yourself?"

Nana replied, "I am reciting a *sloka* (verse) in Sanskrit."

"What sloka?" Baba asked.

Nana replied, "From the *Bhagavad Gita.*"

Baba commanded, "Say it loudly."

Nana then recited the verse from the *Bhagavad Gita (Chapter 4, V 34)*, "Tadviddhi Pranipatena Pariprashnena Sevaya, Upadekshyanti Te Jnanam Jnaninastattvadarshinah."

Baba asked, "Nana, do you understand it?"

"Yes," said Nana.

Baba said, "If you do, then tell me."

Nana responded, "Know that by means of *sashtanga namaskar* (prostration), inquiry and service to the guru, jnanis, who have realized the truth, will teach you jnana, which is knowledge."

Baba said, "Nana, I do not want a paraphrase of the whole stanza. Give me each word, its grammatical meaning, mood and tense." Then Nana explained it word by word.

Baba asked, "Nana, is it enough to merely do prostrations?"

Nana replied, "I do not know any other meaning for the word *pranipata* other than making prostrations."

"What is *pariprashna*?" asked Baba.

"Asking questions," Nana replied.

Baba asked, "What does *prashna* mean?"

"The same—questioning."

"If *pariprashna* means the same as *prashna*, why did Vyasa add the prefix *pari*? Was Vyasa off his head?" asked Baba.

Nana said, "I do not know of any other meaning for the word *pariprashna*."

Baba continued and asked, "*Seva* (selfless service), what sort of seva is meant?"

Nana replied, "Just what we are doing always, like massaging your legs."

Baba asked, "Is it enough to render such service?"

"I do not know what more is signified by the word seva," responded Nana.

Baba asked, "In the next line *padekshyanti te jnanam*, can you read it with another word instead of jnanam?"

"Yes," said Nana.

"What word?" Baba asked.

"Ajnanam," replied Nana.

"Using *ajnanam* (ignorance) instead of *jnanam* (knowledge), can any meaning be made out of the verse?" Baba inquired.

"No, Shankara Bhashya gives no such construction," Nana said.

"Never mind if he doesn't. Is there any objection to using the word ajnanam if it makes better sense?" Baba asked.

Nana replied, "I do not understand how to interpret it by placing ajnanam in it."

Baba asked, "Why does Krishna ask Arjuna to go to jnanis or *Tattvadarshis* to get jnana? Was not Krishna himself a jnani?"

Nana responded, "Yes. He was. But I do not understand why he was sending Arjuna to jnanis."

Baba asked, "Have you not understood?"

Nana was humiliated. His pride was knocked on the head.

Then Baba began to explain:

> *One,* it is not enough merely to prostrate before jnanis. We must do *sarvaswa sharangati,* a complete surrender to the sadguru.

> *Two,* inquiry must be a constant quest for the truth. Questions must not be made with improper motive or an attitude to trap the guru to try to catch mistakes in their answer, or out of idle curiosity. It must be made with devotion, humility and a sincere desire to achieve moksha or spiritual realization.

> *Three,* seva is not service with the feeling that you are free to give or refuse service. You must feel that the body does not belong to you; since you surrendered it to the guru, it exists only to give service to him. If this is done, the sadguru will show you what the jnana referred to in the previous stanza is.

Nana still did not understand what was meant by saying that a guru teaches ajnana. Baba explained:

> How is jnana upadesh, the imparting of realization, to be achieved? Destroying ignorance is jnana. The *Jnaneshwari* commentary of the *Gita* says, "Removal of ignorance is like this, Oh Arjuna, if dream and sleep disappear, you are yourself. It is like that." It also says, "Is there anything else in jnana besides the destruction of ignorance?" Expelling darkness means light. Destroying duality (dvaita) means non-duality (advaita). Whenever we speak of destroying duality, we speak of non-duality. Whenever we speak of destroying darkness, we talk of light. If we have to realize the non-dual state, the feeling of duality in ourselves has to be removed. That is the realization of the non-dual state.

> Who can speak of non-duality while remaining in duality? Unless one gets into that state, how can one know it and realize it? One must enter the non-dual state to know it and realize it.

Again, the *shishya* (disciple), like the sadguru, is really the embodiment of jnana. The difference between the two lies in the levels of consciousness, self-realization, sattva (beingness), and *aishwarya yoga* (divine powers). The sadguru is *nirguna* (formless) *satchitananda* (existence, consciousness, bliss). Even though he has taken human form to elevate mankind and raise the world, his true formless nature is not destroyed even a bit. His beingness or reality, divine power and wisdom remain undiminished. The disciple also is of the same *swarupa* (divine form). But it is overlaid by the effect of *samaskaras* (karmic impressions) from innumerable births, which takes the shape of ignorance, and which hides from his view that he is *shuddha chaitanya* (pure consciousness) (*Bhagavad Gita, Chap 6 V15*). As stated, he gets the impression, "I am a jiva, an individual, lowly and poor."

The guru has to root out these offshoots of ignorance and has to give *upadesh* or instruction. To the disciple, held spellbound for endless births by the idea of being an individual, lowly and poor, the guru imparts the teaching over hundreds of births, "You are God, you are mighty and magnificent." Then, he realizes bit by bit that he is really God. The perpetual delusion under which the disciple is laboring, that he is the body, that he is an individual (jiva) or ego, that God (Paramatma) and the world are different from him, is an error inherited from innumerable past births. From actions based on this misunderstanding, he has derived his joy, sorrow and mixture of both. To remove this delusion, this error, this root ignorance, he must start the inquiry. How did the ignorance arise? Where is it? To show him this is called the guru's upadesh. The following are the instances of *ajnana* (ignorance); the false notions that constitute ajnana:

I am a jiva (individual).

I am the body.

God, the world and the jiva are different.

I am not God.

Not knowing that body is not the soul.

Not knowing that God, the world and the jiva are one.

Unless these errors are exposed to him, the disciple cannot learn the reality of what is God, jiva, the world, and the body, and how they are interrelated and whether they are different from each other, or one and the same. To teach him the correct understanding and destroy his ignorance, the sadguru imparts instruction in jnana or ajnana. Why should jnana be imparted to the jiva, who is a *jnanamurti* (form of knowledge)? Upadesh is merely to show him his error and destroy his ignorance.

Baba added:

Pranipata implies surrender.

Surrender must be of body, mind and wealth.

Why should Krishna refer Arjuna to jnanis other than Himself? The true devotee sees everything to be God (*Bhagavad Gita, Chap 7 V19*). "Any guru will be Krishna to the devotee." And the guru sees the disciple to be God and Krishna treats the disciple as both his *prana* (life force) and *atma* (soul) (*Bhagavad Gita, Chap 7 V18 Jnaneshwari commentary*). As Sri Krishna knows that there are such devotees and gurus, He refers Arjuna to them so that their greatness may increase and be known.

CONSTRUCTION OF THE SAMADHI MANDIR

Baba never talked, nor made any fuss about the things that he wanted to accomplish, but he so skillfully arranged the circumstances and surroundings that the people were surprised at the slow but sure results attained. The construction of the Samadhi Mandir is an instance in point.

Bapusaheb Buti, the famous millionaire of Nagpur, lived in Shirdi with his family. Once an idea arose in his mind that he should have a building of his own there. Some time after this, while he was sleeping in Dixit's wada, he had a vision. Baba appeared in his dream and ordered him to build a wada of his own with a temple. Shama who was sleeping there also had a similar vision. When Bapusaheb was awakened, he saw Shama crying and asked him why. Shama replied that in his vision, Baba came close to him and clearly ordered,

"'Build the wada with a temple. I shall fulfill the desires of all.' Hearing Baba's sweet and loving words, I was overpowered with emotion, my throat was choked, my eyes were overflowing with tears and I began to cry."

Bapusaheb was surprised to see that both their visions were the same. Being a rich and capable man, he decided to build a wada there and drew up a plan with Shama. Kakasaheb Dixit also approved of it. When it was placed before Baba, he approved it immediately. Then the construction work was started under Shama's supervision. The ground floor, cellar and well were completed. While walking on the way to and from Lendi, Baba suggested certain improvements. Further work was entrusted to Bapusaheb Jog and when it was going on, an idea struck Bapusaheb Buti's mind that there should be an open room or platform, in the center of which would be installed the image of *Murlidhar* (Lord Krishna with the flute). He asked Shama to get Baba's permission for this. Shama asked Baba about this when Baba was passing by the wada.

After listening to Shama, Baba gave his consent saying, "After the temple is complete I will come there to stay." Then staring at the wada he added, "After the wada is complete, we shall use it ourselves, we shall live, move and play there, and embrace each other and be happy." Then Shama asked Baba whether this was the auspicious time to begin the foundation work of the central room of the shrine. Baba answered yes. Shama got a coconut, broke it and started the work. In due time the work was completed and an order was also given for making a good image of Murlidhar.

But before it was ready, something happened. Baba became seriously ill and was about to pass away. Bapusaheb Buti became very sad and dejected, thinking that if Baba passed away, his wada would not be blessed by the holy touch of Baba's feet, and all his money (about a lakh of rupees) would be wasted. But the words, "Place me in the wada," which came out of Baba's mouth just before his passing away, consoled not only Bapusaheb, but one and all. In due time, Baba's holy body was placed and preserved in the central shrine meant or designed for Murlidhar, and Baba himself became Murlidhar and the wada became the Samadhi Mandir of Sai Baba. His wonderful life is unfathomable.

Blessed and fortunate is Bapusaheb Buti in whose wada lies the holy and pure body of Baba.

Pranams to Sri Sai

Peace Be to All

CHAPTER FORTY

STORIES OF BABA

B lessed is Sri Sai Sainatha who gives instructions in both temporal and spiritual matters to his devotees and makes them happy by enabling them to achieve the goal of their life. In placing his hand on their heads, Sai transfers his powers to them and destroys the sense of differentiation, and makes them attain the Unattainable Thing. With no sense of duality or difference, he embraces devotees who prostrate themselves before him. He becomes one with his devotees, as the sea with the rivers when they meet in the rainy season, and gives them his power and position. It follows from this that he who sings the leelas of God's bhaktas is equally or more dear to him than one who sings the leelas of God only. Now to revert to the stories of this chapter.

❧

MRS. DEO'S UDYAPAN CEREMONY

"I always think of him who remembers me. I require no conveyance, carriage, tanga, train, nor air transport. I run and manifest myself to him who lovingly calls me."

B.V. Deo was a Revenue Collector at Dahanu. His mother had observed 25 or 30 different vows and an *Udyapan* (concluding) ceremony was to be performed in connection with them. This ceremony included the feeding of 100 or 200 Brahmins. Mr. Deo fixed a date for the ceremony and wrote a letter to Bapusaheb Jog asking him to request Sai Baba, on his behalf, to attend the dinner of the ceremony, as without his attendance the ceremony would not be properly completed. Bapusaheb Jog read the letter to Baba. Baba noted carefully the pure-hearted invitation and said, "I always think of him who remembers me. I require no conveyance, carriage, tanga, train, nor air transport. I run and manifest myself to him who lovingly calls me. Write a pleasing reply to him that three of us, a trio, me, you and a third will attend."

Jog informed Mr. Deo of what Baba said. Mr. Deo was very pleased but knew that Baba never went any place in person except Rahata, Rui and Nimgaon. He also thought that nothing was impossible to Baba as he was all-pervading, and that he might suddenly come in any form he likes to fulfill his words.

A few days before this, a sannyasi with Bengali dress professing to work for the cause of the protection of cows came to the stationmaster at Dahanu to collect donations. The stationmaster told him to go into the town and see the Revenue Collector (Mr. Deo), and with his help, collect funds. Just then, Mr. Deo happened to come by. The stationmaster then introduced the sannyasi to him and they sat and talked on the platform. Mr. Deo told him that a donation list for another charitable cause had already been opened by a leading citizen, Rao Shetty. Therefore, it was not good to start another donation list and it would be better if he would visit again after two or four months. Hearing this, the sannyasi left.

About a month later, the sannyasi returned in a tanga and stopped in front of Mr. Deo's house at about 10 a.m. Mr. Deo thought that he came for donations. Seeing him busy with the preparations of the ceremony, the sannyasi said that he had come not for money but for meals. Deo said, "All right, very good, you are welcome, the house is yours."

The sannyasi said, "Two lads are with me."

Deo said, "Come with them." As there were two hours before dinner, Deo asked where he should send for them. The sannyasi said that it was not necessary as he would come with them at the appointed time. Deo asked him to come at noon. Exactly at twelve noon, the trio came, joined the dinner party and after eating went away.

After the ceremony was finished, Deo wrote a letter to Bapusaheb Jog complaining of Baba's breach of promise. Jog went to Baba with the letter but before it was opened, Baba spoke:

Ah, he says that I promised to come but deceived him. Inform him that I did attend his dinner with two others but he failed to recognize me. Then why did he call me at all? Tell him that he thought that the sannyasi came to ask for donation money. Did I not remove his doubt in that respect and did I not say that I would come with two others, and did not the trio come in time and take their meals? See, to keep my word I would sacrifice my life, I would never be untrue to my word.

This reply gladdened Jog's heart and he communicated the whole reply to Deo. As soon as he read it, Deo burst into tears of joy but then he took himself to task mentally for vainly blaming Baba. He wondered how he was fooled by the sannyasi's prior visit and his coming to him for donations, how he also failed to catch the significance of the sannyasi's words that he would come with two others for meals.

This story clearly shows that when devotees surrender themselves completely to their sadguru, he sees that the religious functions in their houses are properly executed and comply with all the necessary formalities.

HEMADPANT'S SHIMGA DINNER

Now let us take another story that shows how Baba appeared in the form of his picture and fulfilled the desire of his devotee.

In 1917 on the Full Moon morning, Hemadpant had a vision. Baba appeared to him in his dream in the form of a well-dressed sannyasi, woke him up, and said that he would come for meals that day. When he was fully awake, he saw no Sai, nor any sannyasi. He began to recollect the dream and remembered each and every word the sannyasi had uttered in his dream. Though he was in contact with Baba for seven years and though he always meditated on Baba, he never expected that Baba would come to his house for meals. However, being very happy with Baba's words, he went to his wife and informed her that since it was the Holi Festival Day, a sannyasi guest was coming for meals and some more rice should be prepared. She asked about the guest, who he was and from where he was coming. Then not to lead her astray and not to cause any misunderstanding, he told her the truth about his dream. She skeptically asked whether it was really possible that Baba would come to Bandra from Shirdi, leaving the delicate dishes there to accept their coarse food. Hemadpant then assured her that Baba might not come in person, but he might attend in the form of a guest and that they would lose nothing if they cooked some more rice.

After this, preparations for the meal went on and it was ready at noon. The Holi (Festival) worship was done and the *banana leaves* (used as dishes) were spread and arranged with *rangoli* decorations drawn around them. Two rows were made with a central seat between them for the guest. All the members of the family, sons, grandsons, daughters and sons-in-law, came and occupied their proper seats and the serving of the various foods commenced. While this was being done, everyone was watching for the guest, but no one turned up though it was past noon. Then the entry door was closed and chained and the ghee was served. This was a signal to start eating. A formal offering to *Vaishwa Deva* (fire) and naivedya to Sri Krishna were also offered. As the members were about to begin, footsteps were distinctly heard in the staircase.

Hemadpant immediately went and opened the door and saw two men there, Ali Mahomed and Moulana Mujavar. The two men, seeing that meals were ready and all the members were about to begin eating, apologized to Hemadpant and asked him to excuse their interuption.

They said, "You left your seat and came running to us, others are waiting for you, so please take this thing and I shall relate the wonderful tale about it later on at your convenience." Saying this, he took a packet wrapped in old newspaper from under his arm and placed it on the table.

Hemadpant uncovered the packet and saw, to his great wonder and surprise, a beautiful big picture of Sai Baba. Seeing it, he was very moved, tears ran from his eyes and hair stood on end all over his body, and he bent and placed his head on the feet of Baba in the picture. He felt that Baba had blessed him by this miracle or leela. Out of curiosity, he asked Ali Mahomed where he got this picture. He said that he bought it from a shop and that he would give all the details about it some time later and wished that, as all the members were waiting for him, he should go and join them. Hemadpant thanked him, bid them good bye and returned to the dinning hall. The picture was placed on the central seat reserved for the guest and after the proper offering of naivedya, the whole party commenced eating and finished at the proper time. Seeing the beautiful form in the picture, everyone was extremely pleased and wondered how all this happened.

This is how Sai Baba kept and fulfilled the words he uttered in Hemadpant's dream. The story of the picture with all its details, how Ali Mahomed got it, why he bought it and gave it to Hemadpant, is reserved for the next chapter.

Pranams to Sri Sai

Peace Be to All

CHAPTER FORTY-ONE

STORY OF THE PICTURE

Baba knew all the past, present and future, and how skillfully he pulled the wires and fulfilled the desires of his devotees.

At the close of the last chapter, the account of Baba's picture being brought to Hemadpant's house just in time to be placed on the seat of the guest of honor during the Shimga dinner was recounted. Nine years after this incident, Ali Mahomed met Hemadpant and recounted the following story to him:

One day, while wandering the streets of Mumbai, he bought a picture of Sai Baba from a street hawker. He framed the picture and hung it on a wall in his house at Bandra, a suburb of Mumbai. As he loved Baba, he took darshan of the picture every day. Three months before he gave the picture to Hemadpant, he had an operation for an abscess on his leg and lay suffering and convalescing in the house of his brother-in-law, Noor Mahomed.

During those three months, his house in Bandra was closed and no one was living there. Only the pictures of famous living saints like Baba Abdul

Rahiman, Moulanasaheb Mahomed Hussain, Sai Baba and Baba Tajudin were in the house. But the wheel of time did not spare even these, for even pictures have their beginning and end (births and deaths). All the pictures met their fate, but how Sai Baba's picture escaped it, that is something no one was able to explain until now. It demonstrates the all-pervasiveness and omnipresence of Sai and his inscrutable power.

Many years earlier, Ali Mahomed acquired a small picture of Saint Baba Abdul Rahiman. He gave the picture to his brother-in-law, Noor Mahomed, and it lay on his table for eight years. After some time, his brother-in-law decided to take it to a photographer to have it enlarged to life-size. He then distributed copies to his friends and relations, including Ali Mahomed who hung the picture in his Bandra house.

Noor Mahomed was a disciple of Saint Abdul Rahiman. When he went to present the picture to his guru in an open *darbar* (court) held by him, the guru got wild and ran to beat him, then threw him out. He felt terribly sad and dejected. He thought that he lost not only the money he used to reproduce the picture but worse had incurred his guru's displeasure and anger as his guru did not like image worship. He then took the enlarged picture with him and hired a boat to drown the picture at sea. He also requested that his friends and relations return their copies of the picture. After getting six of them back, he had them thrown into the sea by a fisherman.

At the time of this incident, Ali Mahomed lay healing at his brother-in-law's house. Noor told him that his suffering would come to an end if he would also drown his pictures of the saints in the sea. Hearing this, Ali Mahomed sent his manager to his Bandra house and had all the pictures of the saints in his house thrown into the sea.

When Ali Mahomed finally returned home two months later, he was surprised to find Baba's picture on the wall as before. He did not understand how his manager had taken away all the pictures except this one. He immediately took it out and kept it in his cupboard, fearing that if his brother-in-law saw it he would do away with it. While he was thinking of how to dispose of it and who could keep and guard it, Sai Baba himself inspired him to consult Moulana Mujavar and abide by his opinion.

He saw Moulana and told him everything. After mature consideration, they both decided that the picture should be presented to Hemadpant, that he would protect it well. Then they both went to Hemadpant and presented the picture in the nick of time.

This story shows how Baba knew all the past, present and future, and how skillfully he pulled the wires and fulfilled the desires of his devotees.

⚜

STEALING RAGS AND THE READING OF JNANESHWARI

For a long time, Mr. Deo had wanted to read *the Jnaneshwari*, the well-known Marathi commentary on the *Bhagavad Gita* by Jnaneshwar, along with other scriptures. He could read one chapter of the *Bhagavad Gita* daily, and some portion of other books but when he took the *Jnaneshwari* in hand difficulties arose and he was prevented from reading it. He took three month's leave, went to Shirdi and then went to his home at Poud for rest. He could read other books there but when he opened *Jnaneshwari,* some negative or stray thoughts came crowding in his mind and stopped him in his effort. Try however he might, he was not able to read even a few lines of the book with ease. So he resolved that when Baba would create love for the book and order him to read it he would begin, and not till then.

Then in February 1914, he went with his family to Shirdi. Bapusaheb Jog asked him whether he read the *Jnaneshwari* daily. Deo said that he wanted to read it but was not successful and only when Baba ordered him to would he begin. Bapusaheb then advised him to take a copy of the book and present it to Baba and start reading after he blessed it. Deo replied that he did not want to resort to this device, as Baba knew his heart. Did he not know his desire and would he not satisfy it by giving him a clear order to read it?

Deo then saw Baba and offered one rupee as dakshina. Baba asked for Rs. 20, which he gave. At night, he saw Balakram and asked how he secured Baba's devotion and grace. Balakram told him that he would communicate everything next day after Aarati. When Deo went for darshan next day, Baba asked for Rs. 20, which he gave willingly. As the masjid was crowded, Deo went and sat in a corner. Then Baba asked him to come close and sit with a calm mind. Then after the noon Aarati was over and after the men dispersed, Deo again saw Balakram and asked him his previous history, what Baba told him and how he was taught meditation. Balakram was going to reply when

Baba sent Chandru, a leper devotee, to call Deo to him. When Deo went to Baba, Baba asked him who he was talking to and what was he talking about. Deo said that he talked with Balakram and was talking about Baba's renown. Then Baba asked again for Rs.25 as dakshina, which Deo gladly gave.

Then Baba took him inside the Dwarkamai and sitting near the post accused him, saying, "You stole away my rags without my knowledge." Deo denied all knowledge of the rags, but Baba asked him to make a search. He searched but found none. Then Baba got angry and said, "There is nobody here, you are the only thief, so grey-haired and old, yet you came here for stealing." After this, Baba lost his temper, got terribly wild and shouted terrible abuses and scoldings. Deo remained silent and watchful and wondered if he was also going to get a beating. After about an hour or so, Baba asked him to go to the wada.

He returned to the wada and told Bapusaheb and Balakram all that had happened. Then in the afternoon Baba sent for everyone, including Deo, and said that his words might have hurt the old man, Deo, but as he had committed the theft, he had to speak out. Then Baba again asked him for Rs. 12. Deo paid the amount then prostrated before him. Then Baba asked, "What are you doing?"

"Nothing," Deo replied.

Baba replied, "Go on reading the *Jnaneshwari* daily, go and sit in the wada, read some regularly every day and then explain the portion read to everyone with love and devotion. I am sitting here ready to give you the whole gold-embroidered *shella* (valuable cloth), then why go to others to steal rags, and why should you get into the habit of stealing?"

Deo was very happy to hear Baba's words; it was what he had asked for, Baba's command to start reading the *Jnaneshwari*. He had received what he wanted and felt that now he could read the book with ease. He pranammed again to Baba and told him that he surrendered himself to him and that he should be treated like a child and be helped in his reading. He realized then what Baba meant by "stealing the rags." What he had asked Balakram constituted the "rags" and Baba did not like his behavior in this respect. As he was ready to answer any question, he did not like him to ask others so he harassed and scolded him. Deo thought that Baba really did not harass and scold him but taught him he was ready to fulfill his desires, and there was no use asking others in vain. Deo took these scoldings as flowers and blessings and went home satisfied and contented.

The matter did not end here. Baba did not stop with only issuing an order to read. Within a year he went to Deo and inquired about his progress. On April 2nd, 1914, Thursday morning, Baba gave him a dream vision. Baba sat on the upper floor and asked him whether he understood the *Jnaneshwari.* "No," answered Deo.

"Then when are you going to understand?" Baba asked.

Deo burst into tears and said, "Unless you shower your grace, reading it is worrisome and understanding it is even more difficult. I can say this definitely."

Baba said, "While reading you hurry. Read it before me, in my presence."

Deo said, "What shall I read?"

Baba said, "Read *Adhyatma* (spirituality)."

Deo went to bring the book, then opened his eyes and was awakened. We leave the readers to imagine what ineffable joy and bliss Deo felt after this vision.

Pranams to Sri Sai

Peace Be to All

CHAPTER FORTY-TWO

BABA'S PASSING AWAY

This chapter describes the passing away of Baba. The stories in the previous chapter show that the light of the Guru's grace removes fear in mundane existence and opens the path of liberation and turns our misery into happiness. If we always remember the feet of the sadguru, our troubles will come to an end, death loses its sting and the misery of this mundane existence is transformed. Those who truly care about their welfare should listen carefully to these stories of Sai Sainath which will purify their minds.

BABA'S PREVIOUS INDICATION OF HIS PASSING

Up until this point, the readers have heard stories of Baba's life. Now let us listen attentively to the story of Baba's passing. On September 28th, 1918, Baba developed a slight fever. The fever lasted for two or three days; after that

Baba gave up food and began to grow weaker and weaker. Seventeen days later, on Tuesday, October 15th, 1918, Baba left his mortal body at about 2:30 p.m.

Two years earlier, Baba gave an indication of his passing but no one understood it then. In the evening of *Vijayadasami*, the final day of the Mother Divine Festival, Baba went into a wild rage when people were returning from *Seemollanghan* (crossing the border of the village). He tore off his headdress, kafni and waistband and threw them into the dhuni. Fed by this offering, the fire in the dhuni began to burn brighter and Baba shone even brighter still. He stood there stark naked and with his burning red eyes shouted, "You fellows, now have a look and finally decide whether I am a Muslim or a Hindu." Everyone was trembling with fear and none dared to approach Baba.

After some time Bhagoji Shinde, Baba's leper devotee, went boldly near him and succeeded in tying a waistband round his waist and said, "Baba, what is all this? Today is Vijayadasami."

Baba struck the ground with his satka and said, "This is my *Seemollanghan* (crossing the border)." Baba did not cool down until 11:00 p.m. and the people doubted whether the Chavadi procession would take place that night. After an hour, Baba resumed his normal condition, and dressing himself as usual, attended the Chavadi procession as described earlier. Through this event, Baba gave an indication that Vijayadasami was the right time for him to cross the border of life, but no one understood this at the time. Then Baba gave another sign.

DIVERTING THE DEATHS OF RAMACHANDRA AND TATYA

Some time after this incident, Ramachandra Patil became seriously ill and was suffering greatly. He tried every remedy and finding no relief, lost all hope for his life and was waiting for his last moment. Then one midnight, Baba was suddenly standing next to his bed. He grabbed Baba's feet and begged him, "I have lost all hope for life, please tell me definitely when I will die."

Merciful Baba said, "Don't be anxious. Your death warrant has been withdrawn and you will soon recover, but I am afraid for Tatya. He will pass away on Vijayadasami of Shaka (1918). Do not tell this to anybody, nor to him as he will be terribly frightened." Ramachandra got well, but he was nervous about Tatya's life for he knew that Baba's word was unalterable and that Tatya would breathe his last within two years. He kept this hint secret and told it to no one except Bala Shimpi. Only these two people, Ramachandra Patil and Bala Shimpi were in fear and suspense regarding Tatya's life.

Ramachandra soon left his bed and was back on his feet. Time passed quickly and the time was now near. True to Baba's word, Tatya fell sick and was bed ridden so he could not come for Baba's darshan. Baba was also down with fever. Tatya had full faith in Baba and Baba in Lord Hari, who was his Protector. Tatya's illness began to grow from bad to worse and he could not move at all and was remembering Baba continuously. Baba's situation began to grow equally bad. The day predicted, Vijayadasami, was impending and both Ramachandra and Bala Shimpi were terribly trembling and frightened about Tatya as they believed that Tatya's end was near as Baba had predicted.

As Vijayadasami dawned, Tatya's pulse began to beat very slowly and his end seemed near. But then a curious thing happened. Tatya's death was averted. Tatya did not die, Baba passed instead. It seemed to all as if there was an exchange. People said that Baba gave up his life for Tatya. Why did he do so? He alone knows, as his ways are inscrutable. It seems, however, that in the prior incident two years earlier, Baba had given a hint of his passing, substituting Tatya's name for his.

The next morning, October 16th, Baba appeared to Das Ganu in his dream in Pandhapur and said, "The masjid collapsed. All the oilmen and grocers of Shirdi bothered me a lot, so I left that place. I came to inform you. Please go there quickly and cover me with bhakkal flowers." Das Ganu also received the news in letters from Shirdi. So he went to Shirdi with his disciples and started bhajans, singing the Lord's name continuously through the day after Baba's samadhi. Weaving a beautiful garland of flowers studded with Lord Hari's name, he placed it on Baba's samadhi and gave a mass feeding in Baba's name.

CHARITY TO LAXMIBAI

Vijayadasami is regarded by all Hindus as the most auspicious time and it is befitting that Baba should choose this time for his crossing the border. He was ailing some days before this, but he was ever conscious internally. Just before the last moment, he sat up erect without anybody's aid and looked better. People thought that the danger had passed and he was getting well. He knew that he was going to pass away soon and wanted to give some money to Laxmibai Shinde.

BABA PERVADING ALL CREATURES AND THE NINE COINS

"Creatures may be different, but the hunger of all is the same, though some speak and others are dumb. Know for certain, that he who feeds the hungry, really feeds me. Regard this as a self-evident truth."

Laxmibai Shinde was a good and well-to-do woman. She worked in the masjid day and night. Except for Mhalsapati, Tatya and Laxmibai, no one was allowed to step in the masjid at night. One evening when Baba was sitting in the masjid with Tatya, Laxmibai came and saluted Baba. Baba said to her, "Oh Laxmi, I am very hungry."

Off she went saying, "Baba, wait a bit. I will return immediately with bread." She returned with bread and vegetables and placed them before Baba. Baba then gave it a dog. Laxmibai asked, "What is this, Baba? I ran and hurried to prepare bread with my own hands for you. Yet you threw it to a dog without eating a bite of it. You unnecessarily gave me trouble." Baba replied:

Why do you grieve for nothing? Satisfying the dog's hunger is the same as satisfying mine. The dog has a soul. Creatures may be different, but the hunger of all is the same, though some speak and others are dumb. Know for certain, that he who feeds the hungry, really feeds me. Regard this as a self-evident truth.

Although this was an ordinary incident, Baba demonstrated a great spiritual truth and showed its practical application in daily life without hurting anybody's feelings. From this time onward, Laxmibai began to offer him bread and milk daily with love and devotion. Baba accepted and ate it appreciatively. He took a part of it and sent the remainder with Laxmibai to give to Radhakrishna Mai, who always relished eating Baba's remaining food as prasad. This bread story should not be considered as a digression. It shows how Sai Baba pervaded and transcended all creatures. He is omnipresent, birthless, deathless and immortal.

Baba remembered Laxmibai's service. How could he forget her? Just before leaving the body, he put his hand in his pocket and first took out five rupees and then another four. In all, he gave her nine rupees. Nine is symbolic of the nine types of devotion described in Chapter 21 or it may be the dakshina offered at the time of Seemollanghan. Laxmibai was a well-to-do woman and was not in want of money. So Baba might have suggested to her and brought prominently to her notice the nine characteristics of a good disciple mentioned in the 6th verse of Chapter Ten, *skandha* (verse) eleven of the *Bhagwat*, where first five, then four characteristics are mentioned in the first and second couplets. Baba followed the order, first paid five rupees and then four rupees, nine in all. Not only nine, but many times nine rupees passed through Laxmibai's hand, but this gift of Baba she will always remember.

Being ever aware and conscious, Baba also took other precautions during his last moments. In order that he should not be entangled with love and affection for his devotees, he ordered them all to leave. Kakasaheb Dixit, Bapusaheb Buti and others were in the masjid anxiously waiting upon Baba, but he asked them to go to the wada and return after meals. They could not leave Baba's presence, nor could they disobey him. So with heavy hearts they went to the wada. They knew that Baba's case was very serious and they could not forget him. They sat for meals but their minds were elsewhere, with Baba. Before they finished, news came of Baba leaving his mortal body. Leaving their food, they all ran to the masjid and found Baba's final resting place was on Bayaji's lap. Baba did not fall down on the ground nor did he lie on his bed, but sat quietly on his seat, and doing charity with his own hand, left his mortal body. Saints come into human body into this world with a definite mission and after that is fulfilled they pass away as quietly and easily as they came.

Pranams to Sri Sai

Peace Be to All

CHAPTERS FORTY-THREE
& FORTY-FOUR

Baba's Passing Away (Continued)

It is the general practice among the Hindus that when a man is about to die, religious scripture is read aloud to him with the aim that his mind should be withdrawn from worldly things and fixed on spiritual matters so that his future progress is ensured. When King Parikshiti was cursed by the son of a Brahmin rishi and was to die in a week, the great sage, Shuka, expounded on *Bhagawat Purana* to him during that week. This practice is followed even now and the *Gita, Bhagawat,* and other sacred books are read out loud to dying people. Baba, being an incarnation of God, needed no such help but followed this practice to set an example to the people. When he knew that he was soon going to pass, he ordered Mr. Vaze to read *Rama Vijaya* to him. Mr. Vaze read the book once during the week. Then Baba asked him to read it again day and night, and he finished the second reading in three days. Eleven days passed this way. Then he read it again for another three days and was exhausted. So Baba let him stop and be quiet. He abided in his Self and was waiting for the last moment.

For two or three days prior, Baba had stopped his morning excursions and begging rounds and instead sat in the masjid. He was conscious to the last and was advising devotees not to lose heart. He let no one know the exact time of his departure. Kakasaheb Dixit and Bapusaheb Buti were with him daily in the masjid. That day, October 15th, after Aarati, he asked them to return to their residence to take lunch. Still a few remained—Laxmibai, Bhagoji Shinde, Bayaji, Laxman Bala Shimpi and Nanasaheb Nimonkar. Shama was sitting on the steps. After giving nine rupees to Laxmibai, Baba said that he did not feel good in the masjid and that he should be taken to Buti's stone wada where he would be fine. Saying these last words, he leaned on Bayaji's body and breathed his last. Bhagoji noticed that his breathing had stopped and he immediately told this to Nanasaheb who was sitting below. Nanasaheb brought some water and poured it in Baba's mouth. It came out. Then he cried out loudly, "Oh Deva!" Baba seemed to open his eyes and say, "Ah," in a low tone. But it soon became evident that Baba had left his body for good.

The news of Baba's passing spread like a wildfire in the village of Shirdi and everyone, men, women and children ran to the masjid and began to mourn their loss in different ways. Some cried out loudly, some staggered in the streets and some fell down senseless. Tears ran down from the eyes of all and everyone was overcome with sorrow.

People started remembering the words of Sai Baba. Someone said that Baba told his devotees that in a time to come, he would appear as a lad of eight years. These are the words of a saint and so no one should doubt them. In the Krishna Avatar, Chakrapani did this very thing. Krishna, as a lad of eight with a bright complexion and wielding weapons in his four arms, appeared before Devaki who was in prison. In that incarnation, Lord Krishna lightened the burden of the earth.

In this incarnation the Lord, in the form of Sai Baba, came to uplift his devotees. There is no reason for doubt. The ways of the saints are inscrutable. This contact of Sai Baba with his devotees has not only been in this generation, but it has existed for the last 72 generations, generating ties of great love. Sai Baba has only gone temporarily. His devotees hold the firm belief he will incarnate again.

The question then arose how to lay Baba's body to rest? Some Muslims said that the body should be interred in an open space and a tomb built over it. Even Khushalchand and Amir Shakkar shared this opinion. But Ramachandra, the Village Officer, told the villagers with a firm and determined voice, "Your idea is not acceptable to us. Baba's body should be placed nowhere except in the wada." The people were divided on this and discussion regarding this point went on for 36 hours.

On Wednesday morning, Baba appeared to Laxman Mama Joshi in his dream and drawing him by his hand said, "Get up soon. Bapusaheb thinks that I am dead so he won't come. You do the worship and the *Kakad* (morning) Aarati." Laxman Mama was the village astrologer and Shama's uncle. He was an orthodox Brahmin who daily first worshipped Baba in the morning, then all the village deities. He had full faith in Baba. After the vision, he came with all the puja materials, and not minding the protests of the *moulvis* (Muslim priests) did the puja and the Kakad Aarati with all due formalities, then left. Then, at noon, Bapusaheb Jog came with all the others and did the noon Aarati as usual.

Paying due respect to Baba's words, the people decided to place his body in the wada and started digging the central portion of it. Tuesday evening, the Sub-Inspector had come from Rahata and others from different places turned up and they all agreed to the proposal. Next morning, Amirbhai came from Mumbai and the Revenue Collector from Kopergaon. The people then seemed divided in their opinion. Some insisted on interring his body in the open field. The Revenue Collector took a general poll and found that the proposal to use the wada secured double the number of votes. He, however, wanted to refer the matter to the Collector. So Kakasaheb Dixit got ready to go to Ahmednagar. In the meanwhile, through Baba's inspiration, there was a change in the opinion of those who voted against using the wada, and then all the people voted unanimously for the proposal.

On Wednesday evening, Baba's body was taken in procession and brought to the wada and was interred there with proper formalities in the *garbha*, the central portion reserved for Murlidhar, Krishna. In fact, Baba became the Murlidhar and the wada became a temple and a holy shrine, where so many devotees after that will find true rest and peace. Balasaheb Bhate and Upasani, a great devotee of Baba, properly performed Baba's funeral rites.

It may be noted here that, as observed by Professor Narke, Baba's body did not get stiff, though it was exposed for 36 hours and all the limbs were elastic, and his kafni could be taken off without being torn to pieces.

BREAKING OF THE BRICK

Some days before Baba's departure, there occurred an ominous sign foretelling the event. In the masjid, there was an old brick on which Baba rested his hand when sitting. At nighttime, he leaned against it while on his *asana* (meditation seat). This went on for many years. One day, during Baba's absence, a boy who was sweeping the floor took it in his hand and unfortunately it slipped and fell and broke into two pieces. When Baba came to know about this, he bemoaned its loss. "It is not the brick but my fate that has been broken into pieces. It was my lifelong companion. With it, I always meditated on the Self. It was as dear to me as my life. It has left me today," he said.

Some may raise a question here, "Why should Baba express this sorrow for such an inanimate thing as a brick?" To this, Hemadpant replies that saints incarnate in this world with the express mission of saving people in need and when they embody themselves and mix and act with the people, they act like them, outwardly laughing, playing and crying like everyone else, but inwardly they are wide awake to their duties and mission.

72 HOURS' SAMADHI

For fulfilling his mission, he assumed the body and after it was fulfilled, he threw away the body (the finite aspect), and assumed his infinite aspect.

Thirty-two years before this, in 1886, Baba made an attempt to cross the border. On a *Margashirsha Purnima*, the Full Moon in December, Baba suffered from a severe attack of asthma. To get rid of it, Baba decided to raise his *prana* (life force) high up and go into samadhi. He told Mhalsapati, "Protect my body for three days. If I return, fine. If I do not, bury my body in that open land (pointing to it) and fix two flags there as a mark." Saying this, Baba lay down at about 10 p.m. and his breathing stopped, as well as his pulse.

It seemed as if his prana had left the body. All the people, including the villagers, came and wanted to hold an inquest and bury the body in the place Baba had pointed to. But Mhalsapati prevented this. With Baba's body on his lap, he sat guarding it for a full three days. After three days had passed, Baba began showing signs of life at 3 a.m. His breathing commenced, the abdomen began to move, he opened his eyes and stretching his limbs, Baba returned to consciousness (life) again.

From this and other accounts, let the readers consider whether Sai Baba was the three and a half cubits body that he occupied for some years, or was he the Self inside. The body, composed of the five elements is perishable and transient, but the Self within is *the* thing--the Absolute Reality, which is immortal and intransient. The pure being and consciousness, Brahman, the ruler and controller of the senses and mind, is Sai. This pervades all things in the universe and there is no space without it. For fulfilling his mission, he assumed the body and after it was fulfilled, he threw away the body (the finite aspect), and assumed his infinite aspect. Sai ever lives, as also the previous incarnation of God, Dattatreya, Sri Narsimha Saraswati of Ganagapur. His passing away is only an outward aspect, but in reality he pervades all animate and inanimate things and is their Inner Controller and Ruler. This is experienced even now by many who surrender themselves completely to him and worship him with wholehearted devotion.

Though it is not possible for us to see Baba's form in that way now, still if we go to Shirdi, we shall find his beautiful life-like portrait adorning the masjid. This was drawn by Shamrao Jaykar, a famous artist and well-known devotee of Baba. To an imaginative and devoted onlooker, this portrait can even today give the satisfaction of having Baba's darshan. Though Baba has no body now, he lives there and everywhere and will look after the welfare of devotees even now as he did before he was embodied. Saints like Baba never die. Though they look like men, they are in reality God Himself.

BAPUSAHEB JOG'S SANNYAS

"You need not go anywhere in search of me. Without your name and form, there exists in you, as well as in all beings, a sense of

*being or consciousness of existence. That is me. Knowing this,
see me inside yourself, as well as in all beings."*

Hemadpant closes this chapter with the account of Bapusaheb Jog's
sannyas (renunciation). After his retirement from Government Service in
1909, he came and lived in Shirdi with his wife. He had no children. Both
husband and wife loved Baba and spent all their time worshipping and serving
Baba. After Megha's death, Bapusaheb did the Aarati ceremony daily in the
masjid and Chavadi until Baba's mahasamadhi. He was also entrusted with the
work of reading and explaining *Jnaneshwari* and *Ekanath Bhagawat* to the
audience in Sathe's wada. After serving for many years, Bapusaheb asked
Baba, "I have served you so long, my mind is not yet calm and composed, how
is it that my contact with saints has not improved me? When will you bless
me?" Hearing his devotee's prayer, Baba replied, "In due time, the fruit of
your bad actions will be destroyed, your merits and demerits will be reduced to
ashes. I shall consider you blessed when you renounce all attachments,
conquer lust and taste, and getting rid of all impediments, serve God
wholeheartedly and resort to the begging bowl (accept sannyas)."

After some time, Baba's words came true. His wife died before him and as
he had no other attachment, he became free and accepted sannyas before his
death and realized the true goal of life.

BABA'S NECTAR-LIKE WORDS

The kind and merciful Sai Baba said many a time the following sweet
words in the masjid:

Who loves me most, always sees me. The whole world is desolate to him
without me, he tells no stories but mine. He meditates upon me ceaselessly
and always chants my name. I feel indebted to him who surrenders himself
completely to me and ever remembers me. I shall repay his debt by giving him
self-realization. I am dependent on him who thinks and hungers after me and
who does not eat anything without first offering it to me. He who comes to me
like this, becomes one with me, just as a river goes to the sea and becomes
merged (one) with it. So leaving aside pride and egoism with no trace of them,
you should surrender yourself to me. I am who is seated in your heart.

WHO IS THIS ME?

Many a time Sai Baba explained who this 'me' is. He said:

You need not go anywhere in search of me. Without your name and form, there exists in you, as well as in all beings, a sense of being or consciousness of existence. That is me. Knowing this, see me inside yourself, as well as in all beings. If you practice this, you will realize all-pervasiveness, and will attain oneness with me.

Hemadpant pranams to the readers and requests them humbly and lovingly to love and respect all gods, saints and devotees. Has not Baba often said, "Who criticizes and complains about others, pierces me in the heart and injures me, but he that suffers and endures, pleases me most." Baba pervades all beings and creatures and surrounds them on all sides. He wants nothing but love for all beings. Such nectar, pure auspicious ambrosia, always flowed from Baba's lips. He therefore concludes—those who lovingly sing Baba's name and who hear it with devotion become one with Sai.

Pranams to Sri Sai

Peace Be to All

CHAPTER FORTY-FIVE

PRELIMINARY

But ever since his passing away, new leelas have taken place and are happening even now. This clearly shows that Baba is ever-living and helping his devotees as before.

We have described Baba's passing away in the last three chapters. His physical or finite form has no doubt disappeared from our view, but the infinite transcendent form ever lives. The leelas that occurred during his lifetime have been dwelled upon at great length. But ever since his passing away, new leelas have taken place and are happening even now. This clearly shows that Baba is ever-living and helping his devotees as before. The people who had contact with Baba when he was living were indeed very fortunate, but if any of them had not achieved dispassion for the things and enjoyments of the world and did not have their mind turned to the Lord, it was truly their bad luck. What was wanted then and is wanted now is wholehearted devotion to Baba. All our senses, organs, and mind should cooperate in worshipping and serving Baba. It is no use in engaging some organs in the worship and forgetting others. If a thing like worship or meditation is to be done, it ought to be done with all our mind and soul.

The love that a chaste woman bears for her husband is sometimes compared to that which a disciple bears for his guru. Yet, the former love falls far short of the latter, which is incomparable. No one, whether he be father, mother, brother or any other relation, comes to our aid in attaining the goal of life, self-realization. We have to map out and traverse the path of self-realization ourselves. We have to discriminate between the unreal and the real, renounce the things and enjoyments of this world and the next, control our senses and mind, and aspire for liberation only. Instead of depending upon others, we should have full faith in ourselves. When we begin to practice discrimination, we come to know that the world is transient and unreal and our passion for worldly things becomes less and less, and ultimately we get dispassion or detachment towards them. Then we know that the Brahman, which is no other than our guru, is the sole reality and as It transcends and surrounds the seeming universe, we begin to worship It in all creatures. This is the unitive bhajan or worship. When we worship Brahman or the guru wholeheartedly, we become one with Him and attain self-realization. In short, always chanting the name of the guru, and meditating on him enables us to see him in all beings, and it confers eternal bliss on us. The following story will illustrate this.

KAKASAHEB'S DOUBT AND ANANDRAO'S VISION

It is known that Sai Baba had directed Kakasaheb Dixit to read two works of Sri Ekanath daily, *Bhagawat* and *Bhawartha Ramayana*. Kakasaheb read these daily while Baba was living and followed the practice even after Baba's passing. One morning in Kaka Mahajani's house in Mumbai, Kakasaheb was reading the *Bhagawat*. Shama and Mahajani were present and listened attentively to the portion read, the 2nd Chapter, 11th *Skandha* (verse) of the book. There, the nine Naths or Siddhas of the Rishabha family—Kavi, Hari, Antariksha, Prabuddha, Pippalayan, Avirhotra, Drumil, Chamas, Karabhajan—expounded the principles of the Bhagawat Dharma to King Janaka. King

Janaka asked all the nine Naths the most important questions and each of them answered satisfactorily:

1. Kavi explained what is Bhagawat Dharma.
2. Hari explained the characteristics of a bhakti.
3. Antariksha explained what is Maya.
4. Prabuddha explained how to cross Maya.
5. Pippalayan explained what is Parabrahman.
6. Avirhotra explained what is karma.
7. Drumil explained the incarnations of God and their deeds.
8. Chamas explained how a non-devotee fares after death.
9. Karabhajan explained the different modes of worship of God in different ages.

The substance of all these discussions was that in this Kali age the only means of liberation was the remembrance of the Lord's or guru's feet. After the reading was over, Kakasaheb said in a despondent tone to Shama and the others, "How wonderful is the discourse of the nine Naths on devotion. But at the same time, how difficult it is to put it into practice! The Naths were perfect, but is it possible for fools like us to attain the devotion as described by them? We won't get it even after several births, then how are we to get liberation? It seems that there is no hope for us."

Shama did not like this pessimistic attitude of Kakasaheb. He said, "It is a pity that one who has the good luck to have such a jewel as Baba, should cry out so disparagingly. If he has unwavering faith in Baba, why should he feel restless? The bhakti of the Naths may be strong and wonderful, but is not ours loving and affectionate? And has not Baba told us authoritatively that remembering and chanting Hari's name and the guru's name brings liberation? Then where is the cause for fear and anxiety?" But Kakasaheb was not satisfied with Shama's explanation. He continued to be anxious and restless the whole day, thinking and brooding over how to get the powerful bhakti of the Naths. The next morning, the following miracle took place.

A gentleman named Anandrao Pakhade came there in search of Shama. The reading of the *Bhagawat* was going on. Pakhade sat near Shama and whispered something to him. He was mentioning his dream-vision in a low tone. As there was some interruption in the reading by this whispering, Kakasaheb stopped the reading and asked Shama what the matter was. Shama said, "Yesterday you expressed your doubt, now here is the explanation for it.

Hear Pakhade's vision that Baba gave him explaining the saving characteristic of devotion and showing that devotion in the form of worshipping the guru's feet is sufficient." All were anxious to hear the vision, especially Kakasaheb. At their suggestion, Pakhade began to share his vision:

I was standing in a deep sea in waist-deep water. All of a sudden I saw Sai Baba there. He was sitting on a beautiful throne studded with diamonds, with his feet in the water. I was most pleased and satisfied to see Baba's form. The vision was so realistic that I did not think that it was a dream. Curiously enough, Shama was also standing there. He said to me with emotion, "Anandrao, fall at Baba's feet."

I responded, "I want to but his feet are in water, how can I place my head on them? I am helpless."

Hearing this Shama said to Baba, "Oh Deva, take your feet out from under the water." Baba then took out his feet and I immediately grabbed them and bowed to them.

On seeing this, Baba blessed me saying, "Go now, you will be happy, there is no cause for fear and anxiety." He also added, "Give a silk-bordered dhotar to my Shama, you will profit from it."

In compliance with Baba's order, Pakhade had brought a dhotar and requested Kakasaheb to give it to Shama. But Shama refused to accept it, saying that unless Baba gave a hint that he should accept it, he would not. After some discussion, Kakasaheb decided to cast lots. Invariably, Kakasaheb used to cast lots when he was uncertain what to do and would abide by the decision shown in the picked up chit or lot. In this particular case, two chits, on one of which was written 'To accept' and on another 'To reject', were placed at the feet of Baba's picture and a child was then asked to pick one of them. The 'To accept' chit was picked up and the dhotar was accepted by Shama. In this way both, Anandrao and Shama were satisfied and Kakasaheb's difficulty was solved.

This story urges us to give respect to the words of other saints, but at the same time asks us to have full faith in our Mother, the guru, and abide by his instructions for he knows our welfare better than any other person. Carve on your heart the following words of Baba:

There are innumerable saints in this world, but 'our father' is the Father (real guru). Others might say many good things, but we should never forget our guru's words. In short, love your guru wholeheartedly, surrender to him completely and prostrate yourselves before him reverently and then you will see that there is no sea of mundane existence before you to cross and there is no darkness before the sun.

✤

BABA SLEEPING ON A WOODEN PLANK

In his earlier days, Baba slept on a wooden plank, four arms in length and only a span in breadth, with earthen lamps burning at the four corners. Later on he broke the plank into pieces and threw it away. Once Baba was describing the greatness of this plank to Kakasaheb. Hearing this, Kakasaheb said to Baba, "You still love the wooden plank. I will suspend one in the masjid again for you to sleep at ease."

Baba replied, "I won't like sleeping up, leaving Mhalsapati down on the ground."

Then Kakasaheb said, "I will provide another plank for Mhalsapati."

Baba said:

How can Mhalsapati sleep on the plank? It is not easy to sleep up on the plank. Only he who has many good qualities can do so. Only he who can sleep with his eyes wide open can achieve that. When I go to sleep I often ask Mhalsapati to sit by my side, place his hand on my heart and watch the chanting of the Lord's name there, and if he finds me sleepy, wake me up. He can't even do this. He himself gets drowsy and begins to nod his head. When I feel his hand heavy as a stone on my heart and cry out, 'Oh Bhagat!' he moves and opens his eyes. How can he, who can't sit and sleep well on the ground and whose posture is not steady and who is a slave to sleep, sleep high up on a plank?

On many other occasions Baba said, out of love for his devotees, "What is ours, whether good or bad, is with us, and what is another's is with him."

Pranams to Sri Sai

Peace Be to All

CHAPTER FORTY-SIX

BABA'S BODH GAYA TRIP & THE STORY OF THE GOATS

This chapter describes Shama's trip to Varanasi, Prayag and Bodh Gaya and how Baba, in the form of his portrait, was there ahead of him. It also describes Baba's reminiscences of the past birth of two goats.

PRELIMINARY

Chanting your sweet name is the easiest sadhana for devotees.

Blessed, Oh Sai, are your feet. Blessed is remembrance of you and blessed is your darshan, which frees us from the bondage of karma. Though your form is invisible to us now, still if devotees believe in you, they receive living experiences from you. By an invisible and subtle thread you draw your devotees from far and near to your feet and embrace them like a kind and loving mother. The devotees do not know where you are, but you so skillfully pull the wires that they ultimately realize that you are at their back to help and support them. The intelligent, wise and learned fall into the pit of the samsara on account of their egoism, but you save the poor, simple and devout through your power. You play the whole game inwardly and invisibly but demonstrate that you are unconcerned with it. You do things but pose as a non-doer. No one knows your life.

The best course then is for us is to surrender our body, speech and mind to your feet and always chant your name to destroy our sins and karmas. You fulfill the wishes of devotees and to those who are without any desire you give bliss supreme. Chanting your sweet name is the easiest sadhana for devotees. By this sadhana, our negative karmas, and rajasic and tamasic qualities will vanish, and the sattvic, the pure and virtuous qualities, will gain predominance; along with this, discrimination, dispassion and knowledge will follow. Then we shall abide in our Self and our guru, who are one and the same. This is what is called complete surrender to the guru. The only sure sign of this is that our mind becomes calm and peaceful. The greatness of this surrender, devotion and knowledge is unique; for peace, non-attachment, fame and salvation, come in its train.

If Baba accepts a devotee, he follows him and stands by him, day and night, at his home or far away. Let the devotee go anywhere he likes, Baba is there ahead of him in some form or in some inconceivable manner. The following story illustrates this.

⚜

TRIP TO BODH GAYA

Sometime after Kakasaheb Dixit was introduced to Sai Baba, he decided to perform the thread ceremony of his eldest son at Nagpur. At the same time, Nanasaheb Chandorkar decided to perform the marriage ceremony of his eldest son at Gwalior. Both Kakasaheb and Nanasaheb came to Shirdi and lovingly invited Baba to these functions. Baba asked them to take Shama as his representative. When he was pressed to come in person, Baba told them to take Shama with them and, "After going to Benares and Prayag, we will be there ahead of Shama." Now mark these words for they show Baba's all-pervasiveness.

After receiving Baba's permission, Shama decided to attend both these functions then go on to Benares, Prayag and Bodh Gaya. Appa Kote decided to accompany him. They both went first to Nagpur for the thread ceremony then to Gwalior for the marriage ceremony. They went on to Ayodhya and visited the Rama Temple where they stayed for 21 days, next visited Benares, then left for Bodh Gaya by train.

On the train, they both felt uneasy after hearing that there were incidences of plague in Bodh Gaya. They arrived late in the evening at the Bodh Gaya station, and went to stay at the *Dharmashala*, pilgrim lodging. In the morning, the *Gayawala*, the priest who provides for lodging of pilgrims, came to their aid, "The pilgrims have already started. You better hurry." Shama casually asked him whether there was plague in Bodh Gaya. "No," said the Gayawala. "Please come without any fear or anxiety and see for yourself."

They went with him and stayed in his house, which was a large and spacious wada. Shama was pleased with the accommodations, but what pleased him most was the beautiful large portrait of Baba fixed in the central front portion of the building. Seeing this portrait, Shama was overwhelmed with emotion. He remembered Baba's words that he would be ahead of Shama after going to Benares and Prayag, and burst into tears. His hairs stood on end, his throat was choked and he began to sob. The Gayawala thought he was crying because he was afraid of plague.

But Shama inquired where he had gotten the Baba portrait. The Gayawala replied that he had 200 or 300 agents working who looked after the pilgrims to Bodh Gaya and he heard about Baba from them. After hearing about Baba, about 12 years ago he went to Shirdi himself and had Baba's darshan. In Shirdi, he saw the portrait of Baba that hung in Shama's house and was drawn to it. Shama gave the portrait to him with Baba's permission. This was the same portrait. Shama then remembered this former incident. The Gayawalas's joy knew no bounds when he learned that the same Shama who had helped him before was his guest now. Then they both exchanged love and service and were delighted and happy. The Gayawala gave him a royal welcome. He was a very rich man; he sat in a palanquin and made Shama ride an elephant and attended to all his comforts and conveniences.

The moral of the story is this: Baba's words came true to the letter and unbounded was his love for devotees. But leave this aside. He also loved all creatures equally, for he knew that he was one with them. The following story will illustrate this.

TWO GOATS

Once when Baba was returning from Lendi he saw a flock of goats. Two of them attracted his attention. He went to them, caressed and fondled them, then bought them for Rs.32. The devotees were surprised at this conduct by Baba. They thought that Baba was duped in this bargain, as the goats would normally fetch Rs.2 each, at the most Rs.3 or 4 each. They began to take Baba to task for this, but Baba kept calm and cool. Shama and Tatya asked Baba for an explanation. He said he should not store money as he had no home or any family to look after. He asked them to purchase four seers of *dhal* (lentil) and feed the goats at his expense. After this was done, Baba returned the goats to the owner of the flock and gave the following reminiscences about the goats:

Oh, Shama and Tatya, you think that I have been deceived in this bargain. No. Listen to their story. In their former birth, they were human beings and had the good fortune to be my companions and sit by my side. They were brothers from the same womb, loving each other at first, but later on, they became enemies.

The elder brother was an idle fellow, while the younger one was an active chap and earned a lot of money. The elder brother became greedy and jealous and wanted to kill his younger brother and take his money. They forgot their brotherly relationship and began to quarrel with each other. The elder brother resorted to many devices to kill his younger brother but all of his attempts failed. So they became deadly enemies.

Finally, there came a time when the elder brother gave a deadly blow to the younger brother's head with a big stick, and the younger brother struck the elder with an axe, and they both fell dead on the spot.

As a result of their actions, they were both born as goats. As they passed by me, I recognized them at once. I remembered their past history. Taking pity on them, I wanted to feed them and give them rest and comfort. That is the reason I spent all the money for which you criticize me. As you did not like my bargain, I sent the goats back to their shepherd.

Such was Sai's love for the goats!

Pranams to Sri Sai

Peace Be to All

CHAPTER FORTY-SEVEN

BABA REMINISCENCES

B lessed is the face of Sai. If we cast a glance at him for a moment, he destroys the sorrow of many past births and bestows great bliss on us. If he looks at us with grace, the bondage of our karma is immediately snapped away and we are led to happiness. The River Ganges washes away the dirt and sins of all people who go to her for a bath but she longs intently for the saints to come to her and bless her with their feet and remove all the dirt (sins) accumulated in her. She knows that only the holy feet of the saints can purify this accumulation. Sai is the crest-jewel of saints, and now hear from him the following purifying story.

⚜

BABA TELLS THE STORY OF THE SNAKE AND THE FROG

Greed for money drags the greedy man to the lowest level and ultimately brings destruction on him and others.

Sai Baba told this story:

One morning after taking my breakfast I strolled along until I came to a small riverbank. As I was tired, I rested there, washed my hands and feet and had a bath and felt refreshed. There was a footpath and a cart track sheltered by shady trees. The breeze was blowing gently. As I was preparing to smoke my chillum I heard the croaking of a frog. I was striking the flint and lighting the fire when a traveller turned up and sat by my side, bowed to me and politely invited me to his house for meals and rest.

He lit up the pipe and handed it over to me. The croaking was heard again and he wanted to know what it was. I told him that a frog was in trouble and was tasting the bitter fruit of its karma. We have to reap now the fruit of what we have sown in our past life, and there is no use in crying about it. Then he smoked and handed the pipe over to me and said that he would go and see for himself. I told him that a frog was caught by a big snake and was crying. Both were very wicked in their past life and were now reaping the fruit of their actions in these bodies. He went and found a huge black serpent was holding a big frog in its mouth.

He returned to me and said that in about 10 minutes the frog would be eaten up by the snake. I said, "No, this can't be. I am its father, its protector, and am here now. How can I allow the snake to eat it up, am I here for nothing? See how I release it."

After smoking again, we walked to that place. He was afraid and asked me not to proceed further as the snake might attack us. Not minding him, I went ahead and addressed the creatures this way, "Oh Veerbhadrappa, has not your enemy, Chenbassappa, repented yet? Though he has been born as a frog, and though you have been born as a serpent, still you maintain bitter enmity against him. Fie upon you, you should be ashamed. Give up your hatred now and rest in peace." Hearing these words, the snake left the frog quickly and dived into the river and disappeared. The frog also jumped away and hid in the bushes.

The traveller was much surprised. He said that he could not understand how the snake dropped the frog and disappeared by the words uttered, or who Veerbhadrappa was and who Chenbassappa was, and what the cause of the enmity was. I returned with him to the foot of the tree and after sharing a few puffs of smoke with him, explained the whole mystery to him.

There was an ancient holy place sanctified by a temple of Mahadev (Shiva) about four or five miles from my place. As the temple was old and dilapidated, the residents collected funds for its repairs. After a large amount was collected, arrangements were made for worship and plans with estimates for repairs were prepared. A local rich man was appointed treasurer and the entire work was entrusted to him. He was to keep regular accounts and be honest in all his dealings. But he was a first-class miser and spent very little for the repairs, which consequently allowed for very little progress. He then spent all the funds, took some himself and spent nothing from his pocket. He had a sweet tongue and was very clever in offering plausible explanations regarding the poor and tardy progress of the work. The people went to him again and said that unless he lent his helping hand and tried his best, the work would not be complete. They requested him to work out the plan, then collected donations again and sent the amount to him. He received them, but was quiet as before without making any progress.

After some days, Mahadev appeared in his wife's dream and said to her, "You get up and build the dome of the temple. I will give you a hundredfold of what you spend." She told this vision to her husband. As he was afraid that this would involve some expense for him, he laughed it off saying that it was a just a dream, not a thing to be relied and acted upon, or else why didn't God appear to him and tell him? Was he far off from her? This looked like a bad dream with an aim to create ill feeling between husband and wife. So she had to remain quiet.

God does not like big donations collected against the wishes of the donors, but he likes even small amounts when given with love, devotion and appreciation. Some days after, God again appeared in her dream and said, "Do not bother yourself about your husband and the donations kept by him. Don't press him to spend any amount for the temple. What I want is feeling and devotion. So give anything of your own, if you like."

She consulted her husband about this vision and decided to give God the ornaments that had been given to her by her father. The miser felt disconcerted and decided to cheat even God in this. He undervalued the ornaments at Rs.1,000, then bought them himself and instead of giving that amount gave a field to God as a donation. The wife agreed to this. The field was actually not his, it belonged to a poor woman named Dubaki, who had mortgaged it to him for Rs.200. She had not been able to redeem it for a long time. So the cunning miser cheated everyone, his wife, Dubaki and even God.

The land was barren, uncultivated and worth nothing and yielded nothing, even in the best seasons.

The transaction ended and the land was given in possession to the poor priest, who was pleased with the donation. Sometime later, strange things happened. There was a terrific storm and a heavy downpour of rain; lightning struck the house of the miser and both he and his wife were killed. Dubaki also breathed her last.

In the next life, the rich miser was born into a Brahmin family and was named Veerbhadrappa. His devout wife was born as the daughter of the priest of the temple and was named Gauri. Dubaki was born as a man into the family of the attendant of the temple and was named Chenbassappa. The priest was a friend of mine who came to see me often, chatting and smoking with me. His daughter Gauri was also devoted to me. She was growing fast and her father was seeking a good husband for her. I told him not to worry as the bridegroom himself would come seeking her. Then there came a poor boy of their caste named Veerbhadrappa, wandering and begging for bread at the priest's house. With my consent, Gauri was given in marriage to him. At first, he was also devoted to me, as I had recommended his marriage with Gauri. But even in his new life, he was hankering after money and asked me to help him to get it as he was now leading a married man's life.

Strange things happened. There was a sudden rise in prices. By Gauri's good luck, there was a great demand for land and the land that had been donated was sold for one lakh of rupees (100 times the worth of her ornaments). Half the amount was paid in cash and the remaining was to be paid in 25 installments of Rs. 2,000 each. All agreed to this transaction but then began to quarrel over the money. They came to consult me. I told them that the property belonged to God. It was entrusted to the priest and Gauri, who was his sole heiress and proprietress, and no amount should be spent without her consent and her husband had no right whatsoever to the amount.

Hearing my opinion, Veerbhadrappa was angry with me and said that I wanted to establish Gauri's claim and embezzle her property. Hearing his words, I remembered God and kept quiet. Veerbhadrappa scolded his wife Gauri, and she came to me at noon and requested me not to listen to the words of others and not to discard her as she was my daughter. As she had sought my protection, I gave her a pledge that I would cross seven seas to help her. Then that night Gauri had a vision. Mahadev appeared in her dream and said, "All of the money is yours, do not give anything to anyone. Spend some amount for temple purposes in consultation with Chenbassappa and if you want to use it for some other purpose, consult Baba in the masjid."

Gauri told me about the vision and I gave her proper advice in the matter. I told her to take the principal amount for herself, give half the amount of interest to Chenbassappa and that Veerbhadrappa had nothing to do in the matter. While I was talking, both Veerbhadrappa and Chenbassappa came quarreling. I tried my best to appease them and told them God's vision to Gauri. Veerbhadrappa got wild and angry and threatened to kill Chenbassappa and cut him to pieces. Chenbassappa was timid and caught my feet and sought my refuge. I pledged myself to save him from the wrath of his foe. After some time, Veerbhadrappa died and was born as a snake and Chenbassappa died and was born as a frog. Hearing the croaking of Chenbassappa and remembering my pledge, I came here, saved him and kept my word. God runs to his devotees for help in times of danger. He saved Chenbassappa (the frog) by sending me here. All this is God's leela or sport.

⚜

THE MORAL

The moral of the story is that one has to reap what one sows, that there is no escape unless one suffers and squares up one's old debts and dealings with others, and that greed for money drags the greedy man to the lowest level and ultimately brings destruction on him and others.

Pranams to Sri Sai

Peace Be to All

CHAPTER FORTY-EIGHT

WARDING OFF A DEVOTEE'S CALAMITIES

At the start of this chapter, Hemadpant responds to a question whether Sai Baba was a guru or sadguru. Hemadpant answers by describing the signs of a sadguru.

❧

SIGNS OF SADGURU

We do not develop love for anything unless we feel intently about it. Where there is real yearning and feeling, God manifests Himself; this is love and this is the means of liberation.

He who teaches us the *Vedas* and Vedanta or the six *Shastras* (scriptures), he who controls the breath or brands his body with *mudras* (sacred symbols), he who gives pleasing discourses regarding Brahman, he who gives *mantras* (sacred syllables) to disciples and orders them to chant them a certain number of times but does not assure them any result in a definite time, he who by his expansive wordy knowledge explains beautifully the Ultimate Principle, but has himself no experience or self-realization, is not a sadguru. But he who, through his speech, creates in us a distaste for the enjoyments of this world and the next, and gives us a taste of self-realization, who is well-versed in both theoretical and applied knowledge (self-realization), deserves to be called a sadguru. How can he who is lacking in self-realization give it to the disciples? A sadguru does not expect any service or profit from his disciples, even in his dream. On the contrary, he only wishes to serve them. He does not think that he is great and the disciple small. Not only does he love him as a son, but regards him as an equal to him or as Brahman. The main characteristic of a sadguru is that he is the abode of peace. He is never restless or distressed. He has no pride of learning. The poor and the rich, the small and the great, are the same to him.

Hemadpant thinks that it is on account of the accumulation of merits from his past births that he had the good fortune of meeting and being blessed by such a sadguru as Sai Baba. Even in youth, Baba hoarded nothing except perhaps his chillum. He had no family, no friend, no home, nor any support. Since he was eighteen, his control of mind was perfect and extraordinary. He lived fearlessly in a secluded place and always abided in his Self. Seeing the pure attachment of his devotees, he always acted in their interest and so in a way was dependent on them. Those who are attached to him, even today after his mahasamadhi, acquire the experiences he gave to his devotees while he was living in flesh. What devotees have to do is to trim their heart-lamp of faith and devotion and burn in it wicks of love and when this is done, the flame of knowledge (self-realization) will be lit and shine bright. Mere knowledge without love is dry. No one wants such knowledge. Without love there is no contentment, so we should have unbroken and unbounded love. How can we praise love? Everything is insignificant before it. Without love, our reading, hearing and studying are of no benefit. In the wake of love, devotion, dispassion, peace and liberation follow with all their treasures. We do not develop love for anything unless we feel intently about it. Where there is real yearning and feeling, God manifests Himself; this is love and this is the means of liberation.

Now let us revert to the main story of this chapter. Let a man go to a true saint with a pure mind and hold his feet. Eventually he is sure to be saved. This is illustrated by the following stories.

MR. SHEVADE

Mr. Sapatnekar of Akkalkot was studying the law. A fellow student named Shevade had gathered with him and other students to compare their study notes. During their question and answer session it was revealed that Shevade was the least prepared of all for the examination and so the students derided him. He said that though he was not prepared he was sure to pass the examination, as his Sai Baba was there to get him through it successfully. Mr. Sapatnekar was surprised at this remark. He took Shevade aside and asked him who was Sai Baba whom he praised so highly.

Shevade replied, "There lives a fakir in a masjid in Shirdi. He is a great *satpurusha*. There are other saints but he is unique. Unless there is a great store of merit in one's account, one can't see him. I fully believe in him, and what he says is never untrue. He has assured me that next year I will definitely pass. I am confident that I will get through the final examination with his grace." Mr. Sapatneker laughed at his friend's confidence and jeered at him and Baba. When Shevade later passed his exam successfully, Mr. Sapatnekar was quite surprised.

THE SAPATNEKARS

Mr. Sapatnekar passed his examination, settled at Akkalkot and practiced law there. Ten years later, in 1913, he lost his only son to a throat disease. This broke his heart. He sought relief by making a pilgrimage to Pandharpur, Gangapur and other holy places. He found no peace of mind. He also read Vedanta, which did not help. In the meantime, he remembered Shevade's remarks and faith in Baba and thought that he should go to Shirdi and see Baba. So he went to Shirdi with his younger brother and was much pleased to see Baba from a distance. He went close and with pure devotion, prostrated before Baba placing a coconut before him. But Baba immediately cried out, "Get away!"

Sapatnekar hung down his head, moved back and sat to the side. He wanted to consult someone who could advise him how to proceed. Someone mentioned Bala Shimpi's name. Sapatnekar saw Shimpi and sought his help. They bought some photos of Baba and came with them to the masjid. Shimpi took a photo in his hand, gave it to Baba and asked him whose photo it was. Baba said that the photo was of the lover of him, pointing to Sapatnekar. Saying this, Baba laughed and everyone joined in. Shimpi asked Baba why he laughed and beckoned Sapatnekar to come forward and have darshan. When Saptnakar began to prostrate before Baba, Baba again cried, "Get out!" Sapatnekar did not know what to do. They both joined their hands in prayer and sat before Baba praying. Baba finally ordered Sapatnekar to leave immediately. Both devotees were sad and dejected. As Baba's order had to be obeyed, Sapatnekar left Shirdi with a heavy heart praying that he would be allowed to have darshan next time.

Mrs. Sapatnekar

One year elapsed. Still his mind was not at peace. He went to Gangapur, where he felt even more restless. Then he went to Madhegaon and finally decided to go to Kashi. Two days before starting, his wife had a vision. In her dream, she was going with a pitcher to Lakadsha's well. There a fakir with a piece of cloth around his head, who was sitting at the foot of the neem tree, came close to her and said, "My dear lassie, why get exhausted for nothing? I will get your pitcher filled with pure water." She was afraid of the fakir and hurried back with the empty pitcher. The fakir followed her. At this, she was awakened and opened her eyes.

She told this vision to her husband. They thought it was an auspicious sign, so both left for Shirdi. When they reached the masjid, Baba was not there. He had gone to Lendi, so they waited for his return. When he returned, she was surprised to see that the fakir she had seen in her vision looked exactly like Baba. She prostrated herself with devotion before Baba and sat looking at him.

Seeing her humility, Baba was much pleased and began to tell a story to another person there in his characteristically peculiar fashion. He said, "My arms, abdomen and waist have been paining me for a long time. I took many medicines, but the pains did not stop. I got sick of the medicines as they gave me no relief, but I am surprised to see now that all the pains have immediately disappeared." Though no name was mentioned, it was the story of Mrs. Sapatnekar. The pains, as described by Baba, soon left her and she became happy.

Then Mr. Sapatnekar went ahead to take darshan. He was again welcomed with the same, "Get out!" But this time he was more repentant and persevering. He knew that Baba's displeasure was due to his past deeds and resolved to make amends for them. He was determined to see Baba alone and ask forgiveness for his past actions. This he did. He placed his head on Baba's feet and Baba placed his hand on his head. Sapatnekar then sat stroking Baba's leg.

Then a shepherdess came and began massaging Baba's back at the same time. Baba began to tell a story of a merchant in his characteristic way. He related the various vicissitudes in the merchant's life, including the death of his only son. Sapatnekar was surprised to see that the story which Baba related was actually his own and wondered how Baba knew every detail of it. He realized that Baba was omniscient and knew the hearts of all. When this thought crossed his mind, Baba addressed the shepherdess while pointing to Sapatnekar and said, "This fellow blames me and charges me with killing his son. Do I kill people's children? Why does this fellow come to the masjid and cry? Now I will do this. I will bring that very child back again in his wife's womb." With these words Baba placed his hand on Sapatnekar's head, blessing and comforting him saying, "These feet are old and holy, you are carefree now. Place all your faith in me and you will soon get your desire." Sapatnekar was moved with emotion and bathed Baba's feet with his tears, then returned to his residence.

He made preparations for worship and naivedya, then returned to the masjid with his wife. He offered this to Baba and accepted prasad from him. Among the crowd in the masjid, Sapatnekar saluted Baba again and again. Seeing heads clashing against heads, Baba said, "Oh, why do you prostrate yourself again and again? One namaskar offered with love and humility is enough." Then later that night, Sapatnekar witnessed the Chavadi procession as described earlier. In that procession, Baba looked like a veritable Vithal.

When parting the next day, Sapatnekar thought that he should first pay one rupee as dakshina and then if Baba asked again, instead of saying no, he should pay one more, thus reserving a sufficient amount for his journey. When he went to the masjid and offered one rupee, Baba asked for another as this was Sapatnekar's intention. When it was paid, Baba blessed him saying, "Take the coconut, put it in your wife's *oti* (upper fold of sari), then go away relieved and without the least anxiety." He did so, and within a year a son was born to him. When the infant was eight months old the couple came to Shirdi, placed him at Baba's feet and prayed, "Oh Sainath, we do not know how to repay you, so we prostrate before you. Bless us, we are poor and helpless, hereafter let your holy feet be our only refuge. Many thoughts and ideas trouble us in waking and dream states, so bless us and turn our minds away from them to your bhajans."

The son was named Murlidhar. Then two additional sons were also born to them. The Sapatnekars realized that Baba's words were never unfulfilled nor untrue, but turned out literally to be true.

Pranams to Sri Sai

Peace Be to All

CHAPTER FORTY-NINE

Meditation on the sadguru is the best of all. So we should chant Sai's name, think over his sayings, meditate on his form, feel real love for him in our hearts and do all our actions for his sake.

If the *Vedas* and the *Puranas* cannot sufficiently praise Brahman or the sadguru, how can we who are ignorant describe our sadguru Sai Baba? We think it is best to keep quiet in this matter. In reality, the observance of silence is the best way of praising the sadguru. But the good qualities of Sai Baba make us forget our vow of silence and inspire us to open our mouth. Good dishes taste flat without the company of friends and relatives to share the food with us. When they join us, food acquires greater flavor. The same is the case with the *Sai leelamrita*, the nectar of Sai's leelas. We cannot partake of this nectar alone. Friends and brothers have to join us, the more the better.

It is Sai Baba himself that inspires these stories and gets them written as he desires. Our duty is to surrender completely to him and meditate on him. Practicing austerities is better than pilgrimage, vow, sacrifice and charity. Worshipping the Lord is better than austerities, and meditation on the sadguru is the best of all. So we should chant Sai's name, think over his sayings, meditate on his form, feel real love for him in our hearts and do all our actions for his sake. There is no better means than this to break the bondage of samsara. If we can do our part to perform these duties, Sai is certain to help and liberate us. Now let us return to the stories of this chapter.

HARI KANOBA TESTS BABA

A gentleman from Mumbai named Hari Kanoba heard many stories of Baba's leelas from his friends and relatives. As he was a 'doubting Thomas' and did not believe in them, he wanted to test Baba himself. So he came to Shirdi with some of his Mumbai friends. He wore a lace-bordered turban on his head and a new pair of sandals on his feet. Seeing Baba from a distance he thought of prostrating before him but he did not know what to do with his new sandals. He went outside to the corner of the open courtyard and placed them there, then went into the masjid and took Baba's darshan. He bowed reverently to Baba, took udi and prasad from him and returned to where he placed his sandals. When he reached the corner, he found to his dismay that his sandals had disappeared. He searched for them in vain then returned to his lodging very dejected.

He bathed, offered worship and naivedya then sat for meals, but all the while he was thinking about nothing but his sandals. After finishing his meals, he came out to wash his hands when he saw a boy coming towards him. The boy had a stick in his hand on top of which was suspended his new pair of sandals. He told the men who had come to wash their hands that Baba had sent him with this stick in his hand and told him to walk through the streets crying, "Hari Ka Beta! Jari Ka Pheta!" Baba told him, "If anyone claims these sandals, first be sure that his name is Hari, that he is the son of Ka (Kanoba), and that he is wearing a lace-bordered turban, then give them to him."

Hearing this, Hari Kanoba was happily surprised. He went to the boy and claimed the sandals as his own. He told him that his name was Hari and that he was the son of Ka (Kanoba) and showed him his lace-bordered turban. The boy was satisfied and returned the sandals to him. Hari Kanoba thought that as his lace-bordered turban was visible to all Baba might have seen it, but how could he know his name was Hari and that he was the son of Kanoba, as this was his first trip to Shirdi? He came to Shirdi with the sole object of testing Baba and with no other motive. He came to know through this incident that Baba was a great satpurusha. He had gotten what he wanted and returned home very happy.

SOMADEVA SWAMI TESTS BABA

Now hear the story of another man who came to test Baba. Kakasaheb's brother, Bhaiji from Nagpur, went to the Himalayas in 1906 and made an acquaintance with Somadeva Swami of Haridwar. They both wrote each other's names down in their diaries. Five years later, Somadeva Swami came to Nagpur as Bhaiji's guest. There he was happy to hear about Baba's leelas and a strong desire arose in his mind to go to Shirdi to see him.

After receiving a letter of introduction from Bhaiji, he left for Shirdi. When he arrived in Shirdi he saw two large flags flying over the masjid. Generally, we see that saints have different behavior, modes of living and outward paraphernalia. But we should never use these outward signs to judge the value of a saint. But with Somadeva Swami it was different. As soon as he saw the flags flying, he thought, 'Why should a saint take a liking for flags, does this represent sainthood? It means the saint is hankering after fame.' Thinking this way, he decided to cancel his trip and told his fellow travellers that he was going back.

They asked him, "Why did you travel so long? If your mind gets restless by the sight of flags, how much more agitated will you become on seeing the *ratha* (small carriage), palanquin, horse and all the other paraphernalia?"

The Swami became even more confounded and said, "I have not seen sadhus with horses, palanquins and tom-toms. It is better for me to return than see such sadhus." Saying this he started to leave. His fellow travellers pressed him not to go. Instead, they asked him to stop his crooked way of thinking and told him that Baba did not care a bit for flags and other paraphernalia or for fame. It was his devotees that kept up all the paraphernalia out of love and devotion to him.

He was finally persuaded to continue his journey and go to see Baba. Finally, when he saw Baba from the courtyard, he immediately melted inside, his eyes became full of tears, his throat choked and all his evil and crooked thoughts vanished. He remembered his guru's saying that, "Our abode and place of rest is where the mind is most happy and blessed." He wanted to roll in the dust at Baba's feet but when he approached Baba, Baba got wild and cried aloud, "Let all our humbug (paraphernalia) be with us. You go back to your home, beware if you come back to this masjid! Why take darshan of one who flies a flag over his masjid? Is this a sign of sainthood? Do not remain here for a moment."

The Swami was taken aback. He realized that Baba had read his heart and spoken it aloud. How omniscient he was! He saw that Baba was intelligent, noble and pure. He watched Baba embracing one person, touching another with his hand, comforting others, staring kindly at some, laughing at others, giving udi to some and making everyone happy and satisfying all. Why should he be dealt with so harshly? Thinking seriously like this, he came to realized that Baba's conduct reflected his inner thoughts exactly and he needed to take a lesson from it and improve. Baba's wrath was actually a blessing in disguise. Needless to say, later on, his faith in Baba was firmly established and he became a staunch devotee.

Baba Teaches How to Handle the Senses

Once when Nanasaheb Chandorkar was sitting in the masjid with Mhalsapati and others, a Muslim gentleman from Bijapur came with his family to see Baba. Seeing veiled women with him, Nanasaheb wanted to go away, but Baba prevented him from doing so. The women came and had darshan of Baba. When one of the ladies briefly removed her veil to pranam to Baba's feet, Nanasaheb saw her face and was completely smitten with her rare beauty and wanted to see her face again.

Knowing Nanasaheb's restless mind, Baba spoke to him after the woman left:

Nana, why are you getting agitated in vain? Let the senses do their duty; we should not meddle with their work. God has created this beautiful world and it is our duty to appreciate its beauty. The mind will become steady and calm slowly and gradually. When the front door is open, why go by the back one? When the heart is pure, there is no difficulty whatsoever. Why should one be afraid of anyone if there is no evil thought in us? The eyes may do their work but why should you feel shy and shaky?

Shama could not follow the meaning of what Baba said. So he asked Nanasaheb about this on their way home. Nanasaheb told him about his restlessness at the sight of the beautiful lady, and how Baba knew and advised him about it. Nanasaheb explained Baba's meaning:

Our mind is fickle by nature; it should not be allowed to get wild. The senses may get restless, the body, however, should be held in check and not allowed to be impatient. Senses run after objects, but we should not follow them and crave for them. By slow and gradual practice, restlessness can be conquered. Although we should not be swayed by the senses, they cannot be completely controlled. We should curb them appropriately according to the needs of the occasion. Beauty is the subject of sight; we should look at the beauty of objects without fear. There is no room for shyness or fear. But we should never entertain evil thoughts. Making the mind desireless, observe God's works of beauty. In this way, the senses will easily and naturally be controlled and even when enjoying objects you will be reminded of God. If the outer senses are not held in check, and if the mind is allowed to run after objects and is attached to them, our cycle of births and deaths will not come to an end. Objects of the senses are harmful. With *viveka* (discrimination) as our charioteer, we will control the mind and will not allow the senses to go astray. With such a charioteer we will reach *Vishnu pada*, the final abode, our real home from which there is no return.

Pranams to Sri Sai

Peace Be to All

CHAPTER FIFTY

Victory to Sai who is the devotees' support, who is our sadguru, who explains the meaning of the *Bhagavad Gita* and who gives us all powers. Oh Sai, look favorably on us and bless us all.

Sandalwood trees grow on the Malaya mountains and ward off heat. The clouds pour rain and cool and refresh all the people. The flowers blossom in the spring and enable us to worship God. So the stories of Sai Baba are revealed in order to give solace and comfort to the readers. Both those who tell and those who hear the stories of Baba are blessed and holy, as are the mouths of those who tell and the ears of those who hear.

It is a well-established fact that although we may try hundreds of sadhanas, we do not attain the spiritual goal of life unless a sadguru blesses us with his grace. Hear the following story that illustrates this.

✦

KAKASAHEB DIXIT

"I draw to me my man from far off or even across the seven seas,
like a sparrow with a string fastened to its feet."

Kakasaheb was born in 1864 into a Brahmin family. After finishing his primary education, he completed his secondary education at Nagpur. After graduation from college in 1883, he passed his law and solicitor's examinations and started a solicitor's firm of his own.

Before 1909, Kakasaheb had not heard of Sai Baba but soon after that he became one of Baba's great devotees. While he was staying at Lonavla, he happened to see his old friend Nanasaheb Chandorkar. They spent some time talking about many things. Kakasaheb described how when he was boarding a train in London, he met with an accident, slipped and fell and his leg was injured. Hundreds of remedies gave him no relief.

Nanasaheb told him that if he wished to get rid of the pain and lameness of his leg, he should go to his sadguru Sai Baba. He gave all of Baba's particulars and then mentioned Baba's statement, "I draw to me my man from far off or even across the seven seas, like a sparrow with a string fastened to its feet." He also made it clear to him that if he were not Baba's man, he would not be attracted to him or be given a darshan. Kakasaheb was pleased to hear all this and told Nanasaheb that he would go to see Baba and pray to him not to cure his lame leg, but his lame fickle mind and give him eternal bliss.

Some time after, Kakasaheb went to Ahmednagar and stayed with Kakasaheb Mirikar in connection with securing votes for a seat in the Bombay Legislative Council. Balasaheb Mirikar, son of Kakasaheb Mirikar, who was a Revenue Collector of Kopergaon, was also there in connection with a horse exhibition. After the election business was over, Kakasaheb wanted to go to Shirdi and both the Mirikars, father and son, were also thinking about who the right person would be to guide him. Meanwhile, Baba was arranging things for their reception.

Shama received a telegram from his father-in-law in Ahmednagar stating that his wife was seriously ill and that he needed to come. Shama went with Baba's permission, saw his mother-in-law and found her improving.

Nanasaheb Panshe and Appasaheb Gadre happened to see Shama on their way to the exhibition and they told him to go to Mirikar's house to meet Kakasaheb Dixit and take him to Shirdi. Kakasaheb Dixit and the Mirikars were also informed of Shama's arrival. In the evening Shama came to the Mirikars, who introduced him to Kakasaheb.

They arranged for Shama to leave for Kopergaon with Kakasaheb on the 10 o'clock night train. After this was settled, a curious thing happened. Balasaheb Mirikar threw aside the cover on Baba's big portrait and showed it to Kakasaheb. He was surprised to see that Baba, whom he was going to meet in Shirdi, was already there to greet him in the form of his portrait. He was very moved and bowed before the portrait. The portrait belonged to Megha. It had been sent to the Mirikars for glass repair, which had been done, and it was decided to return the portrait with Shama and Kakasaheb.

Before ten, they went to the station and booked their passage. But when the train arrived, they found that the second class was overcrowded and there was no room for them. Fortunately, the guard at the train turned out to be Kakasaheb's acquaintance and he put them up in first class. So they travelled comfortably and landed in Kopergaon. Their joy knew no bounds when they saw Nanasaheb Chandorkar there, who was also bound for Shirdi. Kakasaheb and Nanasaheb embraced each other, then after bathing in the sacred Godavari River, started for Shirdi. After arriving in Shirdi and having Baba's darshan, Kakasaheb's mind melted, his eyes were full of tears and he was overflowing with joy. Baba told him that he was waiting for him and he had sent Shama ahead to receive him.

Kakasaheb then passed many happy years in Baba's company. He built a wada in Shirdi which he made more or less his permanent home. The experiences he received from Baba are so many that it is not possible to relate them all here. The readers are advised to read a special account of them in *Shri Sai Leela* magazine (Vol 12, No. 6-9).

We close this account with the mention of one fact. Baba had comforted him by saying that in the end, "I will take you in an air coach (*Viman*)," which meant that he would make sure he had a happy death. This came to be true. On the 5th of July, 1926, he was travelling in the train with Hemadpant and talking about Sai Baba. He seemed deeply engrossed in Sai Baba. All of a sudden he threw his neck on Hemadpant's shoulder and breathed his last, with no trace of pain or distress.

⚜

SRI TEMBYE SWAMI

We come to the next story, which shows how saints love each other with brotherly affection. Sri Tembye Swami settled on the banks of Godavari. He was a devout jnani and yogi bhakta of Lord Dattatreya. Mr. Pundalikrao, a lawyer of Nanded, went to see him with some friends. While they were talking, the names of Shirdi and Sai Baba were mentioned. Hearing Baba's name, the Swami bowed his hands, then took a coconut and gave it to Pundalikrao saying, "Offer this to my brother Sai, with my pranam and ask him to not forget me, and to always love me." He added that swamis do not generally bow to others, but in this case an exception had to be made. Pundalikrao consented to take the coconut and his message to Baba. The Swami was right in calling Baba a brother, for as he maintained a *dhuni* (sacred fire) day and night, in his orthodox fashion, so too did Baba keep his dhuni ever burning in the masjid.

A month later, Pundalikrao and others left for Shirdi with the coconut. On the way, they were thirsty and stopped at a rivulet to drink some water. As water should not be drunk on an empty stomach, they took out some *chivda* (flattened rice mixed with spice) to eat with it. The chivda tasted pungent and in order to soften its flavor, at someone's suggestion they broke the coconut and mixed it into the dish to make it sweeter and more palatable.

Unfortunately, it was the coconut Pundalikrao was entrusted with. As they neared Shirdi, Pundalikrao remembered that the coconut had been entrusted to him and was very sorry that it had been broken and used in the food. With fear and trembling, he came to see Baba. Baba had already received a wireless message regarding the coconut from Tembye Swami, and so he first asked Pundalikrao to give him what was sent by his brother. He held on to Baba's feet, confessed his guilt and negligence, repented and asked for Baba's forgiveness. He offered to give another fruit as a substitute but Baba refused to accept it, saying that the worth of that coconut was by far many times more than an ordinary one, and that it could not be replaced. But then Baba added:

Now you need not worry yourself any more about this matter. It was on account of my wish that the coconut was entrusted to you and was ultimately broken on the way. Why should you take the responsibility of the actions on you? Do not entertain the sense of doership in doing good, as well as for bad deeds. Be entirely without pride and ego in all things and your spiritual progress will be rapid.

What a beautiful spiritual instruction Baba gave!

BALARAM DHURANDHAR (1878-1925)

Balaram Dhurandhar belonged to the Pathare Prabhu community, of Santa Cruz, Mumbai. He was an advocate of the Mumbai High Court and the Principal of the Government Law School in Mumbai. The whole Dhurandhar family was pious and religious. Balaram served his community and wrote and published an account of it. He then turned his attention to spiritual and religious matters. He carefully studied the *Bhagavad Gita*, and its commentary, *Jnaneshwari*, and other philosophical and metaphysical works. He was a devotee of Vithoba of Pandurang. He came in contact with Sai Baba in 1912.

Six months previously, his two brothers came to Shirdi for Baba's darshan. They returned home and shared their sweet experiences with Balaram and other family members. Then they all decided to go see Baba. Before their arrival in Shirdi, Baba had said openly to everyone, "Today many of my *darbar* (court) people are coming." The Dhurandhar brothers were astonished to hear of this remark by Baba from others as they had not given any hint of their trip to anyone.

While talking to the devotees who were sitting around him, Baba said, "These are my darbar people that I referred to earlier." He also told the Dhurandhar brothers, "We have been with each other for the last sixty generations." All the brothers were gentle and modest and stood with joined hands staring at Baba's feet. They were overcome with *sattvic* (pure) feelings of tears, their hairs standing on end, and throats choked with emotion. Then they went to their lodging, took their meals and after taking a little rest, again came to the masjid. Balaram sat near Baba, massaging his legs. Baba, who was smoking a chillum gave it to him and indicated that he should smoke it. Balaram was not accustomed to smoking but he accepted the pipe and smoked it with great difficulty, then returned it reverentially with a bow. This was the most auspicious moment for Balaram. He had been suffering from asthma for six years. This smoke completely cured him of the disease and it never troubled him again. One day six years later, he did have another attack of asthma. It was precisely the time when Baba took his mahasamadhi.

As the day of this visit was on a Thursday, the Dhurandhar brothers had the good fortune of witnessing the Chavadi procession. Balaram saw the radiance of Pandurang on Baba's face and next morning at the Kakad Aarati time, the same phenomenon, the same radiance of his beloved deity, Pandurang, was again visible on Baba's face.

Balaram Dhurandhar wrote the life of the Maharashtra saint, Tukaram, in Marathi, but did not survive to see its publication. His brothers later published it in 1928. In a short note of Balaram's life in the beginning of the book, an account of Balaram's visit to Baba was given.

Pranams to Sri Sai

Peace Be to All

EPILOGUE

Let this work, the Satcharitra, be in every house and let it be studied daily. Let it ward off the calamities of those who study it regularly with reverence.

When Hemadpant wrote this chapter, he gave his concluding remarks and a promise to provide an index with the contents of all the chapters in verse like those found in original Marathi sacred books. Unfortunately, Hemadpant did not survive to revise and finalize this chapter for the press and the index was not found in his papers (as Chapter 50 was incorporated into Chapter 39, Chapter 51 became Chapter 50, and this chapter [originally Chapter 52] is now the Epilogue). B.V. Deo reviewed the chapter's text and found it to be incomplete and unintelligible in certain places, but it had to be published as it was found. The chief topics dealt with in this chapter are briefly given below.

GREATNESS OF SADGURU SAI

We prostrate ourselves before Sai Samarth and take refuge in him who surrounds all animate and inanimate things in the universe, from a post to Brahman, pots, houses, mansions and even the sky, who pervades all creatures equally without any differentiation, to whom all devotees are alike and who knows neither honor nor dishonor, like or dislike. If we remember him and surrender to him, he fulfills all our desires and makes us attain the goal of life. This ocean of mundane existence is very hard to cross. Waves of infatuation beat high against the bank of bad thoughts and break down trees of fortitude. The breeze of egoism blows forcefully and makes the ocean rough and agitated. Crocodiles in the form of anger and hatred move fearlessly across this ocean. Eddies in the form of the idea "I and Mine" and other doubts whirl incessantly and there are innumerable fish in the form of criticism, hate and jealousy playing in this ocean. Though this ocean is so fierce and terrible, the sadguru Sai is its *Agasti* (destroyer) and the devotees of Sai do not have the least to fear of it. Our sadguru is the boat that will safely take us across this ocean.

PRAYER

Now we fall in full pranam before Sai Baba and holding his feet make the following prayer for the world: Let not our minds wander and desire anything except you. Let this work, the *Satcharitra*, be in every house and let it be studied daily. Let it ward off the calamities of those who study it regularly with reverence.

REWARD OF STUDY — FALA SHRUTI

Now a few words about the reward you get from a study of this work. After bathing in the sacred Godavari and after taking darshan of the samadhi in the Samadhi Mandir in Shirdi (even doing this mentally with reverence and devotion touches the heart of Baba), you should read or hear the *Satcharitra*.

1. If you do this all your threefold afflictions will vanish.
2. Casually thinking about the stories of Sai, you will unconsciously become interested in spiritual life.
3. If you continue reading this work with love, all your sins and karmas will be destroyed.
4. If you wish to get rid of the cycle of births and deaths, read Sai's stories and remember him always and be devoted to his feet.
5. If you dive into the sea of Sai's stories and give them out to others, you will get an ever-new flavor of them and save the hearers from suffering and torment.
6. If you go on meditating on Sai's form, in the course of time it will disappear and you will be led into self-realization.
7. It is very hard to know or realize the nature of the Self or Brahman, but if you approach through the saguna Brahman (Sai's form) your progress will be easy.
8. If the devotee completely surrenders himself to Baba, he will lose his individual ego and merge and become one with him, as the river merges into the sea.
9. If you become merged with him in any of the three states of waking, dream and sleep, the bondage of samsara will be destroyed.
10. If anyone reads it with love and faith after bathing and completes it within a week, his calamities will disappear.
11. Or if he hears or reads it daily and regularly all his dangers will be warded off.

12. By its study, a man wishing for wealth will get it and a pure devotee will get success in his life. He will get the reward according to his faith and devotion. Without these, there will be no experience of any kind.

13. If you read it respectfully, Sai will be pleased, and removing your ignorance and poverty, he will give you knowledge, wealth and prosperity.

14. With a concentrated mind, if you read a chapter daily, it will give you infinite happiness. One who has his welfare at heart should study it carefully, then he will always remember Sai gratefully and joyfully in birth after birth.

15. This work should be read at home especially on Guru Purnima (Full-Moon in July), *Gokul Ashtami* (Lord Krishna's birthday), *Ramanavami* (Lord Rama's birthday) and *Vijayadasami* (last day of Mother Divine festival; Baba's samadhi anniversary day).

16. If you study this one book carefully, all your desires will be satisfied and if you always remember Sai's feet in your heart, you will easily cross the *Bhavasagara* (ocean of worldly existence).

17. By its study, the diseased and sick will receive health, the poor will attain wealth, the mean and afflicted will prosper, and the mind will become quiet and steady.

Dear good and devoted readers and listeners, we also bow to you all and make a special request of you. Never forget him whose stories you have read daily or month after month. The more fervently you read or listen to these stories, the more encouragement Sai gives us to serve you and be of use to you. Both the author and the readers must co-operate in this work, help each other and be happy.

PRASAD YACHANA

We close now with prayer to the Almighty for the following blessing: May the readers and devotees have complete and wholehearted surrender and devotion to Sai's feet. May his form be ever fixed in their eyes and may they see Sai (the Lord) in all beings. Amen!

AARATI

Oh Sai Baba, we wave lights before you, the bestower of happiness to jivas. Give us your servants and devotees, rest under the dust of your feet and burn (destroy) our desires. You remain absorbed in your Self and show the Lord to aspirants. As one feels intently for you, you give him experiences or realizations accordingly. Oh kindhearted one, such is your power! Meditation on your name removes fear of samsara. Your method of work is truly unfathomable as you always help the poor and helpless. In this Kali age, you—the all-pervasive Datta—have incarnated as the *sagura* (the form of) Brahman. Ward off the fear of samsara of devotees who come to you every Thursday (Guru day) so as to enable them to see the feet of the Lord. Oh God of Gods, I pray, let my treasure be the service of your feet. Feed us (the original text has the name Madhav, who is the composer of the Aarati) with happiness as the cloud feeds the chatak bird with pure water, and thus keep your word. Amen!

Pranams to Sri Sai

Peace Be to All

DONATE TO HELP TRANSLATE
THE SRI SAI SATCHARITRA

"Wealth should be the means to work out dharma. If it is used for personal enjoyment, it is wasted." -Shirdi Sai Baba

An effort is underway to translate the *Sai Satcharitra* into many different languages. You can help to bring the reality of Sai Baba's life and teachings to the world through your donations. All donations are tax deductible.

Please go to our website to donate: https://divinelineage.org/donate

Divine Assistants International is a 501[c] (3) non-profit, tax-exempt organization and a 509 (a) (1) and 170 (b) (1) (A) (i) church and public charity. Donations are tax deductible to the extent allowed by law.

SHIRDI SAI SANSTHAN, SHIRDI BABA SAMADHI, SHIRDI, INDIA
WWW.SHRISAIBABASANSTHAN.ORG

ABOUT THE DIVINE LINEAGE
HEALING CENTER

The Divine Lineage Healing Center is a Shiva/Shakti power spot created by Sri Kaleshwar in Mendocino Country, northern California. The Center is a place of healing for the body, mind and soul and is open to the public. Dattatrteya Abhishek and fire homas are performed each New and Full moon at the center's Dattatreya Temple. Our live ustream webcasts of these pujas along with other programs are broadcast every New and Full Moon and other timings.

To learn more: www.divinelineage.org

To visit in person, write us: programs@divinelineage.org

SERVICE TO BABA

It is through the love, devotion and service of many that this work was accomplished. Their loving seva is offered at Baba's feet: William Song, Nityaananda (Clint Thompson, MD), Shakti Thompson, Christinea Johnson, Catalina Peralta, Casey McLerren, Steven and Nina Ketscher, Ramakrishna Jenkins, Terry and Laya Clark, Lynn Berlad, Laina Taylor, E. Hamilton, Lora Stone, William Webster, Robin Strayhorn, Andreas Bittman, Barbara Barnes and Maik Winter.

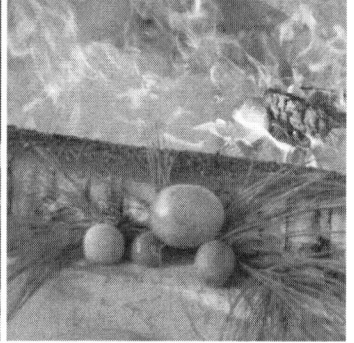

DIVINE LINEAGE HEALING CENTER & DATTATREYA TEMPLE
LAYTONVILLE, CALIFORNIA

LIST OF ILLUSTRATIONS & PHOTOGRAPHS BY CHAPTER

1. Shirdi Baba, original photograph
2. Shirdi murti, 2010
3. Baba with golden sunlight, Andreas Bittman
4. Shirdi village panorama, original photograph
5. Shirdi Baba, original photograph
6. Shirdi Baba, original photograph
7. Shirdi Baba, original photograph
8. Shirdi Baba, original photograph
9. Baba Begging, painting
10. Baba Giving Udi, drawing by Lynn Berlad
11. Formless Baba, watercolor by Christinea Lata Johnson
12. Shirdi Baba, original photograph
13. Baba Cures Leprosy, illustration
14. Baba, Shakti Thompson
15. Shirdi Baba, original photograph
16. & 17. Baba portrait, illustration Robin Strayhorn
18. & 19. Shirdi Baba, painting by Shree Sai Hemant Art
20. Kindness of Baba, painting by William Webster
21. Shirdi Baba, original photograph
22. Dwarkamai, original photograph, circa 1930
23. Baba with Tatya, Mhalsapati and son, original photograph
24. Shirdi Baba, painting by Shree Sai Hemant Art
25. Sai Baba, drawing by William Song
26. Penukonda Baba murti
27. Baba reading sacred texts, illustration
28. Shiva and Baba
29. Shirdi Baba, painting by Shree Sai Hemant Art
30. Shirdi Baba and Durga
31. Always Remember God, illustration

Printed in Great Britain
by Amazon